The Songs of Hugo Wolf

THE SONGS OF

HUGO WOLF

BY ERIC SAMS

Foreword by
GERALD MOORE

LONDON
METHUEN AND CO LTD
36 ESSEX STREET · WC2

TO ENID

Contents

Foreword by Gerald Moore

This is the most important book in the English language on the songs of Hugo Wolf since Ernest Newman proclaimed the composer's genius in 1907. It is the first time, so far as I am aware, that every single song (except the posthumous which the author has rightly omitted) has been translated, examined and elucidated between the covers of one single volume.

To the English-speaking student this work is a treasure to which he will find himself returning again and again: it is indispensable to those of us anxious to gain a deeper knowledge of Wolf.

Through the author's penetration into and intimacy with this composer's style he is enabled to make clear to us how Wolf perceived the communicating function of music and its analogies with language. Yet it is this unique quality of inter-relationship of his muse with that of the poet for which Wolf is condemned in some quarters. Schubert, it is true, sang his songs to all the poetry he could lay hands on; he transfigured an unworthy poem by putting the most glorious music to it. To Wolf, the seed was the word: words inspired him. The finer the lyric, the finer his conception in terms of music. He was generally more discriminating in his choice of poet than any composer before him: his failures, and they undeniably exist, can often be traced to poems that were not worthy of his attention, of the labour – resulting in a 'contrived' composition – that they caused. But the greatness of some of his settings cannot be questioned.

An ardent Wolfian finds himself turning again and again to the Attic type of song, chaste in conception, simple in construction, and holding it in ever-increasing affection. He is seared by the sheer beauty of *Herr, was trägt der Boden hier*; *Grenzen der Menscheit*; *Sankt Nepomuks Vorabend*; *Anakreons Grab*; *Im Frühling*; *Um Mitternacht*; *Auf ein altes Bild*, which Sams in moving language sums up as 'eternal grief in an eternal summer.' He is charmed by the discreet wit and compactness of *Der Musikant*; *Das Ständchen*; *Begegnung*; and marvels at some of the miracles he finds in the *Italienisches Liederbuch*. To have written these songs alone was to have lived to some purpose; one senses their greatness instinctively and finds with pleasure this feeling endorsed by so eminent an authority as the author. Eric Sams, however, is no euphemist; he does not overstate his case. Thus he tells us that one may prefer the strong sweetness of Schubert's *Ganymed* to the blissful masochism of Wolf's, that the latter's *Philine* loses by comparison with Schumann's, that the popular *In dem Schatten meiner Locken* by no means eclipses that of Brahms (a statement which must surely make Hugo turn in his grave). These are suggestions, however, not edicts and the reader will draw from them his own conclusions and, more often than not, find himself in complete agreement.

Our guide will not lead us astray for he is not blinded by his hero and claims for him, in Frank Walker's words, 'a modest place among the immortals'. His judgement is fair, unclouded but not arbitrary. He induces us to think for ourselves.

The fruit of deep study and sympathy with his subject, this book should be on the shelf of every man who professes or calls himself musical.

It is a masterpiece.

Preface

This book discusses all the 242 songs written for voice and piano published in the composer's lifetime, i.e. the contents of the invaluable Peters Edition in twenty-one octavo volumes.

In writing about each song I have tried to translate the German words, to comment on the music in general terms, and to add notes on points of detail. A word or two of explanation may be needed on each of these aims.

Some of the German texts are great poetry, some have no particular merit; some are long, others only a few lines. In some, individual words or phrases are important; in others, only the general mood matters. Accordingly the method of treatment varies. Sometimes it is a literal translation, sometimes a summary, sometimes a paraphrase; sometimes a mixture of all or some of these things. But the aim is always the same – to render in English prose the essence of the words as they appear in Wolf's music.

In the commentaries I try to describe each song, and, so far as possible in so brief a compass, to show the interconnexion between the music and the poem. Inevitably, in so doing, I have also become involved in some attempt at evaluating the intentions and achievements of the songs. To describe music in words is already a difficult task, and the procedure adopted may well also involve a lack of proportion. For instance, there is little to say about some of the finest songs except that they are admirable, while others, less fine, may contain many points that can more helpfully be dealt with by verbal comment. In the last resort these commentaries are simply personal impressions of the songs, evaluated from their effect on one listener who has known them all, and loved most of them, for a long time.

The notes are mainly intended to illuminate various aspects of Wolf's 'musical language' (to use his own phrase). This topic sometimes raises technical points, and here textual references are included.

In the main, then, what follows is a series of separate discussions of particular songs. But one cannot altogether avoid generalization. So the opening chapter attempts a general account of Wolf's song-writing.

I have made no attempt at any serious consideration of Wolf's own personality and the tragic story of his life, important though these matters are to a proper understanding of his music. They have been definitively dealt with in Mr Frank Walker's masterly biography *Hugo Wolf* (Dent, 1951), which should be read by everyone who is interested in Wolf's life and work.

Lastly, I would express my gratitude to all those who have helped me.

I am indebted to Mr Max Hinrichsen for permission to quote and refer to the Peters Edition of Wolf's songs, and for his personal kindness to me.

To Mr Robert Moberly I am grateful not only for the help he gave me by reading and commenting on the text in detail, but for his unfailing understanding and encouragement; and to Mr David Mowatt also for his valuable assistance in critical comment.

Wolf as a Song-writer

Born 13th March 1860 in Windischgraz, Austria; given violin and piano lessons by his father at a very early age; was a music critic in Vienna from 1884 to 1887; early in 1888 suddenly found himself as a composer; and composed in that year alone nearly one hundred songs in rapid succession. These are among the few biographical details that Wolf himself wrote for a friend. He added 'God grant me a long life and plenty of good ideas'.

This is tragic irony. To complete the summary biography:

1888–91: over 200 songs to words by Mörike, Eichendorff, Goethe, Geibel, Keller and Heyse.
1892–94: silence.
1895–97: an opera (*Der Corregidor*), another thirty or so songs, an unfinished opera (*Manuel Venegas*).
1897–1903: madness – death.

Wolf's creative life was perhaps the shortest and most sporadic known to musical history. He did not achieve mastery until he was twenty-eight. In the nine years left to him his songs were written in irregular outbursts, at the rate of one or two, even three, a day. These days add up to less than six months; the main creative periods add up to less than eighteen months. On the achievement of this short span his name and fame rest secure. At the same time his reputation has outstripped his popularity, and his praises are sung more than his songs. Critics agree that his work is admirable; music-lovers are less unanimous about whether it is also enjoyable. These two points may be related. The reasons for which Wolf's songs are highly prized – their literary perception, their fastidious 'declamation', and so on – seem nicely calculated to put people off. It is human to ask what all this has to do with music.

The fact is no doubt that Wolf's songs have lived, and will live, because of their musical excellence. It is also true that the music itself has a unique quality of intimate inter-relationship with words, with language, and with poetry.

★   ★   ★   ★

I

In general, Wolf's songs contain a musical equivalent for the prevailing mood of a poem, or more than one if the mood changes. Against that background particular words and phrases are thrown into relief for particular effect. The total impression is thus one of diversity in unity. This, admittedly, is the essence of all musical form, and need not have any real connexion with the poem set.

We occasionally feel, especially in the earlier songs, that the formal perfection is arbitrarily contrived (e.g. the 1880 *Erwartung*). But mainly it is derived directly from the poem. In the Mörike songs for example a strong central poetic image or idea evokes an iron logic of musical construction (*Auf eine Christblume II, Seufzer, Erstes Liebeslied eines Mädchens*) while a more diffuse poem, whether reflective or narrative, is transcribed into a more flexible and developing formal scheme (*Auf eine Christblume I, Auf einer Wanderung*). The structure of the setting thus reflects that of the poem. Within this general correspondence, there is much subtle variation of rhythm, melody and harmony, to re-create the finer details of the text.

Rhythm, in particular, can be expected to have a central part to play, since it is a factor common to music and poetry. Apart from providing formal shape and continuity (*In der Frühe*, etc.), it can give added meaning. Sometimes this is illustrative, as in the crisp elated rhythm of a song about the exhilaration of a morning walk (*Fussreise*) or the slow throbbing rhythm of a song about a beating heart (*Alle gingen, Herz, zur Ruh'*). A persistent rhythmic figure can also be used evocatively to convey for example the idea of a single-minded preoccupation (*Nun bin ich dein, Mühvoll komm' ich und beladen*). There is an even more intimate link with the moods and meanings of the poem in the rhythmic changes of such songs as *Auf eine Christblume I, Agnes* or *Grenzen der Menschheit*. The possibilities are endless, and Wolf exploits them without ever repeating them; each song creates and sustains rhythmically its own mood and its own world.

It is true that most are in duple or quadruple time, set out in regular two-bar phrases and four-bar sentences, and that this occasionally leads to squareness and monotony where the musical material is not of the finest. This very regularity is however one of the factors that enables Wolf to achieve his superlative perfection of formal construction; and as a technique of setting words to music it is not only defensible but almost inevitable. In German, as in English, scansion is by stress of syllable rather than by length; so the common trochaic foot for example is most directly translated into equal pulses, thus ♩ ♩ rather than ♩. ♩.

Because the whole of Wolf's music responds to poetry, this rhythmic translation pervades the piano part as well as the voice. Not that Wolf's vocal lines are monotonous; on the contrary, they are capable of the most delicate and subtle inflections, and it is precisely the steady rhythmic feeling that makes this possible. Like a *danseur noble* it supports the voice part, which is then left free for rhythmic digression without ever seeming over-elaborate or impeding the forward movement of the song as a whole. This is one aspect of Wolf's 'declamation'.

It is often regarded as self-evident that Wolf takes great pains to match the actual speech-stress of the words he is setting to music, and that this practice is an essential part of his art. This view is wrong and misleading. The rhythm of spoken verse is so individually variable, and so complex, that it cannot be precisely transcribed in the more basic terms of musical notation. Even if it could, the feat would not after all be very musicianly. In fact, Wolf's melodic lines are rarely complex. Certainly he takes pains to lift the musical stress from inessential words in some of the songs. Very often indeed however his accentuation is obviously faulty from the point of view of prosody, just as it often is in Schubert. This is bound to happen to any song-writer who is doing something different from merely holding a mirror up to a poem. Wolf, in his declamation as in his other procedures, is doing very much more than this. If the vocal line hesitates over certain words, or prolongs others, it is in order to enhance them musically, and so to add emotional effect or even new meaning. Sometimes this procedure is reserved for single evocative words, e.g. the prolonged 'geflügelt' (winged) towards the end of *Die ihr schwebet*. More often it is used for larger units, either to underline or to create a mood. Two examples must suffice:

An die Geliebte

Wenn du zu den Blumen gehst

Even these mild complexities are, however, rare in Wolf's songs.

3

They are a special case of the declamation that is at the heart of all his song-writing; the flexible vocal line which is, in Byrd's majestic phrase, 'fram'd to the life of the words'. Even in a strophic song the melody does not necessarily follow set patterns of repetition, but is sensitively deployed to match a changing mood (as in *Der Rattenfänger*) or a new poetic image (as in *Um Mitternacht*).

It may be observed that Wolf in adopting and perfecting this style could be said to be making a virtue of necessity. He is not among the world's most popular melodists, although he could write broad swinging tunes when his text required them (*Fussreise* is a peerless example). His genius lay in writing restrained melodic lines that are not only beautiful in themselves but serve to sustain and enhance the meaning and the emotive power of words, to conduct a current of poetic feeling. In this respect there is hardly his equal in the whole world of music. Perhaps the finest examples are in the Italian songbook (e.g. *Der Mond hat eine schwere Klag' erhoben*, *Wenn du mich mit den Augen streifst*); but almost every song of Wolf's maturity has some such delight to offer.

The penetrating quality of this kind of melody perhaps owes something to the acuity of Wolf's own aural perceptions. He expects from his listeners a sense of tonal values as exact and exacting as his own. All his melody, whether in the vocal line or in the piano themes that are often extended and developed quasi-independently throughout a song (*Auf einer Wanderung*, *Schon streckt' ich aus im Bett*, *Alles endet, was entstehet*), is inseparable from its harmonic context; and harmony is all-important in Wolf's work.

In his lifetime, like most composers, he was attacked for 'dissonance'. His own comment on this was 'The fact that I have been accused of perpetrating chains of unresolved discords leaves me wholly unmoved, for the simple reason that I am in a position to demonstrate how each of my boldest discords can be justified by the most severe criteria of the theory of harmony.' In case this sounds alarming it should be said that Wolf's music is notable for its concord, and that his occasional dissonances do not sound particularly daring nowadays. His rejoinder to his critics shows how deeply he felt himself rooted in the classic tradition; as indeed he was, though no composer of his time could have failed to make use of the extended harmonic possibilities so richly exploited by Wagner. He could have said instead that all his harmonic resources – and they are lavish – are deployed to match the mood of the poem, and this is not only true but vital to his artistic integrity. Of course he has 'fingerprints'; not everyone may share his predilection for

4

four-part harmony, augmented fifths, and cadential second inversions. Nevertheless, the overwhelming impression left by the songs is not one of mannerism but one of deep and original intuitive response. This is at its most marked in key-changes. Modulation in the ordinary sense, e.g. in a piano interlude serving solely as a bridge from one key to the next, is a great rarity in Wolf's work. Instead, the harmony is moulded by the emotive significance of the words. This effect pervades the songs. It is perhaps most easily detectable in the settings of shorter poems. Some have a definite well-established home key or keys from which the tonality diverges at moments of heightened stress or tension. In others, conversely, there is a fluctuating tonality, corresponding to a poetic mood of stress or tension, within which a definite tonality is established as the tension is resolved. *Der Mond hat eine schwere Klag' erhoben* is a good example of the former, *Mir ward gesagt* of the latter. Each type is of course only one particular aspect of a general procedure; an instinctive response in harmonic terms to the emotional tensions and relaxations of poetic language. It is among the most subtle and evocative of all the many intimate correspondences between Wolf's music and words.

This has perhaps particular relevance for interpretative purposes; the harmony is often more helpful than the marked dynamics in determining the emotionally climactic moment of a song. There is for example a whole category of songs in which the introduction or reintroduction of a major tonic chord is delayed, so that its eventual appearance brings an ineffable sense of coming home, of peace and repose (*Verborgenheit*, *Wir haben beide*). Similarly in many songs the late introduction of the major form of a minor tonic suddenly lights up the music, throwing a word or an idea into bright relief (*Wie sollt' ich heiter bleiben*, *Ob der Koran von Ewigkeit sei?*, *Mignon III*). Examples of Wolf's evocative uses of harmony and tonality are endless. They may pervade a whole song, as in the minor – major contrasts in *Wohl denk' ich oft* and more delicately, in *Zitronenfalter* and more subtly still, in *Heut' Nacht erhob ich mich*, or in the moving contrast between chromatic richness and diatonic simplicity in *Anakreons Grab*. They may be reserved for special moments within a song, as in the harmonic play at the refrain 'Ach nein' of *In dem Schatten meiner Locken*, the musical pun that illustrates the verbal pun at the beginning of *Elfenlied*, or the single poignant dissonance for the sudden shadow that falls in the last line of *Auf ein altes Bild*. They can also be used almost pictorially for effects of chiaroscuro (e.g. *Verschwiegene Liebe*, but very many songs have something of this quality) and of colour (*Phänomen*, *Auf einer Wanderung*).

So it is not surprising to find that Wolf appears to have definite verbal associations with certain keys. Many people think of, or even hear, sharp keys as brighter and more colourful than flat keys. Wolf certainly had these associations; his favourite mediant key-sequences for brightening effect add four sharps to (or take four flats from) the key signature with each change. But he had many others more specific. Thus, he tended to use A major for spring songs (*Frühling ubers Jahr, Wandl' ich in dem Morgentau, Gesegnet sei das Grün*), A minor for songs for a woman's voice in various moods of distress or wistfulness (*Das verlassene Mägdlein, Mignon III, Die Bekehrte*) and E flat or A flat major for moods of serene assurance, especially in love-songs (*An die Geliebte, Sterb' ich, so hüllt in Blumen*). He felt C major apt for plainness and directness of expression (*Der Soldat I, Gesellenlied, Königlich Gebet*), D major for moods of blissful contentment or elation (*Fussreise, Der Gärtner, Ganymed*), D minor for discontent or anger (*Prometheus, Das Köhlerweib ist trunken*) and C sharp minor or D flat major for music of night and dream or death (*Um Mitternacht, Alles endet, Komm o Tod*). His B minor songs, especially those ending on the dominant, have an indefinable bittersweet (*Lied eines Verliebten, Sagt ihm, dass er zu mir komme*) while the tonality (not, strictly speaking, the key) of F sharp major is felt to be appropriate to a certain rollicking or boisterous mood (*Erschaffen und Beleben, Nein, junger Herr*). Although there are of course exceptions to these generalizations a study of them may again be helpful for interpretative purposes, and in considering the question of transposition.

They also provide further evidence for verbal associations in Wolf's music. His musical language seems to have a vocabulary more precise than ordinary musical illustration or depiction. These are of course also found. There is plenty of descriptive writing, verging on programme music, in the piano part of Wolf's songs. Thus, there are very many, often brilliant, evocations of stringed instruments (*Das Ständchen, Ein Ständchen Euch zu bringen*) and of military marches or bands (*Der Glücksritter, Sie blasen zum Abmarsch*). Then there are special effects such as widely spaced chords suggesting hollowness and reverberation (*Cophtisches Lied I, Feuerreiter*), processional exits fading in the distance (*Epiphanias, Nun wandre Maria*), and the similar 'disappearing trick' where the music wafts away into thin air (*Waldmädchen, Lied vom Winde*, etc.). In addition there are many still franker examples of imitation; guns fire (*Unfall, Der Jäger*), donkeys bray (*Lied des transferierten Zettel, Schweig' einmal still*), and there is even the swishing of whips

6

(*Gesellenlied, Selbstgeständnis*). All this is part of the song-writer's stock-in-trade, and Wolf sets it out very attractively and amusingly.

Such effects, though not perhaps very subtle, are already very close to language. Wolf seems to go further still in this direction, to pass through the stage of musical depiction to musical statement, a direct expression in music of particular verbal concepts. This appears to be not a conscious process, but yet another aspect of the impact of poetry on an infinitely sensitive musical mind.

There are abundant examples of musical equivalents in Wolf's songs which make this plain. Some have a clear subconscious association, others are puzzling. Some are difficult to formulate precisely. Their existence (if sufficiently accredited) may however tell us something about the meaning or interpretation of a particular song.

They may also be thought relevant to a closer study of the communicating function of music and its analogies with language. Nevertheless, since that would go far beyond the present purpose, no attempt has been made to present them in any of the possible classifications that would be appropriate in the larger context of a general critical work, e.g. frequency, date of appearance in the songs, type of motif (rhythmic, melodic, harmonic), whether occurring in voice or piano or both, degree of correspondence with some definite idea in the poem, or even a Roget's Thesaurus order of the concepts involved. The following list is haphazard. Nor does it set out to be exhaustive; further examples of these and other possible correspondences will be found in the notes to the songs.

1. Worship, submission, self-surrender

A particular rhythm i.e. $\frac{4}{4}$ ♪♩ ♪♪♩ ♪ very often appears, usually in open fifths in the left-hand piano part, in songs of which the words express the idea of worship, whether of God (*Zum neuen Jahre*, middle section) or of the loved one (*Wenn du mich mit den Augen streifst*). The reason for this correspondence is not readily apparent. Yet these persistent figures seem to convey the impression of submission or self-surrender; it is as if the tonic stress had taken refuge by hiding away within the bar-line. Certainly this effect is elusive, and will be lost if there is any suspicion in performance of overt syncopation, thus ♪♩ ♪, etc. A more complex and very compelling example of this rhythmic shift is heard throughout the bass part of *Sterb' ich, so hüllt in Blumen*, where the effect of rapt withdrawal is unmistakable.

2. Childishness, weakness

An analogous rhythm, thus $\frac{2}{4}$ ♪ ♪ ♪ or $\frac{4}{4}$ ♪ ♩ ♪, etc. is found in association with the ideas of childish helplessness or weakness. The reason behind this association is much clearer. These are the weak beats of the bar, and the allusive use made of them is very striking. Thus, on the last page of *Der Genesene an die Hoffnung*, at the mention of the word 'child' ('wie ein *Kind* und sonder Harm') the piano rhythm is displaced by a semiquaver, solely for the one bar in which that word occurs in the voice part. Other examples of this verbal association are in the opening bars of *Der Freund* ('ein sanftgewiegtes *Kind*'), and again in *Nimmersatte Liebe* (at the word 'Mädchen', where the illustration of helplessness is particularly close and apt). More subtly, and movingly, the weak-beat rhythm is heard all through the Harper's song *An die Türen*; the poem depicts a helpless old man 'still und sittsam' (quiet and docile).

3. Smallness

This idea is conveyed by the repeated interval of the minor second, with the two notes played either together or consecutively, usually high in the piano register and in small note-values. The idea of the smallest possible interval lasting the shortest possible time is sufficiently clear. The motif in its basic form is used to illustrate the elf in *Elfenlied*:

and in *Auf eine Christblume I*:

and of course is heard in *Mein Liebster ist so klein*.

4. Laughter, mockery, criticism

Another related effect, this time frankly burlesque, is that of the sharply rising (or occasionally falling) semitone, often in the form of an acciaccatura. This stands for the idea of laughter not wholly free from malice, e.g. throughout *Rat einer Alten*. In this song and others, e.g. *Abschied*, it is also used to suggest the idea of criticism.

5. Unrest, unease

The same basic idea of the rising semitone used in a different context
conveys a very different idea. A repeated piano figuration of the follow-
ing kind,  often corresponds to
a mood of unrest, whether in the form of restless energy (*Genialisch
Treiben*, piano prelude, etc.) or uneasiness of mind (*Storchenbotschaft*,
piano part bar 34) or both (*Der Jäger*, piano left hand *passim*).

6. Manliness

This last motif in turn is related to what seems to be an equivalent for
the idea of manliness or virile force. Here the basic idea is a strongly
rising bass line, sometimes chromatic, sometimes diatonic, usually in
dotted rhythm; in its simplest form thus:

It is interesting that Wolf is not at home with this motif in the 1888
songs. There its use is mainly light-hearted or mock heroic, as in many
of the Eichendorff songs; and when the motif is used seriously, its effect
is bombastic and unconvincing (*Der Freund*). But in 1889 a similar idea,
in a more refined and simplified form, achieves a true expression. In the
climbing octaves of *Prometheus*

(octaves in both hands)

Wolf conveys a shatteringly impressive effect of manly pride and
determination. With this he said his final word on the subject; the motif
is never heard in any of the later songs.

7. Gaiety, élan

In Wolf's many songs in light-hearted vein there is an irresistible sweeping vitality and exultation. His own life and circumstances can hardly
have been very conducive to these feelings, and they must have derived
from some hidden source of strength in his own character. His most
typical musical equivalent is the simplest and most self-evident of ideas
– a scale passage rising to the tonic, usually in the piano treble, thus:

This is put to many fresh and pleasant uses, even expressing various shades of meaning, from swaggering, as in *Der Glücksritter*, to suavity, as in *Spottlied*. Its appearance is often significant. In *Gutmann und Gutweib* and *Ritter Kurts Brautfahrt*, for example, it tells us quite plainly early in the song that the high-flown style is burlesque or mock heroic. In all contexts it is an indication that the composer is in high spirits, enjoying the humour of the verses and his music-making.

8. Freedom

The use of the rising 'horn passage', thus:  is almost a history, in itself, of musical equivalence in Wolf's songs. There is an immediate verbal association with the chase, the huntsman, the open air; and sure enough the first extended use of this motif is in *Jägerlied* of 1888. At the end of Wolf's creative life the same association occurs in *Gesegnet sei das Grün*. In between, this idea takes on a variety of illustrative meanings with the same verbal concepts of freedom, or release from constraint, underlying them all. A clear example is in *Verschwiegene Liebe*, where the brief appearance of this motif at the word 'frei' in the first verse lends point to the verbal context of thoughts flying free.

9. Contentment, the open air

The gaiety of motif 7 above is an evident feature in Wolf's song-writing. Less apparent but no less real is the fact that there is also a series of vocal melodic counterparts for the idea of gaiety or happiness which, like motif 8 above, is usually found in association with the idea of the open air. The many possible variants are best illustrated by actual examples. The following three typical melodies (among others) occur in verbal contexts of feeling of happiness in the open air. All are transposed for ease of comparison.

Der Scholar

Die Spröde

Fussreise

There is apparently no actual verbal association, but the singing lilt that these examples have in common is unmistakably genial and elated.

10. Singing

When Wolf has in mind the idea of singing as such, a different equivalent appears, a chain of rising or falling sixths in the voice part, e.g.:

This pattern, or a melodic line based upon it, occurs typically in songs within songs; whether those that have the word 'song' in the title (*Jägerlied*, opening vocal melody), or those that are about someone singing (*Der Musikant*, opening vocal melody), or even about birds singing (*Der Scholar*, at the words '*singen* alle Vögelein'). The melodic curves of *Lied eines Verliebten* and of *Das Ständchen* have this quality. We may think perhaps of the typical lilt of the waltz or ländler, with which Wolf must have been familiar. At any rate, it is clear from the final section of *Abschied* how easily and pleasantly this motif can be turned into a Viennese dance-strain.

11. Adoration

A near relation of this 'singing' motif – basically thus:

is put to different uses. The sixths in either the voice or the piano part rise and fall more quiescently, more acquiescently; the singing is transfixed. The contexts in which this motif occurs show its meaning; all are songs of adoring love. The significance is perhaps plainest in the piano postludes of *Frage und Antwort* and *Und willst du deinen Liebsten sterben sehen*. The latter song is built up from this idea in masterly fashion.

12. Longing, yearning

This is suggested by a recurring snatch of melody in the right-hand piano part, thus:

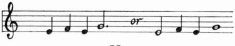

This seems to have occurred to Wolf in a rather unusual way. We gather from his earliest biographer, Decsey, that the first song in which it occurs – *Auf einer Wanderung* – though dated 11th March 1888, was not in fact completed until a fortnight later. It appears that the missing portion was the section beginning 'Ach hier'. The motif that Wolf eventually devised for this passage is not an independent construction. It is derived from the previous material, as described in the notes to this song; but this new variant when it came evidently seemed just right to Wolf for the trance-like mood it depicts. It was again used throughout the later Mörike song *Im Frühling* with transcending effect. The mood of both these songs is one of rapt absorption; and the motif recurs in two Spanish songs of a similar mood – *Bedeckt mich mit Blumen* and (in a more determined version) *Nun bin ich dein*.

13. Love I

This is a musical metaphor. In Wolf's love-music two strands of melody (often in the piano right hand) converge, moving in two-part harmony towards unison. The simplest form

etc.

occurs in the very early and trifling little allegory of love *Das Vöglein* of 1878. Its later uses however are finely wrought and charged with meaning. Their source may well be the postlude of *Lebe wohl*, in which the sad theme of farewell sounds downwards in the treble while the tenor voice strives upwards to meet it. In the *Peregrina* songs this idea is extended into the passionate music that links the two as the postlude to the first song and the prelude and main thematic material of the second.

In this more complex form it recurs in the last song of all, *Fühlt meine Seele*.

In one guise or another it is a marked feature of many of Wolf's love-songs.

14. Love II

The evidence for a second related love theme is offered with more diffidence. One notes here and there in similar contexts a sort of inversion of the idea of the motif quoted above, in which two melodic lines diverge, e.g. in its simplest form

It happens that, musically speaking at least, inversion gives like results.

If these motifs are in fact used thematically, we would expect them to mean another kind of love. There is some ground for conjecturing that an expression of this kind may be a subconscious equivalent for 'agape', the love between parent and child, as distinct from 'eros'. For example there are these diverging melodic lines in *Selbstgeständnis* (e.g. piano postlude) - a song about a parent–child relationship; and in *Der Genesene an die Hoffnung* (piano at the last words 'in deinem Arm') where hope is personified as a maternal and comforting figure. The motif also pervades the music of *Und steht Ihr früh*, a song of ineffable tenderness but far removed from Wolf's typical passionate love-music. We might also hazard as a makeweight that the piano part of *In dem Schatten meiner Locken* is saying in Wolf's language that the singer feels towards her sleeping lover as tenderly as a mother towards her sleeping child.

15. Isolation, loneliness

This is another example of musical metaphor. Again it is a piano figuration. The right hand has repeated chords, from which the left hand moves away downwards, usually in single notes. It is difficult to find an apt verbal equivalent for this motif; yet the passages in which it occurs are clearly related in meaning. To mention first a generalized example -

the descending bass of *Im Frühling* is hardly likely to have any particular thematic significance, although the song is in fact about isolation. This is followed by some interesting, if vague, associations in the Goethe songs. Little is heard of the motif for over a year (no song that might have called for it was written during the interval). Then in *Schmerzliche Wonnen* it occurs, almost absurdly pat, at the words 'when the soul is separated from the body'.

Perhaps Wolf's subconscious associations were becoming more definite from this point on. At any rate there is no mistaking the meaning of the motif that goes grieving through the piano part of *Mir ward gesagt*, a song of which the one single theme is the sorrow of parting. This is deeply felt music; and so we may feel justified in ascribing the same mood to *Auch kleine Dinge* and, even after an interval of another five years, to *Wohl kenn, ich Euren Stand*. If so, fresh light is thrown on the interpretation of these two songs. Again Wolf apparently feels that the inversion of this theme cannot be used to mean the opposite of the idea. Indeed, the inversion (i.e. a steady chordal bass with an upward-tending melodic line in the treble) is not found very often, and seems to have no particular thematic significance.

16. Companionship

In songs expressing the idea of companionship, togetherness, Wolf sometimes uses parallel thirds in the piano right hand. This effect is mainly concentrated in the one supreme example *Nun wandre Maria*. It is amusing to note, however, that the two songs about young soldiers marching off to the wars – *Sie blasen zum Abmarsch* and *Ihr jungen Leute* – have the piano's consecutive thirds in common while being in other respects musically dissimilar.

17. Night and wakefulness

This is offered with some diffidence, because of its unlikely nature. But the three piano passages quoted below are so obviously similar in conception that, knowing Wolf's procedures, one cannot help looking for the verbal idea they have in common.

The first is from *Auf eine Christblume I* and the words are about movement in a nocturnal scene. The same music is later used to describe the activities of an elf at midnight. The second is from *Gutmann und Gutweib* and the words are about the old folk lying in bed, keeping awake. The third is from *Alle gingen* and the words are about the beating heart of a sleepless lover in the night. In each the piano right hand has a steady rhythm, while the bass part goes groping about mysteriously; each is in single notes or in octaves. It seems inescapable, though bizarre, that this music is 'about' the idea of being awake at night. The evident example of sleeplessness in Wolf songs is the superlative *Lied eines Verliebten*; the piano accompaniment throughout takes the basic shape already described. Sleeplessness also suggests the late Byron song *Sonne der Schlummerlosen*; and the piano part in bars 4–5 of that song also conforms to this pattern.

18. Night and sleep

This, after the previous motif, is reassuringly simple and self-evident. A rocking, lulling movement (not unrelated to motif 12 above), usually a shifting semitone in cross rhythm, e.g.:

in the middle register of the piano, occurs in songs about night, sleep, dream. We catch a glimpse of the idea of this shifting movement in the early song *Die Nacht* of 1880. But it is already fully fledged by 1887 in *Nachtzauber*; and in the simplest and most basic form quoted above evokes the idea of Night herself dreaming in *Um Mitternacht*. In *Der Freund* only the opening words are about sleeping – and only the opening bars contain this motif. Its use is evident in *Verschwiegene Liebe*, about night-time, and *Sankt Nepomuks Vorabend*, a nocturnal scene. It requires no very lively sense of metaphor to pass from the idea of sleep and night to that of the serenity of death; a similar motif is heard throughout *Komm o Tod*.

19. Mystery

This is essentially a chordal progression, often dominant sevenths, in slow time, involving a chromatic shift in which two unrelated tonalities are juxtaposed. The corresponding voice part often moves up and down by octaves or fifths. There also are many instances of a change of keyboard register to point the contrast between the two tonalities. The

effect is basically thus:  This or related material is

in part just a Wolfian 'fingerprint'. We know that he greatly admired the Schumann song *Auf das Trinkglas eines verstorbenen Freundes* (Op. 35 no. 6) in which just such a passage occurs, with an impressively mysterious effect. Wolf takes this idea and gives it a bewildering variety of treatment in contexts of which the basic common idea is musically apparent enough but impossible to define in verbal terms, e.g. the music that greets the mysterious apparition of the storks in *Storchenbotschaft* (bar 16), and of the mermaid in *Seemanns Abschied* (bars 13–16); and the mystic refrain of *Cophtisches Lied I*. There is a host of related examples.

20. Deception

A semitonal shift akin to the 'mysterious' motif above but less solemn, and lighter in texture, may suggest the idea of deception or falsity. A good example is in *Geselle, woll'n wir uns*.

This point is not well documented, but for what it is worth similar chromatics are also heard in other songs, e.g. *Lass sie nur gehn* (bars 2–4), in passages where 'pretence' is the idea behind the words.

21. Narration, reflection

A harmonic progression on these lines:

although perhaps more of a mannerism than a meaningful motif, makes
an interesting comparison with the 'singing' motif (10 above). Instead
of lilting sixths in the voice part we have a rather ordinary formula consisting of a gradual semitonal shift in four-part harmony. The contrast
is complete; nothing could be less like 'singing'. This piano motif shows
a rough correspondence in certain of its uses to the idea of 'thinking'.
It occurs in particular where the voice part is about to introduce a new
thought – *Der Knabe und das Immlein* (bars 20–21) – and in general in
the opening bars of many songs in a reflective mood, e.g. *Gebet*.

22. Sorrow

As with motif 15, to which it is closely akin, this is not precisely definable
in words, although its similarity of musical effect in all the contexts in
which it occurs is evident. The basic idea is sorrow or despair induced by
loss or deprivation; its musical expression is a recurring downward-
tending melodic line, usually in the piano right hand, moving by step,
in tones or semitones, never more than three or four notes, never

traversing more than a major third, thus: 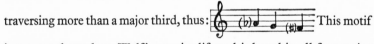 This motif

is present throughout Wolf's creative life and is heard in all four major
songbooks. One of the first examples we meet is the deeply felt *Lebe*

wohl. Here the falling phrase ⟦music⟧ echoes the

sound and sense of this sad word of farewell. In the Goethe volume
this motif is found in the three Harper songs; despair is the theme of
them all. It resounds throughout the only Mignon song which is
specifically about deprivation – *Nur wer die Sehnsucht kennt*. In later
uses the motif has great simplicity and effect, as in the sad slow crotchet
octaves that begin *Wir haben beide*. In the late masterpiece *Wie viele Zeit*
it is introduced, again in a simple form, at the end of the song (in the
postlude) as a new idea. The unmistakable sadness of its presentation

here may perhaps help with the interpretation of that song. There are also many examples of its use in a lighter vein; thus it is parodied in the opening section, where despairing love is derided, of *Frech und Froh II*.

23. Pathos, bathos

Chords of the augmented fifth, e.g. , are frequently heard in songs of strong emotion. Like the preceding example its use may be serious or parodied; it illustrates both tense emotion and maudlin sentiment. (It is perhaps worth mentioning that the German technical term for 'augmented' – 'übermässig' in fact means both 'extreme' and 'extravagant'.) Two examples of its serious use are *Grenzen der Menschheit* (bar 44 et seq.) and *Das verlassene Mägdlein* (e.g. bars 23–26); and two of its burlesque use: *Zur Warnung* (bars 1–2) and *Bei einer Trauung* (*passim*).

24. Increasing intensity

This idea is motif 23 above writ large. Instead of (say) the notes C, E, G sharp together, passages in the tonalities of C, E, G sharp (A flat) major are heard consecutively in ascending order. Again this procedure is sometimes just a 'fingerprint'; but in most contexts it clearly has musical meaning. It appears to be associated in Wolf's mind with the idea of increasing brightness, as in *In der Frühe* and *Morgenstimmung*. The bright vision of *Auf einer Wanderung* and the transfiguration of *Ganymed* are also stated in these terms. This association of ideas perhaps gives added significance to other examples, e.g. *Die ihr schwebet*, *Das Ständchen* and *Schon streckt' ich aus*.

★   ★   ★   ★

We have considered particular aspects of Wolf's style and idiom as they appear throughout the songs. The characteristic quality of his songwriting however lies in the way in which certain of these several aspects are combined in the music of each particular song. *Jägerlied* is a clear and typical example of one possible result. Its date, early in 1888, shows that all the elements of Wolf's style were present from the very beginning of his maturity as a composer. Each song is a separate topic from this point of view; there is endless variety in the ways in which these elements are combined afresh. Yet even in Wolf's short creative life certain shifts in emphasis are detectable. Generally speaking, his musical style varies with each songbook.

In the majority of the Mörike songs for example it is the verbal music of the words that seems to count, and the vocal and instrumental melodic lines that carry the primary musical inspiration, to correspond to this verbal music. In the Goethe volume the proportion of such songs is significantly less; and with the Spanish songs, this trend becomes even more marked. Rhythmical ideas, accompaniment figures, formal constructions, begin to dominate the musical expression. It seems that this aspect of Wolf's work, like the others so far considered, derives directly from the poetry of his songs.

A hypothetical example may make this clearer. Let us imagine some Wolf settings, for voice and piano, of English poetry, say Shakespeare's Sonnets. Some of these have a verbal melody to which Wolf would surely have responded in terms of musical melody as the basic inspiration.

> 'Shall I compare thee to a summer's day?
> Thou art more lovely and more temperate'.

These lines might have begun to sing in his mind, taking shape as a melodic line following the questioning and answering inflections of the words, and bringing out their emotion; perhaps by prolonging each 'more' on a higher note so that the melody can curve down and hesitate gently before 'lovely' and 'temperate'. The idea of a tenderly lulling accompaniment, no doubt in the worshipping rhythm of motif 1 above, might then present itself. The noble serenity of the sonnet could have suggested a basic tonality of E flat or A flat major, perhaps with a brightening allusion to a sharp-sounding tonality (say C flat or F flat major) at the word 'summer'. Against this background we can imagine an endearingly evocative musical treatment of the following line

> 'Rough winds do shake the darling buds of May'

and so on to a fine ringing conclusion at

> 'So long lives this and this gives life to thee'.

This would be Wolf in the Mörike songbook.

Other sonnets however might have been translated in terms of a rhythmic idea in the first place.

> 'Alas tis true I have gone here and there
> And made myself a motley to the view'.

We can imagine how these lines might instantly have suggested a glumly clownish piano figuration. Its interest would of course be partly melodic, since it would have to leap up and down, here and there, and generally make itself a motley to the ear. But the basic idea would have come in the shape of a repeated rhythmic piano figure, quite independent of the stress of the words. These could be left to make their own melodic way following the verbal stress. The piano part might easily be a self-contained solo, of great formal perfection. The bittersweet mood could have suggested the key of B minor, with harmonic tensions relaxing on the dominant in a piano postlude after the last line

'Even to thy pure and most most loving breast'.

This would be Wolf in the Spanish songbook.

The first example assumes a melodic response, the second a rhythmic response, to a poetic idea. Each was imagined as being direct and immediate. In the second example however the music might easily appear less emotionally involved, more deliberately concerned with creating a mood of its own to match the poem, and so more dominant in the partnership with words.

With these points in mind we can trace a development in Wolf's song-writing. What may be called the primary melodic impulse is a striking feature of most of the Mörike and Eichendorff songs and many of the Goethe songs. The coincidental resemblances among songs of this first period are melodic. The favoured four-part harmony is quasi-vocal in character (as in *Gebet*). The songs are almost invariably in two- or four-time, in direct correspondence with the metre. The music is a continuous response to the verbal music and emotion of the words; in particular there are identifiable musical equivalents for poetic concepts.

In the Goethe volume the poetry has more ideas and on the whole (because of Wolf's selection) less beauty of phrase and imagery than Mörike's. In the result, the style is in transition. This collection is musically (as it is poetically) the least homogeneous of all, and technically perhaps the most interesting. There is no clearly definable Goethe style, as there is a Mörike or a Spanish style; the music inclines to one or the other. For example, the late Goethe song *Die Spröde*, which dates from the same period as the first Spanish songs, is like them in style.

The Spanish volume itself marks Wolf's second period. It represents his first sustained attempt at setting verse of no particular quality. He is confronted with a series of rather flat lyrics, each mainly on one particular invariant theme or idea, each in its way formally perfect, often with a cunning rhyme scheme. There is, it is true, much emotion in some of the lyrics of the sacred songs, and intense passion in many of the others. But the effects are broad rather than deep. The content of the poems is never profound, whether emotionally or intellectually; the most frequent concepts are those of action and gesture. In the result, there is little counterweight for the music. The piano parts of some of the songs (including some of the very finest, e.g. *Auf dem grünen Balkon*) stand up as self-contained instrumental solos. Sometimes, as in that song, the vocal melody is a brilliant embroidery on the piano part, sometimes it is tacked on less dexterously. The similarities between the songs are harmonic rather than melodic. Musical equivalents for poetic ideas are fewer and harder to identify. Triple time makes its first large-scale appearance, showing that the metre of the words is (rightly) regarded as of secondary importance.

The Spanish volume was followed after a short interval by the Keller songs, in which the same trends are perceptible. They were the nearest approach to commissioned work that Wolf ever undertook in the field of song for voice and piano, and they took longer to write than usual. One might guess that his difficulties arose because he was still, under the influence of the 'Spanish' style, seeking to impose his own musical ideas, his own interpretation, on Keller's poems. But these poems had ideas of their own, and they did not yield without a struggle. One of them, *Wie glänzt der helle Mond*, had fewer intellectualized concepts than the others, and this Wolf absorbed into a masterly song. In the others, one feels that hidden in the admirable music there are five poems clamouring to be let out.

Six months later, we come to the first Italian songs. It is like coming home. Here, in what may be called Wolf's third and last period, the two previous styles achieve an unexpected and miraculous synthesis. Again the verses are in themselves slight, again the instrumental character of the music is unmistakable; indeed in the later Italian songs the texture suggests string-quartet writing. But the affinities between the songs of this volume are now melodic as well as harmonic, and, in the later songs, rhythmic. What seems to have happened is that Wolf is once again emotionally involved in the lyrics as such, especially in the love-songs. Something in Heyse's verses – perhaps their sense of intimate communal and personal life? – has elicited a response so strong and wholehearted that it takes these simple love-lyrics and forces them to be beautiful. The music in overwhelming the words raises them to its own level of exaltation. They then demand and receive a treatment in terms of primary melodic impulse, just as in the Mörike songs. At the same time the musical technique has become refined. The simplest of means are used; melodies moving by step or in repeated notes, plain harmonies, restrained dynamics, often culminating in a few murmured words and a quiet postlude. The emotive force of the Mörike style is here allied to the formal perfection of the Spanish style; and the result, in the brief compass of these short lyrics, is often transcendent.

⋆   ⋆   ⋆   ⋆

This introduction has attempted to give some general account of the innumerable and complex ways in which Wolf's music responds to different aspects of a poem and to different kinds of poetry.

This is a strange phenomenon, and one that may present difficulties of appreciation from the purely musical point of view. Yet it is also real and rewarding, as anyone who has felt the force of its twofold impact can testify. Wolf's music at its best has a quality of bright wounding beauty, better felt than described. This quality is no doubt derived from the way in which the songs came into being – the intuitive precise pene-tration that reaches the heart of a poem and absorbs and recreates its essence in an illumination of music. Compared with the whole range and resource of all that music has to offer, this may be a limited gift. Yet it is surely precious and enduring; and it wins for Hugo Wolf 'a modest place among the immortals, in the hierarchy of musicians, and the grateful love of inarticulate humanity, for whom he sang of truth and beauty'.*

* Frank Walker: *Hugo Wolf* (Dent, 1951).

THE SONGS
I. The first published songs

In the autumn of 1887, through the generous initiative of a friend, arrangements were put in hand for the publication of some of Wolf's work. From his manuscripts of many years the composer selected the following twelve songs. They contain some favourites, but no masterpieces: these were to come in the following year.

Six songs for a woman's voice

[Peters Edition 3153, Nos. 1–6]

---

1. Morgentau: Morning dew

19th June 1877

Morning breezes have blown away the night. The meadows laugh in their spring array, and a bird sings its sweet dawn-song softly, as if in dream. The rose has heard and is moved; and its petals gently unfolding let fall a dewdrop like a silent tear.

The poem is described as being taken from 'an old songbook'. It has no great merit, and we need not regret its anonymity. But the seventeen-year-old Wolf was evidently much pleased with it, and our first introduction to his work is a charming one. The young composer, though evidently writing under the influence of his great predecessors, shows in this unpretentious song an original and authentic talent of a high order.

The melody is beguiling and the simplicity of the accompaniment conceals much deft art. Towards the end, for example, at 'mehr und mehr enthüllet' (more and more unfolds) there appears a new melody and a new unfolding harmonic progression. These lead gracefully into the final word 'still' (silent), which is lovingly prolonged for two whole bars while under it the right-hand piano part recalls the opening vocal melody. This delightful passage, and indeed the whole song, is redolent of the unaffected freshness of youth; the song is well named.

NOTE. This song has affinities with the incomparably greater *Fussreise* (22) written eleven years later. The basic mood is similar – enjoyment of the freshness of the morning. *Fussreise*, too, is in D major, ends with the same rising scale passage to the keynote, and has as a special feature the harmonic progression from a dominant to a tonic on the mediant of the keynote to the dominant and tonic of the keynote itself (i.e. C♯, F♯, A, D). In *Morgentau* this progression occurs briefly at the word 'Lenzespracht' (spring array); in *Fussreise* it forms the essence of the piano interlude that reintroduces the main theme on the last page, in each case leading back into the original melody. None of these points is common in Wolf's music and the last two are rather rare. This may be just coincidence, or at most a subconscious reminiscence. There is another possible explanation, namely that the idea of morning freshness suggested to Wolf a musical expression of this kind.

25

2. Das Vöglein: The little bird
5th–12th April 1878

The bird flutters down from the tree, and then back again; now near, now hiding; and now close again, teasing.

Try to touch it, and it's gone. Be quiet and patient. If once it comes really close to you it surely won't escape.

And is it so hard to wait, in the flower-filled garden?

Never despair; it will be yours one day. Even then it can only sing for you; but how sweetly it sings.

Hebbel was a dramatic poet of some importance. His lyrics are for the most part well turned but ponderous. The allegory of this early love-song is trite, but the neatly rhymed short lines with their untypically lively rhythm invite musical setting. The words therefore present a mild problem which the young composer solves with some distinction. The music combines graphic allusions to birdsong with a youthful wistfulness that still appeals. The vocal melody has an engaging lilt. But clearly Wolf is still serving his apprenticeship, and this song need not detain us.

NOTE. The theme proposed in the very first bar is an elementary form of Wolf's musical equivalent for love, from which he was later on to fashion so many phrases of exquisite refinement (motif 13).

3. Die Spinnerin: Spinning song
2nd May 1878

How can I go on with my spinning indoors on so bright a day? The wheel stops, the thread breaks. I must go out, mother dear.

The spring sun is peeping through the panes; who could sit indoors and work? I must go and fly with the birds.

I must feel the breeze and find flowers to make a garland for my hair. And if young men come shouting by I'll run away and hide.

But if one young man offered me the very flowers I wanted, what should I do? Might I not smile at him, mother, and stay by his side?

There are several Rückert settings by the mature Schubert; all are superb. But this early Wolf setting of a Rückert poem has little to offer nowadays, save for some interesting anticipations of the mature composer. It must have been exhilarating at eighteen to write a piano part consisting essentially of themes and variations in the traditional vein, interspersed with passionate outbursts of a highly original turn of musical phrase. As Wolf commented later in life on other examples of his early work – 'man spürt schon das kleine Wölferl darin' – you can tell it's a Wolf-cub.

NOTE. Wolf follows Schumann in ending a song of unstilled longing on an unresolved dominant seventh. But this device, though original and effective in Schumann, where it occurs in the short first song of a song-cycle (*Dichterliebe*), is notably less impressive in Wolf's much longer and less inspired song which stands on its own with no sequel.

4. Wiegenlied im Sommer: A summer lullaby
17th December 1882

Sunset; my child in the cradle. One bird still awake sings 'Good night, dear child.'

The cradle rocks gently. What is it the flies are humming? 'Good night, dear child.'

And angels come down and cover my baby with their wings and sing 'Good night, dear child.'

The lullabies of Mendelssohn and Schumann are well known, and those of Schubert and Brahms are world-famous. In none of them do the words count for much; the endearing tenderness of the music is all that matters. Wolf's song worthily follows this great tradition; it should be heard more often.

The essence of Reinick's poem, for what it is worth, is the idea of a rocking cradle. Wolf's accompaniment figure combines two strands of single notes into a gently rocking melodic background over which the voice sings its own irresistibly fresh and sweet melody.

NOTE. The vocal line, especially in the refrain at 'Kindlein, gute Nacht', is an early example of the lifting and dipping melody that the idea of 'singing' often suggested to Wolf (motif 10).

5. Wiegenlied im Winter: A winter lullaby
20th December 1882

Sleep, sweet child. Wild winds are knocking at the window; and if they see a child awake they puff in snowflakes for a white quilt to cover him.

Sleep, sweet child; the night winds will bring you bright dreams about candles shining on the Christmas tree.

Sleep, sweet child. When the sun wakes the winds will blow on your

cheeks; then spring will come and the winds will blow the whole world awake,
so that the sleeping garden bursts into flower.
  So sleep now while the winds blow; sleep, sweet child, sleep.

This companion piece to the previous song has much of the same charm, and more invention; but the invention is not wholly original, or appropriate. The piano prelude sounds as if it is about to turn into a Chopin ballade, an impression not entirely dispelled by what follows. Wolf feels impelled to illustrate the poem; so the winds of Reinick's verses blow through the music.

But in the welcome moments when the piano part stops puffing and blowing there are some wholly Wolfian passages of beatific tenderness in the music, for example the passage on the last page containing the final quiet repetitions of the refrain 'Schlaf' ein, mein süsses Kind'.

NOTES. 1. The persistent flattened sixth (F flat in A flat major) is here used as a passing harmony. In another song, in the same key, inviting sleep, the Mörike *An den Schlaf* (41), it is an integral part of a masterly tonal structure.

  2. We may also compare *Die ihr schwebet* from the Spanish Songbook (140) as another song concerned with winds and a cradled child. This was written only eight years later; in musical accomplishment, it is richer by many lifetimes.

6. Mausfallen-Sprüchlein: Mousetrap magic
18th June 1882

(*The child is to walk three times round the trap and say:*)
        'Little guests, little house.
        Mrs Mouse, or Mr Mouse
        come whisking in tonight
        when the moon shines bright, bright.
            Be very sure
            to shut the door
            behind you!
            and do not fail
            to watch your tail,
            mind you!
            And then we'll sing
            and dance in a ring.
            Take care!
            Beware!
        I think my cat will be dancing there.'

It is easy to see why this delightful miniature, the most characteristic song of Wolf's young manhood, has become popular. The charm of Mörike's verses is real, though hardly possible to communicate in translation, and the gaiety and delicacy of Wolf's setting are evident and irresistible. It gives a very convincing account of mouse-charming. The piano has a series of tiny phrases that come popping up in the treble, like the emergence of a tentative whisker, and are tempted out very slightly further each time by the alluring vocal melody. At the hushed repeated 'Mondenschein' (moonlight) the response becomes more perceptible. Little trills and runs appear, and there is soon a hint of apprehension at the recitative passages – 'mach aber die Tür fein hinter dir zu', etc. (be very sure to close the door behind you). The menaced tail, the dancing and singing, the menacing cat, are all treated in music as appealing as it is witty.

But it seems a pity that this likeable little piece should win plaudits when many far finer Wolf songs, including some in a similar vein, remain in comparative obscurity.

NOTES. 1. To take only one example; musical material similar to that in the piano interlude here after the second 'Dein Schwänzchen' is put to infinitely finer uses in *Gleich und Gleich* (110).

2. The interpretation of this song is often sentimental. Good-hearted sopranos apparently believe that Mörike's child is wholly disposed to innocent merriment. It must surely be possible, without actually singing the song in such a way as to invite prosecution by the R.S.P.C.A., to convey the mischief that is so manifest in the verses and the music.

Six songs to words by
Scheffel, Mörike, Goethe and Kerner
[Peters Edition 3154, Nos. 13–18]

---

7. Wächterlied auf der Wartburg (Neujahrsnacht des Jahres 1200): Watchman's song from the watch tower (New Year's night of the year 1200)

24th January 1887

Sound out, trumpets from the high tower, in the starry night! Praise Him whose hand guides the planets safely through space, and the soul through strife to eternity.

A new century dawns: happy he who goes on his way with a pure heart. Though the times now go in armour there are golden years ahead; and the true-hearted warrior shall find grace.

Let each man act boldly and look to his duty, be he monk, soldier, smith or ploughman. So we ask your blessing, Lord, on this tower, this land: here at the turn of the century we pray for your grace.

Wolf's two songs to words by the popular historical romancer Joseph von Scheffel, this and no. 9 below, were written shortly after the poet's death in 1886. They were no doubt intended as a special tribute. This song, though of no outstanding merit, is vigorous and striking. There is much to admire in the stirring vocal melodies, one of which is later used in effective counterpoint in the piano part, and in the strength of the piano writing generally. But the poem is not good enough to sustain for long at a time the impression of staunch devoutness that it seeks to convey, and the same is true of Wolf's music. In both, the effort to achieve the heights of nobility and grandeur is a little too apparent. Without superlative artistry of performance, the result will sound less like the dawn of a new century than the start of a new school term.

NOTES. 1. There is a typical uncertainty of accentuation at the half-bar which in later songs, especially those of the Spanish songbook, suggests that the piano part is preconceived independently.

2. The piano part at 'Ein Jahrhundert will zerrinnen' (a century is about to pass) is akin to the music later used by Wolf in verbal contexts suggestive of mystery or magic (motif 19).

3. The rising octaves in the piano left hand at 'Dazu Herr dein Segen spende'

(so pour out your blessing, Lord) are later used in contexts denoting manly pride and vigour (motif 6).

4. Ten years later Wolf wrote a theme, which has much in common with the music of this song, expressing the essential nobility of the character Manuel Venegas, in the unfinished opera of that name.

8. Der König bei der Krönung: The King at the Coronation
13th March 1886

Dedicated at the altar to your service, my fatherland; how I am yours. Now let me proclaim the right and the truth, or die. And I pray for peace in my time, so that I may shine like a sun over my fatherland and my house.

The poem is by Mörike, and musically the song is not dissimilar from many of the later Mörike songs of 1888, though well below their general level of achievement. There is something Wagnerian about the hymn-like quality of the moving chords of the accompaniment and their very unhymnlike harmonic progressions. Wolf does not often assume the mantle of Wagner; and when he does it hangs awry. His own essential genius was worlds apart from that of the master he so fervently admired. At the same time, authentically lyrical Wolfian traits of intimate treatment of the text are discernible in this song. The independence and appeal of the melodic line; the slight stress by prolongation on the first word as well as the last in '*wie* bin ich *dein*' (how I am yours) to underline the sense of how whole-hearted the service to the fatherland is to be; and the way in which this simple idea simply stated is transformed musically into an idea of correspondingly greater complexity and richness at the closing words 'dass ich wie eine Sonne strahle dem Vaterland und meinem Haus'; these features are admirable and characteristic. There is good opportunity here for effective and compelling singing.

NOTE. The subject of Mörike's poem is also that of Goethe's *Königlich Gebet* (116). Neither these poems nor their settings are among the best or most typical work of their authors, but it is interesting to compare them.

9. Biterolf (im Lager von Akkon 1190): Biterolf (in camp at Acre, 1190)
26th December 1886

Battle weary and sunburned, far away on a heathen shore, I think of my green-forested homeland. Soft bright starlight, be my messenger, greet my sweetheart far away over the sea.

My sword keeps enemies at bay on all sides, but there is no armour

31

*against my longing for home. Yet despite the heart's lament I shall hold out
undaunted; a soldier in God's cause bears his cross uncomplaining.*

Scheffel's account of the feelings of Biterolf the crusader has moved
Wolf in one respect only, and that the subsidiary one. Love and longing
for a far homeland and an absent sweetheart are emotions that the
composer could understand and transcribe. The piano prelude has
strength and tenderness; and the vocal melody begins memorably.
From 'waldgrünes Thüringland' (green-forested Thuringia) to 'weit
über Meer' (far away over the sea) voice and piano combine in a melting
strain that is all longing and sweetness.

Then the song suffers a decline. The notion of being a doughty and
uncomplaining warrior in God's cause has evidently made no very great
appeal to the composer, and even the accented chords and free harmonic
progressions can do little to help. There are still enjoyable moments
whenever the text relapses into wistfulness: but the contrast between
the appropriateness of this music and the inadequacy of the rest disturbs the balance of the song.

NOTE. A similar patchiness – exquisite treatment of tender sentiments, banal
rendering of forthright sentiments – may be found in some of the Eichendorff
songs (66, 77, 83). The next song is also of interest from a similar point of view.

10. Beherzigung: A lesson learned
1st March 1887

*Cowardice, timidity, hesitation; these cannot avert sorrow, or make you
free.*
   But resistance, determination, strength; these bring the help of the gods!

This is the first of Wolf's published settings of a poem by the greatest
of all German poets, Goethe. Like the early Mörike song (8 above) it
foreshadows the greatness to come. Considered as a purely musical
construction it has great interest and merit; as a restatement of poetic
thought in musical terms it is less convincing. The piano prelude has
chromatically drooping right-hand chords, indicating uncertainty and
diffidence. There is a hectic intensity in the music which suggests that
these are thought of more as personal idiosyncrasies than as common
human failings. The unifying rhythm c ♩♩♫♩ is reiterated in the
left hand while the voice contributes its troubled phrases rising to a
massive climax, for no very clear reason, at 'macht dich nicht frei'
(does not make you free). Then the piano takes up a new theme, in the

same rhythm, now appearing in both hands; and the vocal phrases ring out with great vigour and confidence, the last ('rufet die Arme der Götter herbei') being declaimed three times through an accompaniment of hammered chords that ring out decisively in the piano postlude.

NOTES. 1. This music perhaps tells us more about Wolf himself than about Goethe's poem. It is reasonable to suppose that Wolf intended to give an objective account of the meaning of the text; but the music so exaggerates and distorts the simple contrast of the verses that some special explanation seems called for. Instead of weakness and strength we are given a convoluted shyness and an aggressive brashness, thematically related as if to illustrate the point that they are two aspects of one personal inferiority feeling. This is done brilliantly well. But it is just not what the poem means.

2. The contrast in the poem is a recurrent motif in Goethe's work, and one has only to compare this song with later settings of similar poems, e.g. the later *Beherzigung* (103) and the second *Cophtisches Lied* (100), to appreciate the amazing rapidity of Wolf's development.

3. It may be felt that the device of a thematically unifying rhythm is here carried too far. The same criticism might be levelled at the later use of this device, e.g. in the far finer song *In der Frühe* (36).

4. A rather odd feature of Wolf's work is the use of the chord or tonality of F♯ major, often quite arbitrarily, for feelings of extreme exuberance. Here at 'frei' the chord appears in force.

11. Wanderers Nachtlied: Wanderer's song in the night
30th January 1887

You are the Heaven-sent balm for all pain, twice healing him who is twice afflicted; and I am weary of the world and its joys and sorrows.
Then come, sweet peace, come into my heart.

Goethe's poem is so simple and self-sufficient that musical commentary is superfluous. The only real chance for a composer is to find a melody as limpid and moving as the words themselves. This Schubert achieved in his lovely setting. Wolf's setting is, on the whole, colourless and vague. His melodies are not sufficiently resilient to stand the strain imposed by the emotional tension of the verses. But the song has moments of beauty and inventiveness – the tired drooping piano phrases at the mention of weariness ('ach, ich bin des Treibens müde'), and the way in which, at the final invocation ('Süsser Friede, komm, ach komm in meine Brust') the piano musingly repeats the melodies allotted to the voice for the opening description of the nature of peace.

NOTES. 1. At bars 1–2 etc. is the reflective idea of motif 21.

2. Much of the musical essence of this song, including this motif, is recaptured in the Mörike *Gebet* (40) in a more precise form.

12. Zur Ruh', zur Ruh': To rest, to rest

16th June 1883

Rest you then, weary limbs; and tired eyelids, close. I am alone, the world left behind; the night must come so that I can find the light.

  Take me where in darkest night the light is shining; far away from earth and its sorrows, through night and dream, bring me home.

A moving oration was spoken by Dr Michael Haberlandt at Wolf's funeral. He described the composer's short tormented life, his dedication to his art, and his achievement – for which, the speech concluded, 'take the late, the all too late, thanks of the world with you into your last resting-place. And now, as you sang in one of your loveliest songs . . .' – and the speaker quoted the first part of Kerner's poem above. So this song has a special place in the affection of those who love Wolf's music. Its basic concept is undeniably fine, and a restrained performance can give it a solemnity not unworthy of the last rites of a composer who was buried beside Schubert and Beethoven. Nevertheless it is not among his outstanding successes. The highest level of achievement is not to be expected from Wolf at the age of twenty-three; the time was not yet ripe.

The first page of the song is impressive, with appealing melodies and sensitively modelled accompaniment. Unfortunately, the second part of the poem is much weaker than the first. It has nothing of substance to add; nor has the corresponding music. The young composer worked, perhaps, too hard at filling this poetic void with musical effect. In later years, one feels, he would not have relied on the sequential treatment of melody to such an extent as he does here at 'O führt mich', etc. (Take me), and would have recoiled from the idea of proceeding through night and dream by way of a crescendo up to a fortissimo six-four chord and a sustained swelling top A flat.

II. The Mörike songs

[Peters Edition 3140-3]

Eduard Mörike (1804–75) has been reckoned with Goethe and Rilke among the greatest of German lyric poets. Yet his work is limited in quantity and range, and, like his life as clergyman and teacher, outwardly uneventful. He has little of Goethe's magnificent intellectual vigour, or of Rilke's passionate search for inward truth. Instead his best poems have a quiet, seemingly passive, quality which is easy to perceive but hard to describe. Imagination, religious devotion, realism and humour in the content of the poems, folk-song and the classic tradition in their form, are some of the component parts of this quality. But its precise definition has been the despair of students and examiners for years.

Something of its essence was conveyed by another of Wolf's poets, Gottfried Keller, who when Mörike died said that it was as if a fine June day had passed away with him. There is indeed a quiet radiance about Mörike's poetry, as if it were in a state of grace; and Wolf's response to it brought about a sudden belated and almost Pentecostal release of his creative genius.

The poems chosen are fully representative of each aspect of Mörike's art. This songbook as a whole is unique for its absorption of the essence of one great poet's work into music of a comparable quality.

13 (M 1). Der Genesene an die Hoffnung: To Hope, on recovering from illness

6th March 1888

Day dawned deathly pale: but already I had found you, dear goddess of Hope, and victory was assured.

I had sacrificed to all the gods but you: you stood aside, forgotten at the feast.

Oh forgive me; stand out from your twilight, let me look up once like a child at your moonbright face; take me, just once without pain, in your arms.

Wolf chose this song to stand at the head of the published volume of the Mörike songs, no doubt because the poem had a deep personal significance for him. In 1888 he knew, after long delay, the joy of great achievement.

The prelude begins with slow bleak bass octaves that come groping menacingly up the scale and are still searching as the voice enters with a similar theme. Then warm comforting chords are heard, with a broader vocal line. Voice and piano swell exultantly towards a high G sharp at the repetition of 'der Sieg gewonnen hiess' (victory was assured). Hushed chords now introduce pleading melodies in both voice and piano: the music is all love and gratitude, culminating in the restrained climax at 'mondenhelle Angesicht' (moonbright face) to a vocal phrase as compelling as the poetic phrase. Here the voice soars softly to the high G sharp before falling in a long fluctuating melodic line through nearly two octaves humbly and prayerfully down to the last low notes at 'deinem Arm'. A heartfelt Amen cadence from the piano ends the song.

NOTES. 1. In general Wolf is the most objective of song-writers; but he is human enough to allow his personal emotions to colour the interpretation of his text from time to time. This can detract from the value of the work as a setting of the poet's words. Here, for instance, the repetition of 'bis der Sieg gewonnen hiess', all set about with fanfares, has little justification in the poem; the music of exultation is at odds with the poetry of repentance.

2. The high G sharp to E major harmony at the word 'Sieg' recurs at the same syllable in *Morgenstimmung* (234) written eight years later.

3. A slow rising semitone characterizes the visitation of Hope in this song. This is found again in *Auf eine Christblume I* (32), *Schlafendes Jesuskind* (37) and *Anakreons Grab* (114).

4. The groping bass octaves of the piano prelude are remembered in the prelude to *Alles endet* (241) in the same key (C sharp minor).

5. At 'einmal schaue' etc. the piano part assumes the worshipping rhythm

of motif 1. This is varied for one bar, at the words 'wie ein Kind', to the off-beat rhythm of motif 2.

6. For the melodic lines of voice and piano treble at the last words 'deinen Arm', see motif 14.

7. In this song the music evolves continuously. Each line of the poem is set differently. There is no formal repetition; and yet the song is an organic unity.

14 (M 2). Der Knabe und das Immlein: The boy and the bee
22nd February 1888

In the vineyard on the hill stands a little beehive; and on sultry summer days a bee goes buzzing round the sunflowers.

'Have you come from my sweetheart's garden with a message for me?' says the boy.

'No one sent me. Your sweetheart knows nothing of love; she's only a little girl just out of school. I am gathering honey for her; her mouth is watering already.'

'I wish you would tell her from me that there's nothing in all the world so sweet as hugging and kissing.'

This delicious song begins with the melancholy strain heard again throughout the following song of betrayal and heartbreak. Its effect here however is only one of wistfulness, and even this mood disappears as soon as the imagined dialogue begins. We need not assume that a bee is actually discoursing here, in the style of a Lafontaine fable; it may well be more like a bee in the bonnet. In this enchanting music, in any event, it shares the same bright melodies as the boy's thoughts of his young sweetheart, as if to make the point that the boy is talking to himself. Of course Wolf seizes the opportunities for musical illustration. Little delicate persistent trills buzz in the piano part, and there is a charming piano comment on the prickling foretaste of honey in the staccato quavers that join in with the trills at 'ihm wässert schon der Mund' (her mouth is watering already). [But under all this semi-descriptive writing there is the exquisite portrayal of the hopes and hesitancies of young love. These are blended at the repeated last lines of the poem, 'nichts Lieblichers auf Erden als wenn man herzt und küsst!' Each time these words are sung, the music begins elatedly and then drifts into a sort of wistful shyness, first in the harmony, then in the rhythm, without ever disturbing the flowing shapeliness of the vocal line. The blend of feelings is summed up in the final four bars of piano postlude – two of exultation, two of diffidence.

NOTES. I. Wolf has gone out of his way to emphasize a link between this song and the next – *Ein Stündlein wohl vor Tag*, written on the same day. The intended hint at the possibility of a tragic sequel to the present poem is gratuitously pessimistic, and it seems best to consider each song separately on its own considerable merits.

2. At 'Mein Lieb hat einen Garten' and later, there is the narrative harmony of motif 21.

3. The first two bars of the piano postlude contain a very clear early example of the converging melodic lines of Wolf's love-music (motif 13).

15 (M 3). Ein Stündlein wohl vor Tag: Just before dawn

22nd February 1888

As I lay sleeping, just before dawn, a swallow was singing on a tree by my window; I could hardly hear it, just before dawn.

'Listen to me,' it sang. 'Your lover is untrue. He lies now with another; it is just before dawn.'

Oh say no more, be silent, fly away from my tree. Oh love and truth are like a dream just before dawn.

The simple words of the refrain 'Ein Stündlein wohl vor Tag' and their sad overtones that pervade the poem are reflected in Wolf's strophic setting with its plaintive harmonies that pervade the music.

The melody suggested by the refrain

is heard some twenty times in this short song. Monotony is avoided by subtle variations of pitch and rhythm, e.g. the truncated version which occurs in the tiny prelude and postlude, and in canon in the left hand throughout. Each verse is pitched a semitone higher to match the mounting emotion of the poem in its transition from sleeping to wakefulness; yet the vocal melody is so organized that the last repetition of the refrain theme is at the same pitch as its first appearance, suggesting an endless sorrow.

So, too, with the treatment of the word 'Stündlein' (a little while) in the refrain. The first time we hear it, there is a plain simple harmony to suit sleep; thereafter, a semitonal clash of waking grief. This discord, in an accented form, is incorporated into the beginning of the last verse, at 'O *weh*, nicht weiter sag' (*Alas*, say no more). At this moment, where the words for the first time directly express sorrow, the entry of the voice occurs a bar earlier than the corresponding passage in the second verse, as if grief had compelled its utterance.

With all this refinement it is nevertheless open to question whether Wolf has quite succeeded in matching Mörike's consummate artistry. But it is doubtful whether any music for this poem could do more. The song is masterly.

NOTES. 1. The main theme of this song is also used in *Der Knabe und das Immlein* (see note 1 to 14 above).

2. It might help to note the Peters Edition with, e.g., a D flat in the first bass crotchets of bars 11 and 14, and an E natural at the first crotchet in the piano treble in bar 28, although the fact that these notes are tied makes the reading reasonably clear. In older Peters Editions an E natural needs to be marked in the voice part at 'weh' in bar 28.

16 (M 4). Jägerlied: Huntsman's song
22nd February 1888

How delicate is the tread of a bird in snow when it walks on the mountain-tops; more delicate still is my sweetheart's dear hand, writing me a letter from far away.

How swift and high is the flight of a heron in the air; but the thoughts of true love fly far higher and swifter still.

This, although perhaps not among the greatest of the Mörike songs, is particularly radiant with the mastery that suddenly shone into Wolf's song-writing in February 1888.

The time-signature of $\frac{5}{4}$ is unique in his work. In the piano part, at least, it is very precisely used, being conceived not as so often in terms of $2 + 3$ or $3 + 2$, but as an indivisible metrical unit throughout. The needs of the vocal accentuation, however, mean that this rhythm must not be taken too literally. A slight stress on the first beat of each bar for the pianist, and the natural stress of the words for the singer, are all that is required.

Of the song's sixteen bars, half are for piano solo; two to introduce the text, two to reintroduce it, and four to round it off. The whole is constructed with an exquisite intuitive craftsmanship.

This work is perhaps the first of all Wolf's songs to show his uncanny power of re-creating poetry in musical terms. It is so typical and so revealing in this respect as to be worth dwelling on for a moment, here and in the notes below. In general, one imagines Wolf reading this poem and being taken (as all who read it in German must surely be) with the sound and sense of the first line 'Zierlich ist des Vogels Tritt im Schnee' – the delicate movement of a bird walking on snow. This idea is given musical shape in the piano prelude

We need not assume that there is any deliberate intention of *depicting* this idea musically. But there is a fascinating correspondence between the poet's concept and the musician's, which lies beneath the words and beneath the music. Wolf also brings out a point that is only latent in the poem, namely, that there is something slightly unaccustomed and stilted about the bird walking in the snow, and also about the girl's handwriting. This in no way detracts from the delight of the nature-lover – or the lover – but it lends a certain new quality to this delight. If this is right, the piano introduction should be played with a con-strained delicacy, and not with the heartiness that may be suggested by the title.

NOTES. 1. There are other details of the music which may have a conceptual, or verbal, connotation, e.g.:

(a) The melody of piano and voice in bar 3 has the engaging lift and dip found in other Wolfian melodies in association with the idea of singing – a song within a song (motif 10).

(b) The piano left-hand harmony at bar 4 occurs in reflective or narrative passages (motif 21).

(c) The mediant key-changes in bars 9–11 are thematic in contexts sug-gesting yearning, aspiring; particularly in association with the idea of increasing intensities of light (motif 24).

(d) The piano's horn passages at bars 15–16 are elsewhere found in associa-tion with the idea of freedom and the open air (motif 8).

2. The interplay of musical and verbal concepts could be charted on this basis (bearing also in mind the composer's expression marks). The following attempt may be of interest to some readers and performers.

		Wolf	Mörike
Bar	1 2	A bird stepping on the snow!	
,,	3	The sight sets me singing about	a bird stepping on the snow,
,,	4	which makes me think	here on the mountain,
,,	5	tenderly, of	her hand, even more delicate,
,,	6	more delicate! how sweet,	writing to me far away,
,,	7 8	like a bird stepping on snow.	

41

Wolf	*Mörike*
Bar 9 And if a bird were to rise,	a bird high in the air
,, 10 soaring into the bright sky,	remote and free
,, 11 high and sunlit, it would still be	far less high and swift than the thoughts
,, 12 of the love I bear for her,	of my true love.
,, 13 And I go on singing,	
,, 14 singing,	
,, 15 in the open air:	
,, 16 a huntsman.	

3. Other points worth noticing are the ways in which the singing curve of the voice part for a bird in the snow (bar 3) is counterpoised by the upward curve of the melody for a bird in the air (bar 9), and the harmony of bars 5–6 is troubled at the mention of the loved one's hand, as if that hand were touched. The blend of simplicity and subtlety charged with emotion so exactly akin to that of the poem is Wolf at his most characteristic.

17 (M 5). Der Tambour: The drummer-boy
16th February 1888

(*A drummer-boy posted to France in the Napoleonic wars indulges in a little wish-fulfilment fantasy.*)
    '*If only my mother were a witch, and could cast spells; then she could be the regiment's vivandière and I'd have midnight feasts when the camp is quiet. My drum would be a dish heaped high with steaming sauerkraut, the drumsticks knife and fork, my sabre a long sausage and my shako a tankard full of Burgundy. The moon would shine to light the feast; and even though I suppose it would shine in French it would still remind me of my sweetheart far away in Germany . . . oh dear, now I've spoilt the fun . . . All the same, if only my mother could cast spells! . . . If only she could!*'

This is the song that began Wolf's creative outburst of 1888. It is not itself one of the really great songs, but gives plentiful promise of the greatness to come. It is notable for prodigality of thematic material. In four pages there are enough march tunes and rhythms for half a dozen songs. It is also notable for a deftness and wit of writing that compresses all this fertility of invention into a homogeneous whole and embellishes it on every page with illustrations of the text. The music shows how much Wolf must have enjoyed this unpretentious and good-humoured poem.
    The drum-roll in the piano that begins the song and gives it its

essential character is obvious enough, as is the drumbeat that accompanies the mention of 'die Trommel' later in the poem. But such piano passages as the delighted commentary at the thought of heaped sauerkraut; the sad echoes of the words at the repeated 'ach weh' (oh dear); and the way in which the tonality gets lost on the last page with the little tune slipping vaguely from key to key in a reverie of home and beauty, particularly the latter – all these are evidence of a new and lively impetus in song-writing, of compelling originality and power.

NOTES. I. The gay rising piano phrase at 'Marketenderin' is motif 7.

2. Fertility of invention is a feature of those of Wolf's songs which stand at the beginning of a new cycle of creativity. There is another example in the Eichendorff songbook (74, note 3); the Italian song *Dass doch gemalt* (195) is even more striking.

18 (M 6). Er ist's: Spring is here
5th May 1888

The sky is like a flutter of blue ribbons, there are sweet familiar scents in the air. Violets are already dreaming of their time to come. Listen! do you hear the soft sound of a distant harp? That is Spring himself.

The poem is paraphrased; as a setting of words, this song is not among Wolf's outstanding successes. Perhaps he chose to read into the poem the fervour and triumph which he presumably felt in this particular Spring of 1888, when he was producing masterpieces of song at a rate hardly paralleled in musical history. Such a feeling might explain the arbitrary repetitions of the text, and the way in which a shy and tender evocation of the personified spirit of Spring is concluded by a sustained high G over a thunderous accompaniment. Yet the song is a splendid *tour de force* for voice and piano, its conclusion in particular being of the utmost brilliance and energy. Setting Mörike's poem aside, the music can be greatly enjoyed for its own sake – the racing pulse of the accompaniment, the soft treble harp chords, the excitement and the dipping and soaring and final quietude of the postlude, and the free melodies and strong climaxes of the voice part.

NOTE. At 'Veilchen träumen schon' etc. both voice and piano have something of the 'mystery' of motif 19.

19 (M 7). Das verlassene Mägdlein: The girl left lonely
24th March 1888

At cockcrow, before the faint stars fade, I must stand at the hearth and kindle fire.
The flames shine, the sparks fly; I watch them, sunk in sorrow.
Suddenly I know that I have been dreaming all night long of you, my faithless lover.
Then tear on tear falls. So my day dawns; would it were over.

Mörike's few folk-song lines evoke a whole world of love and loss. The warm brightness of flames and dreams, the cold darkness of the house and the truth, make a poignant contrast which is fused into one single emotion as the poem passes from night and unawareness to daybreak and tears, evoking in this brief transition a lifetime of joys past and sorrows now and to come. This is among the great lyrics of the world, and the task of finding music to match it is a daunting one.

We know from a letter something of how Wolf came to attempt it. 'On Saturday I wrote, without having intended to, a setting of *Das verlassene Mägdlein*, already set to heavenly music by Schumann. If I set it again, it was almost against my will. But perhaps just because I was suddenly caught up in the magic of this poem, the result was outstandingly good, and I think that my song can stand comparison with Schumann's.'

It is not easy to see how any musical setting could do full justice to the fusion of contrasts in Mörike's poem. But Wolf renders as many aspects of it as are simultaneously translatable into musical terms, and the result is a masterpiece of its kind. The music is similar in inspiration to 15 above, and is again dominated by variants of one plaintive theme. It begins bleakly in A minor with a drooping vocal melody. Then it turns brighter in A major with a rising melody and a slightly livelier rhythm for a moment as the flames sparkle. In the third verse, beginning 'Plötzlich, da kommt es mir' (Suddenly I remember), wistful harmonies and a rising motif are added in the piano part. The enduring love which is hinted at but not directly expressed in the poem is indicated in the music, e.g. at the word 'geträumet' (dreamed). Here the voice part lifts, and lightens, and hushes; without any real change in texture or mood, a sudden tenderness invades the music.

This, like the poem, is essentially simple. Also, like the poem, it goes deep. But its quality may not be as immediately apparent as in many of

44

Wolf's songs. To savour it fully, one needs to have listened with attention and imagination to a great performance.

NOTES. 1. The augmented triad is used, as often in Wolf's songs, to convey pathos (motif 23). This aspect of his harmonic idiom may sound somewhat laboured nowadays.

2. The key of A minor is often found associated with a particular wistful mood, mostly in songs for a woman's voice.

3. Schumann's setting (Op. 64 no. 2) is valuable both as a comparison and in its own right.

20 (M 8). Begegnung: A meeting
22nd March 1888

What a storm there was last night! It lasted till daybreak. How clean that unbidden broom swept all the chimneys!

And startled down the wind-swept streets a girl goes walking, the colour changing in her cheeks like a wind-blown rose.

A handsome lad goes up to her; they stare at each other awkwardly, joyously.

He seems to be asking how she has found time to braid her hair – wasn't it disarranged in that storm last night?

Then he stands entranced, still dreaming of her kisses, as she rustles away round the corner.

One imagines that a chance encounter witnessed by Mörike from his window one morning gave rise to the idea of this fresh little poem. Wolf's treatment, in what is perhaps the most thematically compact of all the Mörike songs, derives from deep understanding of his poet. The idea that love is like the wind is a recurrent image in Mörike's verse. Almost any other song-writer would have gone in for good solid storm-effects in the piano part, in order to make play with the rather obvious double-meaning of the two kinds of storm. Wolf goes beyond this, to find a unity of theme and concept that refreshes and refines our appreciation of the poem. The gentle sighing accompaniment, even at its most dramatic in the prelude

45

never rises above a forte; and reaches that level only some eight times in over sixty bars. All is restraint, discretion, and allusion. A slightly different figuration, a new key, a change from minor into major, and voice and piano are suddenly bright with melody well suited to express the morning's freshness and the girl's charm, as she appears at 'Da kommt ein Mädchen'.

The sighing winds reappear in the piano interludes, and are delicately recalled as the brief meeting is described at 'Er scheint zu fragen', etc. (he seems to be asking). In the last verse the piano resumes its melodies. The vocal countermelody at first lingers dreamily on the same note, at 'der Bursche träumt noch von den Küssen' (the lad is still dreaming of her kisses), and then wells up in delight. The postlude, with typically Wolfian felicity, takes the piano's melodies that heralded the girl's arrival on the scene, and sets them sighing in the same way as the wind-theme already quoted, as the girl whisks round the corner and out of sight, herself a breeze.

NOTE. The verbal accentuation of this song is inexact. This feature in Wolf's songs often suggests that the composer is deliberately subordinating the natural stress of the words to an instrumental preconception, here no doubt the accompaniment figure.

21 (M 9). Nimmersatte Liebe: Insatiable love
24th February 1888

Love is not to be stilled with kisses. You might as well try to fill a sieve with water; you could pour water in for a thousand years; it would never be full. You could go on kissing for ever; love would never be satisfied.

Lovers are always in search of new delights; today we kissed till our lips were sore. She was quite still, like a lamb under the knife, but her eyes implored me – go on, the more it hurts, the better!

Love is like that, and always has been; even for King Solomon himself, with all his wisdom.

'Yet another new song' wrote the delighted Wolf to a friend in February 1888. 'You'll go wild with delight when you hear it' – one reason for this being, he explained, that at the end it bursts out into a rollicking students' song. So indeed it does, after the music has duly explored, with rather more delicacy than the poem, one aspect of amorous experience. The piano prelude begins with a repeated phrase

which so clearly mimicks speech that we are surprised not to find words written in. Since they are not, the precise sense remains conjectural; but its effect of pleading is apparent enough. The vocal line looks as if it should be taken quite fast. But Wolf asks for a 'very moderate' tempo; the words are meant to be heard. The piano first shares in the melody, then – to enhance the idea of vain endeavour towards a love fulfilled or a sieve filled full – has softly syncopated chords which proceed in increasingly yearning leaps ranging from a fifth to two octaves at 'tust ihr nie zu Willen' (love would never be satisfied). At this point the voice has a characteristically beautiful Wolfian melody of small compass but great effect. The brief expressive piano interlude is again akin to speech; this time the sense is easier to follow since the right hand is playing a subtle variant of the vocal phrase just heard. Excitement grows with the search after new delights in the next verse. The melody becomes more chromatic and intense. The pulse of the piano part quickens with small repeated semiquaver chords. The chords that accompany the following expressive phrases, linking pain with pleasure, are masochism itself in their musical weakness – repeated notes, in augmented fifths, shifted off the beat – weakness of melody, harmony and rhythm. At the end the promised students' song arrives; not perhaps as rollicking as all that, but contrived with brilliant technical assurance. This section is marked 'Mit Humor'; and we may safely assume that one point about Solomon had not escaped Wolf's attention – namely that he is popularly known for the number of his wives as well as the extent of his wisdom. Here Wolf reorganizes the material of the first part of the song and displays its latent possibilities for the depiction of forthright jollity as well as romantic yearnings. This delightful burlesque of popular song is handled with a wit and restraint that suggest a latent genius for comic opera. The piano postlude offers the same pleading comments as the prelude, this time with a quiet but decisive full close.

NOTES. I. The striking passage at 'Das Mädchen hielt in guter Ruh',' etc. combines two typical aspects of Wolf's thematic procedures.

(*a*) the chain of augmented fifths, here standing for maudlin sentiment (motif 23).

(*b*) the chords on the off beat standing for childish helplessness (motif 2).

2. The rhythms used throughout the song are an interesting study. For ♪ ♩ ♪ in particular see motif 1.

3. For affinities with the somewhat earlier love-song *Frage und Antwort* see 47 note 2.

22 (M 10). Fussreise: A country walk
21st March 1888

When I go out walking the woods in the early morning, drinking in the air and the sunlight, then, like the birds singing in the trees, like golden grapes feeling the first morning sun, I feel what Adam must have felt in the dawn of creation – the bliss of those first mornings in the Garden of Eden.

So the old Adam that stern preachers condemn can't be so bad after all; it is still the love and praise, world without end, of God the Creator and Preserver.

And with God's grace my whole life would be just such a walk on just such a morning.

Delightedly, Wolf wrote to a friend 'I have to retract my opinion that the *Erstes Liebeslied eines Mädchens* is the best song I have ever written; for what I wrote this afternoon, *Fussreise*, is a million times better. When you have heard this song, you can have only one wish – to die.' It is an odd way of putting it; but one sees what he means. The song creates and communicates a very real sense of release, exaltation and abiding delight.

Some may feel that, here as elsewhere in the Mörike songs, in *Neue Liebe* (42) for instance, Wolf's vision is more secular than that of Mörike's poem paraphrased above. But somehow the authenticity of the music takes it outside praise and blame, and turns this kind of comment into pedantry.

The brief prelude, with its easy melodic lilt and rhythms that sound throughout the song's 83 bars, sets the scene. This, one recognizes, is just how a man might feel, walking at peace with himself and the world, in love with life (or just in love), invigorated with the morning air, humming a little tune, about to break into a song.

At the inevitably right moment, the voice strikes in with its fine swinging melody. The piano, not to be outdone, joins in zestfully at the same moment; and the two set off together with a light step, their tunes blending into one exhilaration as the melodic curves go lifting and dipping into the words 'Hügel auf und ab' (uphill and down). The freshness and immediacy of this music, achieved by the simplest of means, have an irresistible forward impetus. This, like the thought of the words, carries through and over the piano interludes; the song walks on air. When the piano prelude theme resumes, lively in the higher octaves, the voice strikes in as before, alighting gently on the word 'dann' (then) as if it had never really left off. It sweeps on in the same melodies, lovingly extended and brightened, first to 'Morgensonne' (morning sunshine) and then, through an interlude now delicately altered to suggest small stirrings of exultation, to 'Paradieseswonne' (bliss of the Garden of Eden), with a joyous echo from the piano.

After this recreation of the feeling of the morning the next section provides something of a contrast. The voice drops in pitch, and the music becomes quieter and more reflective – 'also bist du nicht so schlimm, o alter Adam' (so you aren't so bad after all, old Adam). But it becomes elated again once the depressing teachings of 'die strengen Lehrer', the stern teachers and preachers, are decisively rejected. The accompaniment, having thoughtfully tried out various harmonies, is ready to join in the singing again at 'liebst und lobst du immer doch' (you still love and praise) on to the strong F sharp major climax at 'deinen lieben Schöpfer und Erhalter' (your beloved Creator and Pre-server). And with this thought, as the voice ends its melodic curve, the brisk walking accompaniment is contented. For eight bars it breathes pure delight, leading back happily to the original key of D major to rejoin the voice in the repetition of the opening themes with which, in a paean of rejoicing, the song ends. In the postlude the swinging tunes stride past and away with a light heart, leaving lightened hearts behind them.

NOTES. 1. The correct tempo of this song is a matter of some uncertainty. Much depends on taste and technique; but certain points seem clear. The music is idealized; it is not about the act of walking, but about the feeling of walking on air. This is reflected in Wolf's direction 'ziemlich bewegt' (rather quick) and his use of quaver and semiquaver rests throughout, and single notes rather than chords in the continuous bass rhythmic figure. The texture looks light and crisp on the printed page, and must surely sound so in performance. Once the sturdy plodding of hobnailed boots gets into this song, the exhilaration dies forlornly out of it.

2. At 'Hügel auf und ab' is the finest example of the lilting melody that moments of elated contentment suggested to Wolf (motif 9).

3. Some parallels between this song and the much earlier *Morgentau* (1), and also the contemporary *Gebet* (40) and *Selbstgeständnis* (64), are suggested in the notes to those songs.

4. Note the occurrence (at bar 7, etc.), in this song of freedom and the open air, of the horn passages of motif 8.

5. The climax at 'Lieben Schöpfer', etc. has the tonality of F sharp major, which Wolf often reaches at moments of great elation.

23 (M 11). An eine Aeolsharfe: To an Aeolian Harp
15th April 1888

Aeolian harp, leaning on the ivied wall: play me your sweet lament again.

The singing winds come flower-filled from the green grave of him I loved so much, blowing into my heart, how sweet, sweet, and into the harpstrings; quickening with my yearning and dying away again.

But there comes a sudden gust of wind, and the harp cries aloud, to my sweet terror; and the ripe rose, shaken, strews all its petals at my feet.

Aeolian harps were dear to the nineteenth century; there is something romantic in every sense about a stringed instrument played by the wind. But Mörike's poem, and Wolf's music, go far beyond mere romance. The song begins, without piano prelude, in soft invocation. Coaxing arpeggio chords provide the accompaniment. All this is beautifully drawn, in melodic recitative of the utmost quietude; there is hardly any rhythmic impulse, no breath of wind in the air. So the song continues as far as 'Klage' (lament). Then, in a magic moment, the most delicate of breezes strays into the song. Successive harp notes drift up slowly and softly on the piano, barely audible at first (*pppp* is the composer's direction) then gaining slightly in strength and immeasurably in sweetness as slow chordal melodies are added high above them. In between the voice weaves its own independent melodies. At every turn the music mirrors the indescribably rich and sweet melancholy of the poem, compounded of grief for a dead brother, surrender to the radiance of summer, and, over and through all, the wind-blown music latent in the words that Wolf finds and releases and sets singing anew.

The composer wrote this music without ever having heard an Aeolian harp. He later found one on a country walk, and was delighted to discover that the instrument sounded just as he had imagined it.

NOTES. 1. Brahms' early setting of the same poem, Op. 19 no. 5, is by no means negligible.

2. The words 'wie süss' are heard four times in the third page of this song,

thrice with a falling semitone – the interval used in the same kind of rhythmic and harmonic context for the same words at bar 8 of *Der Genesene an die Hoffnung* (13) dated five weeks earlier.

3. One of the prevailing rhythms, $\frac{4}{2}$ ♩♪ ♩ ♪♪ etc. is allied to the self-surrendering rhythm of motif 1.

24 (M 12). Verborgenheit: Seclusion
13th March 1888

Would that the world would leave me alone to know my own joy, my own sorrow. I grieve without knowing why; sunlight shines through my tears.
 Through my gloom bright joy shines blissfully into my heart. Would that this world would leave me alone to know my own joy, my own sorrow.

It is perhaps a pity that this song should have attained so wide a popularity when many greater Wolf songs remain comparatively unknown. Wolf himself expressed dissatisfaction with it in later years. One can see why. There are some very untypical touches of sentimentality in the music. Without the utmost restraint on the part of singer and pianist the result can easily suggest a drawing-room ballad cosiness which is false to Mörike, and unfair to Wolf. For *Verborgenheit* is not wholly unworthy of its composer. It has tenderness, even nobility; its melodies are memorable, and its structure shapely and effective.

Two bars of quiet prelude lead to the entry of the voice with a simple melody entwining and interchanging with the countermelody of the sustained top notes of the accompaniment. There is a climax at the word 'Wonne' (joy) matched with diatonic harmonies. The simultaneous joy and sorrow of the middle section is interpreted by an increased flexibility of harmony, though the strong melodic impulse never falters. As joy triumphs, the real climax, a transmuted version of the first, arrives at 'wonniglich' (blissfully). The tonic chord of E flat major shines out splendidly, greatly heightened in effect by the fact that it is being heard for the first time for some fifteen bars. Then quietude supervenes and the song ends as it began, in gentle intercession.

NOTE. Avoiding or delaying the tonic chord to give added effect to its later use is a feature of Wolf's song-writing, particularly effective in the Italian songs, e.g. 205 and 224.

25 (M 13). Im Frühling: In spring
8th May 1888

Here I lie on the hill of spring, the clouds my wings, a bird flying by. Tell me my love, my own for ever, tell me where you live, that I may live with you. But like the breezes you have no home. My sunflower heart lies open, yearning in love and hope. What is it you want of me, Spring? When will my longing be stilled?

I see the cloud moving, and the river; the golden kiss of the sun drives deep into my veins. My dazed eyes close as if in sleep, my ears hear nothing but the hum of the honey bee . . . .

I think of this and that, I yearn without knowing why. It is half joy, half lament. Tell me, my heart, what memories are you weaving here in the darkling shade of golden-green boughs?

Memories of past days that lie too deep for words.

In this typically Wolfian masterpiece the radiance of a great poem is rekindled in music. The song flows in an endless stream of melody from start to finish, and every bar testifies to the depth and authenticity of the composer's response to the poet's mood. The first four bars are a sensuous but direct equivalent for the opening line, as to the piano's idling melodies the voice adds its own – 'Hier lieg' ich auf dem Frühlingshügel'. Then voice and piano pursue their own separate dreaming and wistful ways, though all the music grows out of these first few bars, branching and flowering out into new melodies. The last of these begins to sing the persistent yearning phrases that are the heart and joy of this song, at the first mention of love – 'Ach, sag' mir, alleinzige Liebe'. They fade sadly after 'ihr habt kein Haus' (you have no home) and lead back to the opening strain again. At the mention of the sunflower, 'Der Sonnenblume gleich', the first melody is gently opened out. In the piano part, octaves are added. The phrases are expanded; the vocal melody broadens, the harmonies are a little brighter, a little higher; and voice and piano flower as before. At the next mention of love – 'Lieben und Hoffen' – the yearning melody returns and sings on and on in the right hand, unwilling to cease; through the invocation to Spring 'Frühling, was bist du gewillt?', then softly, lullingly, down into the left hand when the voice resumes with the words 'Die Wolke seh' ich wandeln' (I see the cloud moving). It is now a lullaby melody, with new melodic inventions and gently falling right-hand chords, until voice and piano drift together into the trance of which Mörike speaks; closing dazed eyes, 'als schliefen sie ein' (as if falling asleep), hearing only the sound of the bee, as in the piano interlude the melodies go drowsing and day-dreaming on. Then this interlude stirs, rouses, and drifts gently back to the first strain again. Now at 'ich denke dies und denke das' (I think of this and that), the voice enters a bar later than at the outset, as if awareness were returning only gradually. The mutual flowering and brightening of voice and piano follow as before, growing again into the persistent yearning theme. The last question 'was webst du für Erinnerung?' (what memories are you weaving?) is asked and answered in a broad vocal line to slow solemn harmonies that have been at the heart of the music throughout, as the answer lies at the heart of the poem – 'Alte unnennbare Tage!' (literally, 'old unnameable days').

NOTES. 1. The theme described as 'yearning' in the comments above (piano r.h. bars 13–20 et seq.) is found in similar contexts in other songs (motif 12). Its lullaby use here emphasizes its musical affinities with the themes that Wolf found appropriate in contexts expressive of night and dream (motif 18).

2. Throughout the song this persistent 'yearning' theme is associated with a steadily falling bass line in the piano – a figuration similar to that associated in later songs with the idea of 'loneliness' (motif 15).

3. See 37, note 3.

26 (M 14). Agnes: Agnes' song
3rd May 1888

Summer's roses have soon faded, all too soon. If my lover had kept faith, kept faith with me, it would not grieve me so.

Girls are singing happily, happily at the harvest. But I am sick, sick at heart; there is no more joy for me.

I creep through the valley, through the valley as if lost in dream, to the hillside where he vowed to be true.

There I weep alone, while the ribbon he gave me plays in the wind.

At first hearing, the vocal melody takes precedence and the piano part 'accompanies'. Wolf has seen that the gracefully cadenced repetitions of the poem –

> 'Rosenzeit, wie schnell vorbei,
> Schnell vorbei,
> Bist du doch gegangen!' –

call for this treatment. The vocal line has wistful appeal; and when Mörike's lines are allowed to speak in terms of simple melody, plainly harmonized, as at 'Schnitterinnen singen' the result is enchanting. But there is great grief in the poem, and Wolf would not be Wolf if he did not feel this and provide an equivalent for it. So the piano part, though kept in the background, is inflected with great subtlety. Wide rising discordant intervals (minor ninths) are heard in the slow piano prelude, and form the bass of the piano part throughout the first verse; while the treble has light chords which follow the rhythm of the vocal melody, mainly in contrary motion. In the second verse the minor ninths disappear and a new falling motif sounds in the piano treble to a new rhythm ♩ ♪ ♪ ♪ ♪, etc. This echoes the vocal line at the word 'gegangen' (gone) in the first verse. It is as if, while the voice is singing of the reapers at the harvest, the accompaniment were saying to itself 'gone, gone', softly and insistently, a nagging pain. This same rhythm becomes incorporated into the bass in the third verse and makes the recurring leaps of the minor ninth more poignant and desperate than before. In this verse the falling phrase already noted occurs at the word 'verloren' – and the piano takes up this strain again in the last verse with a similar effect. 'Lost, lost' say the repeated drooping phrases of the piano part that sound throughout the verse and bring the song to a close in the short postlude.

NOTE. Wolf's setting is perhaps over-stylized. Brahms' pleasant treatment of the same poem (Op. 59 no. 5) goes to the other extreme; it is homespun. One feels that the essence of Mörike's poem is not wholly captured by either.

27 (M 15). Auf einer Wanderung: On a journey
11th March 1888

I came into a friendly little town, with the red light of sunset lying about its streets. Then I heard a voice singing. I cannot say why, but it sounded like golden bells, or a choir of nightingales; quickening the air, refreshing the roses.

Long I stood, surprised by joy.

I remember no more until outside the town the world lay broad and bright with the skies surging in a tumult of crimson, the little town lying behind me in a golden haze, the sound of the millstream among the alders, the mill in the valley. For a moment I had lost my way in a dream. Oh Muse, you have touched my heart with a breath of love.

Mörike's poems often take place in a timeless world or a timeless moment (as also in, e.g., *Im Frühling* and *Um Mitternacht*). This poem distils an essence of pure joy in one such moment, and Wolf finds for it a musical equivalent of matchless perfection.

The music grows out of the lilting four-bar piano prelude. This sets the mood of the first part of the song; light and carefree, yet somehow expectant and incomplete. It is really an accompaniment figure and is so used but, as in so many of Schubert's songs, its four-part harmony contains independent melodies. Into this gay background one of these melodies (the 'tenor' part) enters as the vocal line – 'In ein freundliches Städtchen tret' ich ein'. Expectancy increases. Slight harmonic and rhythmic changes bring a new depth and colour into the music of the next line. The lilting melodies become bright in D major, mellow in D flat. Then, at the crucial words, 'eine Stimme scheint ein Nachtigallenchor' (a voice sounds like a choir of nightingales) the music takes a magical turn. It enters briefly into the neutral C major. There the piano's melody shifts off the beat to the half-bar like a catch in the breath; and its first three notes sing and tail off as if overwhelmed. This moment of surprise by joy now sounds out in E major in the piano part at this first quiet climactic moment of the song. Here Wolf directs the pianist to reduce the tone still further from *pp* to *ppp*. This allows the voice to shine out on the sustained first syllable of the word 'Nachtigallenchor', creating a vivid impression of tone contrast. All the very considerable emotive force of the music is now concentrated on the one notion of utter amazement and delight that a circumstance so naïve as hearing a voice singing at sunset could on this one occasion seem so sweet to one listener.

All this is indicated with the utmost restraint. Only at the following words 'dass die Blüten beben' (so that the blossoms quiver) is the pent-up emotion allowed to come out; and then it bursts out, overflowing with excitement and gratitude. Then in a piano interlude that moment of singing is savoured again, anticipating the explanation in the voice part 'Lang hielt' ich staunend' (Long I stood amazed). The piano has gradually returned to the gay strolling themes of the prelude, now no longer jaunty but miraculously transformed by slight changes into a mood of ineffable dreaminess. This wandering tranced music again anticipates and illustrates the voice's explanation: 'I do not know how I reached the gate of the town.'

Now the mood changes from dream to vision. A new though related theme is heard in the piano. As the voice sings in expressive phrases of the crimson sunset, the golden haze, this theme is extended lovingly over sixteen bars, shifting up in Wolf's characteristic bright chain of mediant key-changes from B flat through D and F sharp to B flat an octave higher. The tumultuous excitement mounts, then subsides as the piano finds, for the first time since the opening bars, the home tonic of E flat major; and broadens into spread harp-chords, to herald Mörike's final invocation to the Muse. The postlude softly resumes all the musical themes that we have heard, now made richer by their verbal associations. The piano is as it were reliving the poem, like an inward voice whispering 'surprised by joy'.

NOTES. 1. Like the poem, the music is a single essence, undergoing changes.

The strolling theme of the prelude (a) etc.

is ie. shifted half a bar and tails off thus (b):

yielding a new theme of which a variant is (c)

This in turn becomes (d) etc. for the visionary

moment of the song, and in augmentation (e) etc.

for the invocation of the Muse.

(Essential notes only are shown, in the same key and register for ease of comparison.)

2. This song also affords a good illustration of one aspect of Wolf's harmonic procedures. He is here using key-change and -contrast as a painter uses a palette; e.g. on the first two pages, a warm C flat (B) major tint for sunset red, the brightness of D major, the mellowness of D flat major and later the clarity of E major for the first climax. The result has a chromatic look on the printed page. But it is worth noting that of the *sixty-four* notes sung by the voice up to the quiet climax of 'Nachtigallenchor' only *two* do not form part of the ordinary major scale of the key being used at each successive moment. These two notes are the B flats on the word 'Stimme' (voice) – the idea from which all the emotion of the poem derives.

3. According to Wolf's first biographer, Ernst Decsey, the last section took fourteen days to complete after the rest of the song. The trancing effect of this belated inspiration ((d) above) so appealed to Wolf that he used it, transformed in various ways but still recognizable, in other later songs where the mood is also one of something approaching auto-hypnosis (motif 12) – notably in the later Mörike masterpiece *Im Frühling* (25).

4. Mediant key-change often suggests transcendence in Wolf (motif 24).

5. The two bars marked 'ausdrucksvoll' in the last line of the postlude recall the invocation to the Muse in a way characteristic of motif 14, which may suggest the idea of filial affection.

28 (M 16). Elfenlied: Elf-song
7th March 1888

Night in the village: and the watchman cries 'Eleven!'* A little elf was asleep in the wood, just at eleven.

And he thinks that the nightingale or someone must have called his name from the valley.

So he rubs his eyes, gets up, peeps about, stumbles sleepily downhill through the hazelwood, and comes to a stone wall bright with glow-worms.

'Why are the little windows lit up? It must be a wedding: I'll just peep in.'

'Ouch!' – he bangs his head hard. Poor little chap: but you can't help laughing at him.

The four pages of this song are a dazzling *tour de force* teeming with playful wit and invention. As in no. 17 there is material enough for half a dozen songs, and there are some particularly good examples of Wolf's intuitive skill in finding musical equivalents for details in the text without marring the artistic unity of the whole. Thus, in the first two lines the composer seeks and finds the musical equivalent of a contrast of meaning (the pun on 'Elfe'), a contrast of states of being (the night-watchman, the elf) and a contrast of distance (the village in the valley, the wood on the hill). These are rendered by a change of key, a change of texture and a change of dynamics, all within the infinitely simple thematic framework of a rising scale and a falling octave (on the word 'Elfe'). Then, when the voice part describes the first confused thoughts of the waking elf the octaves persist in the piano part as if to say 'someone called me'. As the elf rubs his eyes ('reibt sich der Elf die Augen aus'), the piano indicates some small dazed activity. Then the top notes of the falling octaves in the right hand are accented, implying – 'someone *did* call my name; I'm *sure* of it'. As the elf totters down into the valley in answer to this summons, the hitherto unchanged octaves also begin to move downward, interspersed with little occasional uncertainties. Now the music brightens from F into G major and the piano part takes on a soft sparkling appropriate to glow-worms: the essence of the verse and of the piano texture are so ideally matched here that it is as if the music were being set to words. The elf's subsequent enthusiasm and disillusion are graphically illustrated; and the song ends with a brief page of comment from the poet or the singer. ('Gukuk', a dialect word for

---

* *Elf* = eleven in German.

'cuckoo', is hopelessly untranslatable, but the tone is one of affectionate teasing.)

There is no question here of 'great' music. The subject is slight, the treatment not profound. We are given however one aspect of the song-writer's art in brilliant perfection.

NOTE. The treble minor seconds in, e.g., bars 22–25 are characteristic (motif 3).

29 (M 17). Der Gärtner: The gardener
7th March 1888

A summer day: the young gardener pauses in his tending of the palace gardens to see the princess herself riding by on a white horse, the scarlet plumes nodding on her bonnet, the sanded paths glinting gold in the sun. 'For just one plume,' he thinks, 'I would give all my flowers.'

And the princess rides by.

The lovely poem here paraphrased has two aspects, the picture and the mood. Wolf's painting is finely done, with an immediate charm and appeal that have made the song world-famous. Its freshness is never spent; it catches and fixes to perfection a fleeting and gracious moment. But the mood, elusive in the verses, somewhat eludes the music. The dancing rhythm of the prelude dominates the song and tells, no less than the opening words, of the princess riding down the avenue; but there is little musical equivalent for the humble adoration of the un-noticed gardener. As a result the song needs to be sung with more consciously heightened feeling, and more deliberate underlining of the words, than is normally necessary in Wolf, if there is to be any question of emotive effect.

A permissible alternative, which is certainly more usual and possibly preferable, is to perform or study this song as if it were a nursery-rhyme or fairy tale of 'a fine lady upon a white horse'; and a very enchanting one it makes.

NOTE. This setting has somewhat unfairly eclipsed Schumann's (Op. 107 no. 3).

30 (M 18). Zitronenfalter im April: Lemon butterfly in April
6th March 1888

Cruel sun, to wake me before my time; the flowers I feed on will not bloom till May.

Unless some kind girl will offer me a little honey from her rosy lips, I must die miserably; and May will never see me in my yellow dress.

The voice part is all melody; the accompaniment is melodic commentary. The song begins with a little jerky yet dainty phrase suggesting the uncertain movements of a newly emerged butterfly. As the voice part enters, the piano tune takes on an upward lilt as though striving for flight. The tonality lightens hopefully into the major and there follows a notional flight, delicately sketched in. The high, drifting staccato phrases in the piano rise, fall and gradually fold at the repetition of the last words 'in meinem gelben Kleid'.

The grave delicacy and grace of this music are a perfect match for one aspect of the poem. But as in *Der Gärtner* (29 above) there is perhaps more charm than poignancy.

NOTE. The theme of the verses and the minor/major changes of the music make this song a perfect companion piece to Schubert's *Die Rose* (Op. 73), which makes of a greatly inferior poem a by no means inferior song.

31 (M 19). Um Mitternacht: At midnight
20th April 1888

Night came in serenely to the eastern shore; and now leans dreaming against the mountain side. Her eyes see the golden balances of Time at rest in equipoise.

In the silence the streams are heard singing to Night, their mother, of the day, the day that is gone.

She pays no heed to their age-old lullaby; she is tired of it. The dark blue of the sky, the equal yoke of the fleeting hours, hold sweeter music for her.

Yet the streams sing on. They sing in sleep, in dream, of the day, the day that is gone.

Strophic songs are rare in Wolf; this one is a treasure in music. Mörike's poem is a masterpiece, and the setting no less so. The piano begins in a low register with a gently rocking quaver rhythm that lulls through the whole song; the very music of sleep and dream and night. From this background the slow calm rising melody of the voice comes in as inevitably and serenely as Night herself. The lullaby accompaniment and the voice rise brightening at the mention of the singing streams – 'und kecker rauschen die Quellen hervor'. Stressed sustained notes sing out in the piano as pitch and harmonies deepen again into the word 'Tage' with a pang of regret for the bright day ended. The piano echoes lovingly – 'Tage'. Now the music has found the lower register again. The shades close, the memory merges into the night, as at 'vom heute gewesenen Tage' (the day it has been today) the voice twice falls in octaves, ending on a low G sharp. This in its context is an infinitely evocative and moving moment.

In the second verse the variants of the voice part though slight are most memorable. At 'Bläue süsser noch' (blueness sweeter still) the vocal line arches to reach the highest and brightest note in the song. At the last word of 'gleichgeschwungenes Joch' (equally balanced yoke) the long note heard at 'ruhn' (rest) at the end of the first verse is held still longer, in a sustained equipoise. In the postlude the lullaby music sings itself to sleep.

NOTE. The characteristic accompaniment theme (the alternation of tones and half tones in cross-rhythm) is found in several contexts associated with the idea of sleep, dreams and night (motif 18); so is the key of C sharp minor.

32 (M 20). Auf eine Christblume I: To a Christmas rose I
21st April 1888

Here in a drear wintry churchyard I first find this flower I had sought so long; close kin to the lily, the Christmas rose.

Who tends you, whose grave do you grace? You make death beautiful.

In the dark grove overspread with snowlight, there is your magic kingdom.

For you are the fair child of the moon, not the sun; your food is the cold balmsweet air.

Your delicate scent is like the bridal robes of the Blessed Virgin touched by the hands of angels. Five crimson drops would become you fair as signs of Our Lord's suffering; but like a child you wear white for Christmastide.

The elf, on his way to dance at midnight in the moonbright glade, stands in awe at your mystic glory. He looks long at you from a distance in inquiring silence; and flits by.

In the long and untranslatable poem summarized above the Christmas rose has appealed to two major aspects of Mörike's complex creative personality; a romantic love of magic and dreams, and a visionary Christian insight into mystery. Both aspects are treated with the same high order of poetry, and they can be unified to some extent by familiarity and sympathy with Mörike's mind and art. But they are not perhaps wholly fused in this strange and elusive poem. Wolf's music re-creates not only the beauty of the verses but their exquisite diffuseness and duality. In the result, this long song is a succession of memorably beautiful moments rather than an organic whole.

The poem's imaginative musings on a mystic flower are matched by rich melodic and rhythmic variations on an intangible theme. The slow semibreves that accompany the opening invocation to the Christmas rose are gradually unfolded by a series of rhythmic changes into repeated staccato quaver octaves at 'Im nächtigen Hain' (In the dark grove). The slow opening strain resumes at 'Schön bist du', as the flower is again invoked, and is again rhythmically transformed into the gentle crotchet and quaver movement of the following verses. In the last verse the music of the previous nocturnal scene reappears, with the repeated quavers further transformed into elfin semiquaver triplets, which tail off and are lost just before the final chord.

NOTES. I. Rising semitones characterize hope in *Der Genesene an die Hoffnung* (13). They play a large part in this song (e.g. right hand at bars 14–16) and are found again associated with the Christ child in *Schlafendes Jesuskind* (37). From the same motif is spun the peace and beatitude of *Anakreons Grab* (114).

2. The vocal melody at 'lieblich fiel ihr Teil' and later is akin to that found in the second *Christblume* song (33) at 'nie soll er kosten deinen Honigseim' and in *Auf ein altes Bild* (35) at 'frei spielet auf der Jungfrau Schoss'.

3. At 'so geschah ihm Heil' is the 'mystery' motif 19.

4. The piano part at 'im nächtigen Hain', etc. and later is the nocturnal music of motif 17. In the elfin music of the last page this is combined with the 'smallness' idea of motif 3 in the right-hand semiquaver triplets.

33 (M 21). Auf eine Christblume II: To a Christmas rose II
26th November 1888

Within the wintry ground there sleeps, itself a flower seed, a butterfly that will cradle its velvet wings in the nights of the coming spring. It shall never taste your honey dew.

But who knows? Perhaps, when you bloom again next winter, its frail ghost dizzy with your slight fragrance will circle unseen around you?

This was the last of the Mörike songs to be completed. One ventures to guess that its conception was contemporary with that of others of its type: and that Wolf had the general idea of this music in his mind for many months before being able to formulate it to his satisfaction. The idea of Mörike's lovely poem is again elusive; indeed this quality is part of its poetic excellence. Again Wolf has distilled the essence of a poem only to show, perhaps, that there is no viable musical equivalent to some aspects of great poetry. In finding some music for the idea of the ghost of a butterfly Wolf may have succeeded in producing only the ghost of a masterpiece.

Yet this song is full of great mystery and beauty, and will richly reward closer acquaintanceship. The piano part consists of one tiny

phrase  repeated some twenty

times; and it will be seen that this phrase itself is in essence a two-fold repetition of an even simpler germ-theme. Its rhythmic and melodic shape remains constant throughout. But it is treated with such subtle variation of pitch and harmony that the repetition passes unnoticed, as the butterfly hovers unseen. Against this quiet background the voice shines out in melodic phrases of striking beauty. In each verse they begin delicately and hesitantly and move in increasing simplicity to the last line, which is matched by a melodic line as memorable as Mörike's own – tranquil and resigned at 'nie soll er kosten deinen Honigseim' (it shall never taste your honeydew), questioning and wistful in the closing words. In the postlude the piano theme is heard in its original form for the first time since the song began. Having achieved this poised restatement, it unfolds and vanishes.

NOTE. The melody at 'nie soll er kosten deinen Honigseim' also occurs at 'frei spielet auf der Jungfrau Schoss' in *Auf ein altes Bild* (35).

34 (M 22). Seufzer: A heartfelt sigh
12th April 1888

How truly I longed to tend and cherish the fire of your love, O Lord. But I have failed to tend it, and failed to cherish it. I am dead at heart; I feel the pangs of Hell.

'Slow and sorrowful' is the composer's direction. But there is more than sorrow in the music; there is torment. The Latin verses on which Mörike bases his poem express keen regret; in Mörike the mood is sombrely remorseful, and in Wolf tortured. The prelude has poignant dissonances which must have seemed very startling in 1888, and have not yet lost their power to compel attention. They are followed by a four-bar sequence of chromatically rising octaves leading to the entry of the voice, which laments over a discordant accompaniment. At 'wollt' ich es hegen, wollt' ich es pflegen' (I longed to tend and cherish it) the piano repeats the poignant opening chords. At 'hab's nicht geheget' (I have not tended it) it repeats the chromatically rising octaves. The voice reaches a climax at 'bin tot im Herzen', etc. (I am dead at heart), and an anguished postlude brings this striking song to a close.

NOTE. The tenderness (and some of the sense) of the poem is squashed by the rigidity of the musical construction.

It will be seen that the piano part provides a frame for the voice. Further, the vocal part is itself framed, by bars 9–12 and bars 23–24. At the centre of this layer-cake appears the musical equivalent for the central idea of Mörike's poem 'I longed to . . .; I have failed to . . .' This is extrapolated and announced as the prelude; the voice tells its story; the postlude borrows and meditates on part of the last vocal phrase 'the pangs of hell'. It must be admitted that by these means Wolf achieves an extraordinary degree of emphasis. The content of the poem is set out in voice, in piano solo, and again in both together; and these three aspects are welded in the final unity of the 31 bars of the song as a whole. This iron musical framework for a central poetic idea is a striking anticipation of the style of the Spanish songs, particularly the sacred songs (e.g. *Mühvoll komm' ich und beladen*, 143).

35 (M 23). Auf ein altes Bild: An old painting
14th April 1888

The meadows are green and lush by the cool lake. See how happily the Child without sin is playing on the Virgin's lap.
  How blissfully the trees grow in the sunlit wood.
  One of them will be the Cross.

'The song I have just finished', Wolf wrote to a friend, 'is without doubt the crown of my work so far. I am still in the grip of the enchantment of the mood of this song; there is still a green summery haze shimmering around me.'

Of the six lines of Mörike's poem, five describe the picture. Only in the last two words 'Kreuzes Stamm' (the upright of the Cross) does the foreknowledge of suffering lend poignancy to the spectator's delight. So in Wolf; we are in the presence of mystery, not of tragedy. The mood is quiet, gentle, undemonstrative. With a modal tonality and slow rhythms the melodies of voice and piano move by step in contrary motion; all within a very limited compass. This gives the song an other-wordly quality of timelessness, as Wolf himself suggests – a motionless summery haze. The little gentle phrases of voice and piano lead up to one stab of pain at the last word where a transient discord is introduced and resolved in the piano part. The piano postlude relives the timeless scene: and if the song has made its proper effect there is eternal grief in that eternal summer.

NOTE. See note to 33.

36 (M 24). In der Frühe: Near dawn

5th May 1888

*No sleep has yet come to cool my eyes; and already it is near dawn. I
am tormented by my doubts and fears.*

*Fear no more, doubt no more, my soul. Rejoice! Already, round about,
the matin bells are waking.*

The quietude and humility of this song, as well as its position in the
volume, seem to indicate that Wolf is interpreting the poem, no doubt
rightly, as being religious in its inspiration. The heavy chords in the
piano that begin the song establish the basic features of the music – a

fine rising phrase in the right hand 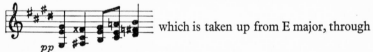 which

permeates the whole work, over a throbbing rhythm in the left hand that
persists unchanged throughout. The voice joins in with a wonderfully independent and strong melodic line. At the mention of daybreak the piano
gradually abandons its chromatics; and steadier rhythm and harmonies
allow a little light to come in. The first themes return to darken the
music again; but at 'Ängste, quäle dich nicht langer' (fear no more,
doubt no more) the key changes, and the harmonies brighten. The
original piano theme first heard in D minor is now heard in a new form

which is taken up from E major, through
G major and B flat major to D major. All the while the voice sings
its reassuring phrases, welcoming the morning, as light comes welling
in to the words and the music, bringing comfort and peace of mind.

NOTES. 1. The pervading bass rhythm ♪ ♩ ♪ is a Wolfian characteristic. It is
often used as an accompaniment figure in songs where the verses describe the
surrender of the self in worship (motif 1).

2. In the second part of this song the chain of mediant modulations is typical
(motif 24). It is associated in Wolf's work with the idea of aspiration or striving
or mounting excitement, and often as here in contexts suggesting increasing
intensity of light (cf. also *Ganymed*, 135).

3. The text at bar 11 should read 'Ängste', not 'Ängst'ge'.

37 (M 25). Schlafendes Jesuskind: The Christ-child asleep
6th October 1888

(A meditation on a painting by Francesco Albani (1578–1660))

Son of the Virgin, child of Heaven: lying asleep on the wood of sorrow that the pious painter has placed – a meaningful allusion – under your light dreams.

You flower; even in the bud, darkling and sheathed, still the glory of God the Father. And behind this brow, these dark lashes, if only one could see the delicate interplay of pictures in those dreams!

Son of the Virgin, child of Heaven.

Our understanding of the 'wood of sorrow' in Mörike's beautiful poem is helped by a similar descriptive passage in Goethe's *Wilhelm Meisters Wanderjahre* (Chap. II) – '. . . a wonderfully beautiful picture. You observe a quantity of timber lying dressed; it is just to be put together, and by chance two of the pieces form a cross. The Child has fallen asleep on the cross. . . .'

Both poem and music are meditations on a theme: each enriches and illumines the other, to our lasting delight. 'Very sustained and solemn', the composer directs. After a meditative prelude the voice enters softly, with a reverence that characterizes the music throughout. The gradual change from tenderness to hidden strength at the phrase 'Blume du', etc. (You flower . . .) is unforgettable. In the piano part of the following section the same music is subtly changed to suggest the delicate interplay of images in the Child's dreams. The last vocal phrase, 'in sanftem Wechsel malen!', ends on a slight rising inflection as if reluctant to leave its contemplation. The hymnlike prelude is repeated; and Wolf takes the liberty, amply justified by the results, of repeating Mörike's first words and the music for them. He directs the singer to sing 'Son of the Virgin, child of Heaven', as if rapt in deep contemplation. A fine performance of this moving moment, with the words barely audible, as if only the mind and heart were singing, must be rare in the conditions of the concert hall. Perhaps the whole song can be better savoured in the intimacy of domestic performance.

NOTES. 1. Note the illustration in the music at 'deinen leichten Träumen unterlegte' (laid under your light dreams) where the descending vocal melody is taken over and continued without a break by the piano.

2. The piano part at bar 7 also occurs in *Wo find' ich Trost* (43, bar 7) dated the same day and in the Heine song *Wo wird einst*, dated early in 1888 (236, bar 3) apparently with no particular thematic significance.

3. The piano bar marked 'sehr ausdrucksvoll' before the words 'Blume du' on the other hand is clearly a meaningful motif, though its use is not noted anywhere else except in a remarkably parallel passage in *Im Frühling* (25, bars 1 and 2, etc.).

4. The rising semitones in the piano part at bars 19–20 are elsewhere used by Wolf in similar reverential passages (see 32 note 1).

38 (M 26). Karwoche: Holy week
8th October 1888

It is the week that saw the crucifixion of Our Lord. Over the bright spring-time falls the shadow of the Cross. Yet the trees still blossom, the violets smell sweet, and all the birds sing songs of praise.

Be silent, birds on the green meadows. Muffled bells are tolling, the angels are singing soft dirges. Be silent, birds high in the blue skies.

These violets shall adorn no maiden's hair today. My love has plucked them to take to the church of the Virgin, there to wither on the high altar.

And there, dazed with sad music and overcome by incense, she seeks the Bridegroom in the vaults of death; and love and spring, everything, is lost forever.

The poem refers to Mörike's love for Luise Rau, more fully and directly described in *An die Geliebte* and *Lebe wohl*. In some mysterious way these verses seem to have set Wolf thinking in terms of the piano music of Chopin; certainly Mörike's nostalgic blend of lament and delicacy in these verses comes very close to a verbal counterpart of some of the musical language used by Chopin, whom Wolf much admired. But the total effect of the song is curiously muffled. There is a series of beautiful equivalents; sometimes emotive, as in the sweet and sad first pages, and sometimes pictorial, as in the sweeping phrases and trills of the song-birds after 'Jubellieder' (songs of praise). But the work does not quite cohere, in spite of its sensuous appeal. The first strain is repeated at the end, for the sake of musical form rather than for any particular aptness of reference to the poem; and the way in which it is managed is, to judge by Wolf's usual standards of fastidious refinement, clumsy.

NOTE. This is one of the songs in which no clearly identifiable Wolfian 'finger-print' of style occurs. In some songs this is because he is being absolutely original, and surpassing himself. In this one, it is suggested, the reason is that he is being derivative.

39 (M 27). Zum neuen Jahr – Kirchengesang: A hymn for the New Year

5th October 1888

Like a seraph softly and shyly treading the earth with rosy feet, so the morning nears. Sing welcome in jubilation, ye faithful; and you my heart sing too.

May the new year begin in Him who moves moons and suns on the blue canopies of the sky. Guide and lead us, Lord; into Thy hands be laid beginning and end and all things. All things!

The decorative frieze of consecutive thirds high in the piano over and around the vocal melody in the opening and concluding sections of this song has been compared to 'cherubs blowing silver trumpets'. More prosaically, a carillon of bells heralding the new year may be suggested. In any event this piano part admirably matches the jubilation of the poem. The song is notable for its melodic and harmonic simplicity. The musical material is all drawn from the same source. In the middle section at 'In Ihm sei's begonnen' (may it begin in Him) the delightful vocal melody that informs the first part of the song is transferred to the piano right hand over a new syncopated bass while the voice has new melodies to announce.

As in other Mörike songs, both religious e.g. *Neue Liebe* (42) and secular e.g. *Der Gärtner* (29), a part of the poem's content is left unexplored. Here its humility is not wholly rendered, except perhaps in the middle section. But performers may safely rely on the aspect of the verses that is most evident in the music; the concluding section, where voice and accompaniment sing out together in an overflowing of joy, is overwhelming in its appeal.

NOTES. 1. Consecutive thirds have been noted (motif 16) as sometimes expressing companionship, but their use here is clearly decorative and allusive rather than thematic. A similar use of thirds and sixths is found in *Sankt Nepomuks Vorabend* (105).

2. The bass rhythm ♪♩♩ in the middle section is typical of songs in a moment of self-surrender (motif 1).

40 (M 28). Gebet: Prayer
13th March 1888

Thy will be done: it is enough to know that both joy and sorrow flow from Thy hands. But I pray not to be overwhelmed with either; believing the middle path to be the true way.

The concept of the 'golden mean' is classical rather than Christian (both traditions are strong in Mörike). Wolf's setting is perhaps an outsider's conception of the particular blend of devout feeling expressed in the poem. It is for the most part a four-square four-part hymn tune, quite simply harmonized, with a faint air of religiosity about it. But in the closing lines, which form a comment on the prayer rather than a part of it, the music becomes free of constraint and full of understanding. It is clear that what moves Wolf is not so much the hymnlike qualities of the poem as the idea of both joys and sorrows in moderation. Wolf's own unhappy life would have been profoundly alleviated by such a disposition of fortune. So it comes about that the end of the poem is lovingly and prayerfully illuminated by the music; at the last words 'doch in der Mitten liegt holdes Bescheiden' (a phrase impossible to translate, but approximating to 'for in between lies sweet serenity') the piano's independent melody intertwines with the voice, then soars like a violin obbligato and finally falls gently into a hushed and heartfelt Amen.

NOTES. 1. Appealing though the concluding passage is, it is not what Wolf would have chosen at a later stage in his brief creative life. In the Italian Songbook devices such as these are refined to a new essence of the song-writer's art (e.g. throughout the masterly *Wenn du mich mit den Augen streifst*, 224).

2. Very remarkable is the thematic kinship between this song and *Fussreise* (22) which is also a prayer with non-religious aspects that caught Wolf's fancy. The similarity lies mainly in the feeling of the music in each case: but there are strong parallels in the harmony (compare bars 6–8 here with no. 22 bars 24–26) and at one point an identity of vocal line (here bars 17–20: no. 22 bars 43–46).

3. The *Wanderers Nachtlied* (11) of 1887 is almost a study for this song. The opening rhythm and harmonies (note motif 21 in both) and the treatment of the final section are closely akin. The two poems themselves have much in common, and a comparison of the texts and music is illuminating from the point of view of Wolf's developing mastery.

41 (M 29). An den Schlaf: To Sleep
4th October 1888

Sleep, sweet sleep; although nothing is so like to Death as you are, I bid you welcome to my couch.
  For without life how sweet it is to live; so far removed from death, how easy to die.

Like *Seufzer* (34) the poem is a rendering of Latin verses. Underlying the play on words there is a suggestion of despair; but Wolf treats the poem mainly as a heartfelt appeal to Sleep for sleep. After a short piano prelude, the dreaming mood of which continues as the voice enters with its quiet invocation 'Schlaf! süsser Schlaf!', the treatment of the song for both voice and piano consists in the creation and relaxation of harmonic tensions, like little rehearsals for sleep. The second part of the song, beginning at 'Denn ohne Leben' (For without life), is announced in a new key, and here the music remains until the slow final relaxation of the piano postlude, without returning to the original tonality – as if sleep had indeed intervened.

NOTE. The new key is that of the flattened sixth above the tonic A flat; a note also important in the early *Wiegenlied im Winter* (5). In that song, as befits a simple lullaby, the use of this note is melodic; here its significance is incorporated into the harmony. Both interval and chord are also a feature of some of the A flat major songs of the Italian Songbook in a similar mood, e.g. *Und willst du deinen Liebsten* (203).

42 (M 30). Neue Liebe: New love
4th October 1888

In the long night I pondered; can two people really belong to each other in this life? I had to say 'No'. Then I can belong to no one, and no one to me? But out of the darkness in me a flame of joy leaps up. Why should I not be at one with God today? A sweet terror fills me. How strange that I should have thought it strange to be at one with God Himself here on earth.

Mörike's poem is devotional. But our enjoyment here is of the music as such rather than of that perfect relationship of music to poetry which represents Wolf's art at its highest.
  The first pages tell of loneliness, in long superb melodic lines that pass to and fro between voice and piano. At 'so kann ich niemands heissen?', etc. (then I can belong to no one?, etc.) the two melodic lines are heard together until piano and voice fall to a lower register at 'Aus

F   69

Finsternissen' (from the darkness) and rise again in pitch and tone and intensity to glow out splendidly at 'Freudenschein' (flame of joy). Now the lagging rhythms and themes heard in the prelude revive and stand up strongly in the piano part. But the song begins to decline from this point on, despite the dramatic effects of great chords and rolling tremolandi. The music that follows is not notably inferior, but seems essentially more like a love-song than a revelation of union with God. Of course there is still much to admire. The way in which the conclusion of the song is made to relive a moment of great joy, in a sweeping crescendo from *ppp* to *fff* at 'Gott selbst', with the long final vocal phrase falling through an octave and a half in pitch and a correspondingly wide dynamic range until it merges into the solemn postlude, is wholly compelling.

NOTES.1. The music of the last section is akin to Wolf's love-music (motif 13) suggesting that subconsciously the composer is accepting the dilemma posed by the poem but rejecting the offered solution.

2. The thematic affinities between this song and the next two, different though their poetic themes are, might suggest that Wolf at this time was undergoing some strong personal emotion which spilt into – and sometimes spoiled – the religious songs.

43 (M 31). Wo find' ich Trost? Where shall I find salvation?
6th October 1888

I know a true and faithful love; ever-renewed, ever-forgiving. That love once drank the bitter cup of death for me; hung on the Cross to atone for my sins, till they sank in a sea of mercy.

Why is it then that I am cast down and writhe in torment, crying 'Watchman, what of the night?' and 'What shall save me from death and sin?'

Confess your wickedness, my heart. Confess that your pure love and faith have passed away long since.

This is why I am cast down and writhe in torment. Watchman, watchman, what of the night? What shall save me from death and sin?

The music contains many stereotypes and is by no means flawless either from a purely musical point of view, or as a setting of words. But dramatically this is a work of shattering effect. The basic design is simple and strophic. After a short prelude, and an introductory verse set to a tender and worshipping strain, the story of the Passion is told. Here the stern chords and ominous rising octave phrases in the piano seem to anticipate the sense of guilt and unworthiness described in the second verse. There is an expressive interlude, the pleading of that ever-present love; then a moment of torment swept away into insignificance by a huge despairing cry 'Hüter, ist die Nacht bald hin?' (Watchman, will the night soon be over? – the German counterpart of Isaiah xxi. 11) to widespread chords interspersed with ringing repeated notes in octaves; the knocking on the door, the summons itself. The voice confesses unworthiness, unreadiness; is there still time? 'Watchman, what of the night?' The outburst of despair is again answered by the inexorable summons, clarion at first, then in the postlude dying away, returning in a grinding dissonance, then fading into inaudibility.

NOTES. 1. For the piano part at 'war getreu' and similarly later, see 37, note 2.

2. At 'hing am Kreuz' in both voice and piano appears the 'mystery' of motif 19, here used without any particular sensitivity.

3. This song has some affinity with *An die Geliebte* (44) and *Lebe wohl* (48) where similar material is used (e.g. the first bar of piano interlude in all three) with more compelling effect. Wolf's mastery of musical equivalence is more apparent in themes of human love than in those of divine love; at least this is so in the autumn of 1888. Only two years later he was emotionally capable of writing the profound music (e.g. in the sacred songs of the Spanish volume) that this song only suggests.

44 (M 32). An die Geliebte: To the beloved
11th October 1888

Sometimes, when my whole being is mute with wonder as I look at you and delight in your infinitely precious being, then truly I hear the soft breathing of the angel that dwells within you.

And an amazed, a questioning, smile rises on my lips. Am I deceived by a dream, or is it true that in you my boldest, my only wish is fulfilled, to my eternal joy?

Then I plunge ever more deeply into the nature of things. I hear from afar off, out of the darkness of God, the melodies of the springs of fate. I lift my dazed eyes to Heaven. There all the stars are smiling. I kneel to listen to their song of light.

Mörike's sonnet is addressed to Luise Rau. It is not only fine verse but a masterpiece of formal construction. The emotion underlying the words is intense throughout; its expression is gradually heightened from contemplation to tenderness and then from vision to transfiguration. To this challenge Wolf responds superbly. There is great strength latent in the quiet simple rhythms with which the piano part begins, an absolute assurance of devotion. This strong support enables the voice part to linger out its long expressive melodic line by dwelling on the worshipping words 'stumm' (mute), 'heil'gen' (saintly), 'Engel' (angel), ignoring or even contradicting the bar lines without ever troubling the calm surface of the basic rhythm.

There has been much critical discussion and explanation of the subtleties of Wolf's declamation. The effect of its sensitive flexibility here is akin to that of a rubato passage written out in full detail. The unbroken calm of the piano part is maintained by the deep bass octaves, which continue in an expressive piano interlude. But they cease when the voice resumes at 'Und ein erstaunt, ein fragend Lächeln' (and an amazed, a questioning smile). There is less certainty in the music and even greater tenderness. At 'von Tiefe dann zu Tiefen' (from depth to depths) the piano plunges down with a new tremolando figuration, then rises as eyes are raised heavenwards. This treatment of the words is perhaps over-dramatic; but if this is a defect it is richly compensated by the effective contrast that follows. Soft repeated chords shine out in the piano; high, distant, clustered, gently pulsating – 'Da lächeln alle Sterne' (all the stars are smiling). The voice finds a quiet climactic note and bows down from it in the long falling final phrase 'ich kniee, ihrem Lichtgesang zu lauschen'. In the postlude the soft treble chords shine out brighter, fade, and cease.

NOTES. 1. As in *Der Genesene an die Hoffnung* (13, note 7) the music evolves continuously. But taken as a whole the song is perhaps not so convincing in its formal construction as the poem. Just as in the *Peregrina* songs (45–46) and *Gebet* (40), the individual felicities foreshadow passages of exquisite refinement in the later Italian songs. Compare, for example, this song at 'dass nun in dir', etc. with the whole of *Wenn du mich mit den Augen streifst* (224) or this song from 'da lächeln alle Sterne' with the corresponding close of *Gesegnet sei* (190) dealing with the same verbal idea.

2. The beauty of a face, especially of eyes, was one to which Wolf's musical response was, throughout his creative life, invariably sensitive and profound. From this Mörike song of 1888 to the last song of all (242) in 1897, any poem, or any phrase in a poem, that speaks of such beauty elicits a music so heartfelt that it is difficult to resist the conclusion that an overwhelming personal emotion went into the making of it.

3. For affinities with other Mörike songs see *Wo find' ich Trost* (43, note 3) and *Neue Liebe* (42, note 2).

4. The pervading rhythm ♪ ♩ ♪, etc. of the first part of the song is the self-surrendering motif 1.

45 (M 33). Peregrina I
28th April 1888

Your brown eyes are a mirror reflecting an inward gleam of gold, drawn up from where it dwells in the deep sorrow of your heart. Innocent child, you invited me to plunge into this dark night of your gaze. You want me to consume us both in fire; smiling you offer me death in the cup of sin.

46 (M 34). Peregrina II
30th April 1888

Why do I suddenly think of you, my love, and weep as though my heart would break?

Yesterday in the brightly lit children's room where I thought to lose myself in noise and mirth, I saw you in vision; you came in and joined us at the meal.

We sat apart in speechless sorrow; until at last I broke out into loud sobs, and hand in hand we left the house.

The two poems are the first and fourth of a series of five. Like many of the others in this songbook, they appear in Mörike's novel *Maler Nolten* (Nolten the Painter), a discursive autobiographical work owing much to Goethe's *Wilhelm Meister*. They relate to Mörike's youthful love for a young girl, Maria Meyer, of great beauty and temperamental instability. She had an incurably wandering disposition in every sense (hence his name for her, 'Peregrina'). In his novel she appears as the mysterious gypsy girl Elisabeth. Although this experience moved him profoundly the poems retain an air of self-contained privacy. Wolf treats them almost as consecutive diary entries, capturing their secretive essence in the linking phrases that form the postlude to the first song and are continually heard in one form or another throughout the second.

The first is stately and solemn, the dotted crotchet and quaver rhythm supporting a sensitively flexible vocal line. In the last few lines the piano part expands into expressive melodies and new rhythms to match the passionate outburst of love and renunciation in the voice, and is eloquent of great love in the postlude.

The second song takes this love-music as prelude, now verging towards the minor; its rhythm faltering, its melody hesitant, all lost love and regret. This music underlies and underlines an expressive vocal line throughout, now heard in its original form to match a passionate avowal, now extended and made rarefied and tenuous as the moments of a

73

remembered vision are relived. After the heartbroken final phrase 'Hand in Hand verliessen wir das Haus' the piano is left singing its tender song as the vision fades.

NOTES. 1. These two songs mark an interesting stage in Wolf's development. Their thematic material is treated in a style that is highly wrought, perhaps overwrought, in its correspondence with the inward tensions of Mörike's poems. For the simpler and more direct verses of the Italian Songbook Wolf in later years found more direct and perhaps more convincing techniques. But whatever view one takes of the success of these two songs, they were certainly deeply felt by the composer, and they open up a new wellspring of feeling. For instance, the first lends its rhythmic structure to *Der Mond hat eine schwere Klag' erhoben* (193, note 2) and its melody at 'tief aus dem Busen scheint er's anzusaugen' to the parallel verbal phrase 'am liebsten grüb' ich es tief aus der Erden' in *Was für ein Lied* (209). Again, the second song lends its love theme (motif 13) and its general atmosphere of passionate yearning to the last song *Fühlt meine Seele* (242); while its rhythm $\mathbf{c}$ ♩ ♫ ♬ heard at bars 26 and 28, which though simple is rare in Wolf's songs, assumes great importance in similar contexts in the Italian songs (see 224, note 2).

2. Motif 11 is hinted at in the voice part of the first song at 'Willst, ich soll kecklich', etc. In the second, the off-beats of motif 2 (q.v.) appear (at the mention of children!) in the passage beginning 'ach gestern'; here the verbal accentuation, elsewhere so sensitive, seems to have gone astray, suggesting that the piano part was the dominant conception in both songs.

47 (M 35). Frage und Antwort: Question and answer
29th March 1888

You ask me where this unhappy love came from and why I cherish its bitter sting in my heart? Tell me, why does the wind blow, and where is the hidden source of the spring?

Try and see if you can check the wind in full flight, or conjure the stream to be still.

There are three verses to the poem, one to each of the sentences above. The first verse is a real question. The second, a rhetorical question, is part of the answer. But it is verses one and two, not two and three, that Wolf takes together and treats similarly. The prelude seems to hover on the verge of articulate speech. It is wistful and uncertain, with expressive chromatic harmonies. The voice has an unusually wide-ranging melody, poised over a harmonically shifting accompaniment. This scheme is repeated, perhaps less appropriately, in the second verse; and the piano then repeats the delicate questioning of the prelude. But the musical answer when it comes proves to have been worth waiting for, and the more effective for having been delayed. The vocal melody is broad, free and self-contained. It overrides the natural stresses of Mörike's fine phrases, and yet it enhances them and makes them even more memorable. The piano has direct and affirmatory chords in a new rhythm. The slight alterations of their basically diatonic harmonies, as the voice floats down from a soft high A flat, gives the last line a lingering sweetness. The postlude sings the answer again, in a quiet close.

NOTES. 1. Both question and answer are about the nature of love. Most of the piano part is in the worshipping rhythm of motif 1; and the melody of the postlude is associated in other songs with the idea of adoring love (motif 11). This theme pervades the later Italian song *Und willst du deinen Liebsten sterben sehen* (203). A comparison between the two songs and their postludes is instructive.

2. But there is a much closer comparison with *Nimmersatte Liebe* (21). There is a sense in which something of the same feeling underlies both poems; at any rate Wolf seems to have thought so. There are evident affinities in the mood of the music in each case, for instance the pleading preludes. But perhaps the most obvious passages for comparison are 'tust ihr nie zu Willen' in the earlier song and 'Zaubergerte du die süssen . . .' in this one. There is the same harmonic progression, in the same key (A flat major), with almost the same vocal melody.

48 (M 36). Lebe wohl: Farewell

31st March 1888

'Farewell', you said. You do not feel the sadness in the word. You said it with a light heart. 'Farewell.' I have said it many times, in endless anguish. I have broken my heart in saying it.

The music shares Mörike's own suffering and loss in parting from his sweetheart Luise Rau. It is all concentrated in the simple phrase heard in the first bar. These mourning semitones, falling in farewell, pervade the highly wrought piano accompaniment and fill it with the sad sound of 'Lebe wohl'. The voice has passionate phrases rounded and moulded to the sense and sound of the words. The wealth of sad rich melody culminates in a crying climax at 'nimmersatter Qual' (endless anguish) which can be unforgettable.

NOTES. 1. In the piano postlude the 'Lebe wohl' theme becomes part of a figuration which is used in Wolf's love-music (motif 13), here heard for the first time in this form. It dominates, e.g., the second *Peregrina* song (46) dated a month later.

2. The descending chromatics here matched to the words 'Lebe wohl' are used in later songs, particularly in the Goethe volume, as a musical expression of grief or deprivation (motif 22).

49 (M 37). Heimweh: Longing for home
1st April 1888

With each step I take, going away from my loved one, the world changes; and my heart is reluctant to go on.

Here even the sunlight is cold, everything is unfamiliar and false, even the flowers.

'Forget-me-nots grow here too' the stream seems to say. Yes, they are lovely everywhere; but so much more lovely there. And I go on my way, blind with tears.

Both the mood and the scene remind us of Schubert; the forget-me-nots and the rippling brook of *Die Schöne Müllerin*, the cold sunlight and the sad reluctant journey of *Die Winterreise*. Wolf in his different way approaches the achievement of Schubert at his most masterly.

After one bar of prelude the sad slow piano rhythm and the beautiful vocal line move together downhill and away. They look back wistfully, then move away again with lagging steps. With this reluctant departure goes a great burden of sad love. We are made to feel as if the melodies are pressed down, the tonality flattened into the minor, at 'weiter von der Liebsten' (away from my loved one). The harmonies are warmer at 'Mein Herz', etc. (my heart) with a memorable melodic line, rising hopefully, trying to escape and return, but falling again as it is forced to go on. The following piano interlude in turn takes its melody pleadingly upwards before lapsing again as the voice sings 'Hier scheint die Sonne kalt' (here the sunlight is cold). The piano echoes this, and the succeeding phrases about the strangeness of the world, with unfamiliar harmonies. The first themes resume, with the brook trilling its attempted consolation in the piano part, and breaking off as the comfort is rejected – 'aber nicht wie dort' (but not as they are there).

Now the sad journeying chords and melodies pass through a wistful reverie of key change, and rejoin the original key with overwhelming effect at 'die Augen gehen mir über' (my eyes brim with tears). The grieving postlude continues its lone journey.

NOTES. 1. Original though this song is, it is so close to the spirit of Schubert as to invite comparison. For instance, the piano's echoes of vocal phrases and its suggestion of the flowing water of the brook are wholly Schubertian in conception, and Wolf's falling farewell melody cannot fail to recall *Gute Nacht*, the first song of the Winterreise cycle.

2. The formal construction will repay study. The general ABA form is evident enough, but the bar-by-bar identity of harmonic structure between

bars 1–16 and 35–50, in conjunction with the varied melodic line and the quite different effect of these two passages, makes an object-lesson in craftsmanship.

3. The deprivation of motif 22 resounds throughout.

50 (M. 38). Lied vom Winde: Song of the wind
29th February 1888

'Where is your home?' says the child to the passing winds.
 'Who knows?' say the winds.
 'Wait a bit, winds; tell me where love lives?'
 'Love is like the winds; it has no home. And now we must be off. If I see your sweetheart I'll blow a kiss for you. Goodbye, child.'

Here pictorialism runs riot. With a rush of chromatics the winds come whirling on stage in the first bar. Whispering tremolandi convey their reply to the child's questioning, then the chromatics rush off again in unabated vigour. Another pause, and another departure, this time a final one zephyring up into thin air in the postlude.

This school-of-velocity chromatic *étude* with vocal obbligato, though most effective in its way given the necessary virtuoso performance, seems alien to Wolf's usual tact and delicacy. For once there are few melodic felicities in the vocal line; the text is arbitrarily repeated; worst of all, the poem paraphrased above, one of Mörike's freshest and most attractive, is sadly misrepresented in the music. No one would suppose on hearing this song that the words were more about the nature of love than the behaviour of winds. This comparison, a favourite one of Mörike's, is found again in *Begegnung* (20) where it is treated with much greater understanding and restraint.

NOTES. 1. One is tempted to find excuses for this song; its technical brilliance and its paucity of content suggest an early idea refurbished in February 1888, at the era when Wolf was sure of his master-craftsmanship.

2. The postlude of this song disappears into thin air, like those of *Nixe Binsefuss* (57) and *Der Rattenfänger* (96), but here this effect is more obvious and less rarefied.

51 (M 39). Denk' es, o Seele! : Think on this, my soul
10th March 1888

There is a little fir-tree growing green in a wood – who knows where? and a rosebush – who can say in what garden? They are already appointed – think on this, my soul – to root and grow on your grave.
 There are two little black colts grazing in the fields. They come trotting

gaily home to the town. One day they will tread slow step by step with your hearse; perhaps even before they cast the shoes that I now see shining on their hooves.

Mörike's short story *Mozart on the way to Prague* has been described as the loveliest and brightest in all literature. It recounts an imagined incident. During a halt in a coach journey the composer strays into the grounds of a great house, is recognized after some misadventures as the famous young musician from Vienna, and is persuaded to stay and make music for a wedding celebration. After his departure the young bride, while rearranging the music, chances to pick up an old songbook which falls open at a 'Bohemian folk-song'. The imagined words of this song are given in Mörike's poem. She weeps to read them, somehow knowing that Mozart has not long to live.

The setting is delicately lyric and sombrely dramatic by turns. It creates a world of its own, or more precisely of Wolf's own; the drama seems to go far beyond the quiet sadness of the poem. In the piano prelude is heard a passing bell and then a light sigh. This is repeated. The voice enters to a gentle $\frac{6}{8}$ ballad strain. There is a pause; then the tolling bass octaves reappear at 'Sie sind erlesen schon' (they are already appointed), and the harmonies and texture darken and deepen. The piano part again tolls and sighs until the opening ballad-theme is set cantering at 'zwei schwarze Rösslein', etc. Then follows the slow measured tread of the cortège in $\frac{2}{4}$ time. The voice declaims, and the piano chords gather strength as they go. They burst into fortissimo tremolandi, then hush awe-struck. A postlude rounds off the song, with the sorrowful flow of the prelude transformed rhythmically into a wistful funeral march.

NOTE. In the $\frac{2}{4}$ section the music has resemblances to that of *Heimweh* (49) dated some three weeks later. The dragging reluctant rhythm common to both is in each case related to a Schubert song of the Winterreise cycle – in *Heimweh* it is akin to *Gute Nacht* (both describe a journey away from the loved one) and this passage of this song is akin to *Der Wegweiser* (both are about a journey towards the grave).

52 (M 40). Der Jäger: The huntsman
23rd February 1888

Three days of ceaseless rain, and no sunshine; and I've had three days of quarrelling, and no love. We've fallen out, my love and I. The bickering and bitterness are a pain in my heart. So I welcome the thunderstorm and plunge out exultantly into it.

Now she'll be sitting at home, happy with her family; I hear the leaves whispering in the dark forest. Now she'll be weeping in her own little room; and I am at home here like the animals, hidden in the darkness.

No sign of a stag anywhere! I'll fire a shot all the same, to pass the time. The sound and its echo refresh the marrow of my bones.

But as the thunder peals around, a sudden sorrow overwhelms me and my heart sinks.

My love and I have quarrelled, and the bickering and bitterness are a pain in my heart. So away to her house to put my arms round her and make up and kiss and love again!

Wolf was very displeased with a critic who praised the song but was tactless enough to call it a 'Liedchen' (ditty). The composer complained that one might as well call *Tristan und Isolde* a little operetta. Certainly the song is extended, even diffuse, in construction; but one has a certain sympathy with the critic. There is a homeliness about the poem and its setting that almost justifies the term 'Liedchen'.

The restless bass rhythm announced by the piano makes a somewhat harsh comment on the situation; but the opening melody is simplicity itself, almost a folk-song strain. The rhythmic figurations become more boisterous and less surly at the welcome to the thunderstorm – 'Willkommen denn', etc. The original rhythm returns, its asperities somewhat softened, at 'Nun sitzt sie wohl daheim' (now she'll be sitting at home). At the mention of the whispering leaves in the forest ('Blätter flüstern') the rhythm, as if suddenly reminded of the central character's plight, briefly resumes its harshness; only to soften even more than before at 'Nun sitzt sie wohl und weinet', etc. (now she'll be sitting weeping) and then to resume, as if reminded by the words 'in Finsternis geborgen' (hidden in the darkness). The song, admirable so far, now strikes a bad patch, in which operatic conventions supervene. At the verse beginning 'Kein Hirsch' (no stag), which is perhaps the weakest in Mörike's not very successful poem, the central figure steps out of his solitary mood and on to a stage. The unquiet lover alone in the night becomes the stock character of the professional huntsman. The result is jarring in the poem; in the song it is a disaster. In the piano part a gun fires, an attempt at manly sentiment misfires, and, for the mention of thunder, the harmonies of the original piano theme are set shaking and pealing in sympathy in a way just right for a Weber opera, but just wrong for a Wolf song. The balance is somewhat redressed by the reappearance of the original theme in voice and piano for Mörike's repetition of his second verse; and the song rattles off to a gay and racy conclusion with a spirited postlude.

NOTES. 1. The piano left hand throughout typifies unrest (motif 5).
   2. The piano at 'Gesunder Knall', etc. has the manly motif 6.

53 (M 41). Rat einer Alten: The old woman's advice
22nd March 1888

(*An old woman is haranguing her neighbour and his young daughter over the garden fence.*)

   '*I was young once,*' she says, '*so I understand these things; and now I'm old, so there's a lot in what I say.*'

   (*To the neighbour, with a meaning glance at the daughter, she says:*) '*It's no use putting a fence round your garden when the berries are ripe. Gay little birds know the way in.*'

   (*To the young girl – a piece of advice:*) '*Love and respect for your sweetheart will make him your slave. Be frank but tactful, rise early, work hard; a healthy body, clean linen, these things become a young girl and a young wife.*'

   (*And she repeats her credentials:*) '*I've been young once, and now I'm old; so I know all about it.*'

It is easy to criticize this song. The piano part is little more than conventional accompaniment. The voice has the same basic melody, save for the opening and closing strains, to cover all the changing sentiments and moods expressed. The accentuation is uncertain. The situation is not made clear in the music. In general, there is a certain stiffness and insensitivity of treatment, quite uncharacteristic of the composer. Indeed one begins to suspect that the melody was conceived independently, perhaps even with some other poem in mind. Wolf told a friend that he found this the least satisfactory of all the Mörike songs; and he went so far as to consider excluding it from later editions.

We may agree that as a setting of words the song is second-class Wolf. Yet by more usual criteria it is surely first-class music. The sheer melodic appeal of the vocal line may well be thought to outweigh any possible defects of construction or treatment. Nor are the characteristic touches wholly lacking. Grace-notes cackle and chirrup throughout the song. They are there in the incisive rhythm of the first and final sections, to suggest laying down the law. They are gay and decorative for the metaphor of the birds and berries (at 'schön reife Beeren'). They are didactic but, in warmer major harmonies, half-affectionate in the advice to the young girl at 'Aber mein Dirnchen', etc., until the first strain reappears and the clinching chords round off the song.

NOTE. Acciaccature are used by Wolf to indicate didacticism, criticism, or mocking laughter (motif 4). As all of these occur in this song, it is not surprising that the device is found here, if anything, too often.

54 (M 42). Erstes Liebeslied eines Mädchens: A girl's first love-song

20th March 1888

Love is blind, love goes fishing; how can a frightened child tell what her net has caught? Is it a sweet eel to eat, or a poisonous snake to kill me? See how it twists and turns, slipping from my hands to my heart, whipping inside me, biting. It is agony and bliss together; it will kill me soon.

'Today,' wrote Wolf, 'I have produced my masterpiece. This is by far the best song that I have ever achieved. By the side of it all the rest is child's play. The music is strikingly characteristic and at the same time intense enough to lacerate the nervous system of a block of marble.' Other songs even finer were to follow; but Wolf's own description of this one is hardly exaggerated. The poem has been the subject of much Freudian commentary. Wolf himself described it as a striking example of the excesses to which Mörike could be tempted when he dealt with the daemonic aspect of reality. It is remarkable for its blend of innocence with passion. Wolf's song is in essence, in the piano part, the eightfold repetition of a sixteen-bar theme which is itself repetitive. The essential innocence of the poem is suggested by this basic simplicity of structure and by naïve snatches of melody throughout. The passion is reflected in the texture of the music as well as in its speed. Thus the piano right-hand theme is always preceded by a quaver or two quavers' rest, like a sharp gasp; the syncopations of the vocal line sound like a fighting for breath. The incandescence of the mixture is evoked by the brightening key-changes that carry the theme through an octave during the course of the song, and by the shine of sustained high notes, coinciding with the last words of the lines of the poem, e.g. 'Schlange' (snake), 'Lust' (delight), 'Ring', etc. The central symbol of the cause of all this tumult appears throughout the song. Small sforzando chords graphically describe a ring; and the postlude has a frantic lithe whipping movement which is mercifully cut off by a final fortissimo chord.

NOTE. Two Wolfian themes are present in an adolescent stage of development:
(*a*) The 'love' music, e.g. in the first piano bars, of motif 13.
(*b*) The brightening mediant key-changes of motif 24.

55 (M 43). Lied eines Verliebten: A lover's song
14th March 1888

In the dark hours, long before dawn, my heart wakes me to think of you.

My eyes are bright awake at midnight, brighter than matin bells; but when have you ever thought of me, even by day?

If I were a fisherman I should rise and carry my nets down to the river, and bring the fish to market with a light heart.

Already the miller's lad is hard at work; it would do my heart good to be working with him.

But I poor wretch must lie here idly grieving on my bed, with nothing in my head but thoughts of an unruly little girl.

The essence of Mörike's poem is in the opening lines:

> 'In aller Früh, ach, lang vor Tag,
> Weckt mich mein Herz, an dich zu denken'.

This is the poem's only direct mention of the love that inspires it; but these few words set the tone of all that follows. Wolf matches them with a melody that is among his very finest inspirations. For eight bars of piano prelude we have an unforgettable tune, announced in single notes in the left hand and accompanied by throbbing off-beat chords in the right. It sings out successive phrases of unrest and love, linked together in a long upward spiral of melody that traverses two octaves before coming to rest. Then it begins again with a wholly different effect as the voice enters with a downward-tending countermelody, itself almost equally memorable.

Throughout the song the vocal melodies are subtly framed to the inflection of the words. They rise questioningly at 'mein gedacht?' (thought of me?). They take an upward turn for the activity of the fisherman and the miller, and again at the end of the song. The piano melodies, though varied, persist in essentially the same rhythm and shape as in the prelude; and the two strands, vocal and instrumental, now dividing, now joining, give new life and meaning to each other and to the words. As ever, Wolf highlights certain moments and thoughts. He has a C sharp major triad for the brightness of matin bells, and a staccato treatment of the piano's melody for the miller's lad at work. Subtly, the piano postlude echoes the prelude, only to break off sharply and unexpectedly as if to deny the solace of the theme. These details in no way disturb the perfect organization of this song, which with its twin streams of clear fresh melody is among the most enduring delights of the Mörike songbook.

NOTES. 1. The inspired piano prelude theme is described above as being compounded of love and unrest. It is clear from later songs that its melodic phrases had, or came to have, thematic significance for Wolf. Their shape and feel at, e.g., bars 1, 3, 5, etc. are heard again in later love-songs (122, 164), and at, e.g., 2, 4, 7 have the 'unrest' idea of motif 5.

2. The tonality of B minor ending on the dominant also conveys a bittersweet mood in one or two of the Spanish songs (171, 175).

56 (M 44). Der Feuerreiter: The Fire-rider
10th October 1888

'Do you see? There, at the little window? It's his red cap again. There must be something weird afoot; he's moving up and down!'

All at once, everyone's jostling over the bridge, down to the meadow. Listen! the fire alarm bell is shrilling – behind the hill, behind the hill, the mill's on fire!

Look! There he rides raving sheer through the gate. It's the Fire-rider, on his bony mare. Through the smoke and heat he rides cross-country like the wind. The bell peals on and on – behind the hill, behind the hill, the mill's on fire!

So often he had smelt the red smoke from miles away and ridden out to conjure the flames blasphemously, with a fragment of the One True Cross, but this time – look out! There from the rafters the Devil is grinning at you in the flames of hell. May God have mercy on your soul!

Behind the hill, behind the hill; he's running wild in the mill!

Soon the mill burst into ruins. But the rash rider was never again seen from that hour.

People and carts come thronging back home away from all that horror. And the little bell rings itself out – behind the hill, behind the hill . . . fire . . .!

Later on the miller found by the cellar wall a skeleton, with a cap on, seated bolt upright on the bones of a mare. Fire-rider, how coldly you ride in your grave! Hush! It's all flaking away in ash.

Rest in peace, rest in peace, down there in the mill.

Mörike was adept in the poetry of magic and dream. This ballad is all black magic and nightmare. It is remarkable alike for its vividness and its obscurity, like the strange fire-lit scenes it describes. The origins of the poem have been traced back to various earlier legends. These have

antiquarian interest, but in an important sense it is Mörike's own per-
fervid creative imagination that has given legendary force to this bizarre
narrative by making it seem so true and compelling. Wolf's imagination
in turn was fired and fused into music of nerve-flaying intensity. The
resultant song rivets our attention and compels our acceptance with a
force that all but outmatches the poem. It is formidably difficult for both
performers; but a fully achieved performance is one of the most impressive and memorable things in music. Very literally, it must be heard
to be believed. It does not inspire affection; no human emotion is involved in this extraordinary gallimaufry of fire, crowds, bells, hoof-
beats, madness and annihilation.

We begin with generalized emotions and crowd scenes – alarms and
excursions. The initial impulse is therefore mainly rhythmic and dynamic. The drumming octaves in the piano part mutter apprehensively, a
shiver of excitement and fear. The voice breaks in with an agitated
whisper – 'do you see it? the red cap?' Tension mounts as the piano
figure rises and bursts out on top of a new piano theme crowded with
thronging rhythms – 'Und auf einmal welch Gewühle' (and suddenly
what a crowd). To this is added, high in the treble, a persistent ringing
note at 'Horch! das Feuerglöcklein gellt'. This is the fire alarm bell,
which breaks out into insistent tremolandi as voice and piano come
storming up to the frantic cry – 'The mill's on fire!'

The excitement and drama of the voice part derive from the masterly
organization of the music as a whole. In the twenty-six bars of piano
part heard up to this point a group of themes, each adapted superbly
to a particular illustrative purpose – excitement, crowds, alarm bell –
has been fused into one single impulse that climbs in a great uninter-
rupted sweep over three octaves in pitch and from pp to fff in volume.

Now the Fire-rider himself appears. Great octaves ride raving down
the bass with rising figures in the treble that cut and crack like a whip-
lash – 'Schaut! da sprengt er wütend schier', etc. In contrast to the
first descriptive group of themes, this bold motif typifies one individual.
It is more melodic and extended, and stands out from the music as if in
an extra dimension. The thronging crowd rhythms reappear at 'Quer-
feldein!' (cross-country) with the Fire-rider's music riding sheer through
and over them. Again the bell notes ring out and voice and piano reach
another frantic climax at 'hinterm Berg, hinterm Berg, brennt es in der
Mühle!'

Now the tension relaxes into a ballad-like strain with a broad vocal
melody and orthodox accompaniment. But not for long. The harmonies

become contorted, the repeated quavers ominously insistent. The voice recounts the horror in the mill and chants 'Gnade Gott der Seele dein' ' (God have mercy on your soul). This leads to the true dynamic climax of the song, where fresh power previously held in reserve is suddenly unleashed. With a tumult of jagged chords in dotted rhythm the Fire-rider's theme is sent jerking and tearing in unbridled and terrifying violence 'running wild in the mill!' ('hinterm Berg, rast er in der Mühle!') In the piano interlude these chords resolve into octaves that plunge down from the heights of the piano to the depths. The right hand takes over the insistent rhythm as in the left hand the Fire-rider's theme broadens out and hushes at the re-entry of the voice. There is a sudden brief outburst from the piano as the mill collapses ('barst in Trümmer'). Then the voice falls suddenly to its lowest register and intones the fate of the rash rider, who was never again seen from that hour. Under pianissimo chords his theme duly disappears and is not heard again.

The thronging crowd rhythms resume, with a downward turn for the return home at 'Volk und Wagen im Gewühle', and, after the refrain, the bell rings itself out in a brilliantly conceived piano interlude. The repeated bell notes in the treble break off, resume at irregular intervals, and fade, while the bass chords have a stammering version of the melodies and rhythms allotted to the refrain 'Hinterm Berg', etc., with an effect of vague disjointed speech – 'The mill . . . burning . . . fire . . .'

After a long pause, the folk-ballad accompaniment resumes, somewhat more leisurely in rhythm, to a new melody. All this was long ago, it seems to say, reassuringly; all forgotten. But suddenly the warmth dies out of the music, a great chill strikes into it and from it. The anguished harmonies that told of the encounter in the mill reappear, softly and haltingly, to describe its aftermath. Groups of quiet, detached, strange, widely spaced chords are heard interspersed by whispers from the voice part. The compelling music of the warlock, the ride, the fire, is turned into dreams and nothingness; cold bones under drifting ash.

The voice intones its final requiescat through the tolling bell notes of the accompaniment – 'Ruhe wohl, ruhe wohl drunten in der Mühle!'

NOTES. I. The details of the subtle and perfect organization of this song repay careful study. A technical analysis would be beyond the scope of this book, but the following passages are perhaps of outstanding interest.

(a) the excited crowding rhythms in bars 15–18, traversed by the Fire-rider music in 35–38, and set running and returning home in 84–87;

(b) the transition of the Fire-rider theme from its arrival at bar 27 et seq.

through its use in diminution at 63 et seq. and final disappearance after 83;

(c) the harmonic identity, and rhythmic variation for dramatic effect, of bars 47–62 as compared with 103–120.

2. The 'mysterious' harmony of motif 19 is heard at bars 55–56 and at 111–112.

3. For what looks like a deliberate reference to this song in the Goethe Songbook see 132, note 2.

57 (M 45). Nixe Binsefuss: The fairy Reedfoot
13th May 1888

The fairy comes dancing on the moonlit ice past the fisherman's house, singing and laughing.

'*I am the fairy Reedfoot, looking after my fish. I can see them all through the ice, and I often count them. So take care! Keep your nets away or I'll shred them to bits for you.*

But your daughter is a good girl and she's got a fine young man. For a wedding present I'll give her a magic lucky fish all made of real silver.

And now farewell, my child. The morning cock crows in the village.'

(And she fades in air.)

There is no precise English equivalent for 'Nixe'. She is certainly not a mermaid, as some translations suggest, but rather a water-fairy or water-sprite. 'Reedfoot' or 'Bulrushfoot' is Mörike's idea of an appropriate name for such a being. Typically, the poem here paraphrased is full of such fantasies, which become lost or blurred in translation. Fortunately this music re-creates them for us. As in *Elfenlied* (28) a slight theme and treatment are made memorable by the sheer brilliant perfection of Wolf's evocative writing. With a wisp or two of chromatics in the piano prelude the fairy drifts diaphanously on to the scene. The voice then enters with an ingratiating melody, and the piano deserts its chromatics for an accompaniment figure which is a study in transparency. Staccato bare fifths and bare octaves are heard in the treble left hand, and the same basic motifs are set delicately dancing in the right. Even the look of the music on the printed page conveys the impression of lightness and airiness. The gossamer chromatics stop and stand in air as the fairy begins her song – 'Ich bin die Nixe Binsefuss'. Under the light treble chords the sharp grace-notes and runs hint at anger. An icy breeze sweeps into the upper register of the piano at the wintry threat to the nets. But the dainty accompaniment is momentarily more mellow at the thought of the little daughter, ('Dein Mägdlein zwar', etc.) and tender for the promised wedding gift ('Drum häng ich ihr', etc.). Then it becomes sharp and fey once more. In a piano interlude the dancing accompaniment figures suddenly fade and become with very little change a sharp cock-crow. The drifting gauze of the original theme returns in staccato bare fifths and octaves. With the last words, 'Der Morgenhahn im Dorfe schreit!' the chromatics reappear, flit up the piano, and vanish, leaving the ice empty in the cold light of dawn.

NOTES. 1. Wolf seems to have imagined the figure of Nixe Binsefuss as being tiny (minor seconds staccato, motif 3) and diaphanous (as the bare fifths and octaves indicate) – a rather more conventional conception than Mörike's. For the use of bare octaves in a verbal context of transparency see *O wär' dein Haus durchsichtig* (226).

2. The petulant acciaccature are motif 4.

3. A minor is often used for a woman's voice in any mood approaching that of distress.

4. See 59, note 1.

58 (M 46). Gesang Weylas: Weyla's song
9th October 1888

(*The goddess Weyla sings.*)

You are my land, Orplid, shining afar; your sunlit shores send up sea-mists that moisten the cheeks of the gods. Ancient seas rise renewed around you, my child; kings serve and worship you.

This is less a song than an incantation, and one of great magic. Orplid is an imagined island, Weyla its imagined tutelary goddess. Yet in the context of the poem, and with the added powers of persuasion of Wolf's setting, these romantic fantasies assume reality. We are privileged to attend a mystic ceremony as it takes place in Mörike's magic world.

The song begins with four hushed arpeggio chords in solemn equal measure. These establish the mood and rhythm of ritual harp-music, which sounds throughout the piano part. Then the voice enters with its incantation, and the atmosphere of solemn witchery is complete. The music becomes more obscure and tense as mists and mystery cloud the rhythm and harmony. After a hushed emotional climax at 'Uralte Wasser steigen verjüngt' (ancient seas rise renewed) the mists disperse, the harmonies resolve and the plain harpchords resume. In the graphic final phrase the voice lifts and shines out royally on a high F at 'Könige' (kings); and then bows down, leaving the harp-notes to die away as the song ends.

NOTES. 1. It must be very tempting to shout the word 'Könige', or at any rate to sing it with a powerful increase of volume well above the forte marked by Wolf; but to do so misses the point completely.

2. The 'mysterious' harmonic progression at 'uralte Wasser steigen' is one aspect of motif 19.

59 (M 47). Die Geister am Mummelsee: The ghosts of the lake
18th May 1888

What is that procession winding down the mountainside so late at night, splendid with torches? Can it be for a feast or a dance? The singing sounds so gay.
'Oh no!'
Then tell me, what can it be?
'What you see is a funeral cortège. What you hear is a lament for the dead wizard-king. They are carrying him home.'
Then it must be the ghosts of the lake! They glide down into the valley, on to the lake. They float over the water with a murmur of prayers. Oh look – the shining woman . . . the coffin . . . Now the lake opens its green gate and they sweep down into it, a stairway of phantoms. Do you hear? they are singing him to rest there below.
How sweet the waters burn and glow in green fire. The mists ghost away. Hush – what is that moving? The lake divides again, and – help me, help! – they are coming back! There's rustling in the rushes, a great wind in the reeds – now quick, run, they're after me, they've caught me!

Wolf was here perhaps attempting the impossible. This dream-poem from Mörike's fantasy world appears in his novel *Maler Nolten* as a colloquy for two fairy children in a shadow play. An effective musical treatment can hardly avoid being dramatic and setting the ballad in a human context. Such a procedure was absolutely right for Schubert in *Erlkönig* but it seems out of place in this poem, in which both the menace and the action are removed several stages further in the world of the imagination. Nevertheless, the good tunes and the opportunities for dramatic effect make this ballad a certain success for the gifted singer and accompanist.

It abounds in enjoyable moments. At 'Sie schweben herunter' (they glide down) and later at 'die Wasser wie lieblich' (how sweet the waters) appears a bass counter-melody. Its rhythm – c ♩♩♪♩♩♪|♩♪♩♩ – is derived from the rhythmic idea conveyed by the opening words of the German text 'Vom Berge was kommt dort um Mitternacht spät', and its new heavily-accented version reinforces the impression of growing menace. There is great solemnity at the repeated 'sie singen ihn unten zur Ruh' (they are singing him to rest there below), and a sparklingly brilliant piano part (which needs correspondingly brilliant execution) at 'Die Wasser, wie lieblich sie brennen' (how sweet the waters burn) etc. Most impressive of all is the spectacular climax. With a sudden diminuendo the repeated last words of the poem, 'sie wittern, sie haschen mich schon!', become last words in another, more sinister, sense.

NOTES. 1. The ballad-writing of Carl Loewe (1796–1869), whose work Wolf greatly admired, exerts a perceptible influence on this song and others in the Mörike volume (e.g. 57).

2. In the piano at 'Totengeleit' is the 'mystery' of motif 19.

3. The piano part at 'sie wittern, sie haschen', etc. is analogous to the section of *Abschied* (65) beginning 'Alle Hagel!'

60 (M 48). Storchenbotschaft: The storks' message
27th March 1888

The shepherd has a little hut on wheels high up in the hills. There it stands, wet or fine; and there are many who'd be glad of such a night's lodging. A shepherd wouldn't wish to change beds with a king.

Sometimes there are odd noises at night, it's true. But the shepherd just says a prayer or two, and goes off to sleep. When ghosts or goblins knock, he doesn't answer.

But one night it really went too far. The shutter was banging, the dog whining. Our shepherd lifts the latch, and what does he see but two storks, man and wife.

This happy pair bows politely; they are clearly trying to say something. 'What on earth do they want? But perhaps it's good news.'

'You've come from my home town? you've been visiting my dear girl? Is the baby crying, and the mother even more so, wishing I were with her – wanting christening presents arranged; something to eat, perhaps, and a little purse with money in? Well, tell her I'll be back in two or three days, and give my baby a kiss from me, and stir his broth for him.

But just a minute – why are there two of you? It can't be – no – surely not – not twins?' The storks clap their wings in delight. They nod, curtsy, and fly off.

This song is one of the supreme examples of high spirits in music. Understandably, it is a universal favourite. A shepherd's bagpipe tune is announced by the piano. In the first verse it is sung sturdily through by the voice to a swinging accompaniment. In the second verse ('und käm' ihm zur Nacht', etc.) the air is repeated in the voice, while the piano has a variation of the same basic accompaniment embellished with odd murmurings and knockings. In the third verse ('Einmal doch', etc.) the piano has another variation, this time frankly apprehensive. The latch is lifted. To mysterious chords, and an angular vocal line, the two storks appear ('Da stehen zwei Störche'). The shepherd's tune re-appears, first with baffled harmonies, then in the major key with an absurd yodelling effect as the storks make their bow. Voice and piano express exasperated bewilderment, followed by a lively cross-examination in which the words, the bagpipe tune and the storks' nodding and bowing motif combine hilariously in music as enjoyable as it is effective. 'You've been to my home?' – big octave nods of agreement – 'visiting my girl?' – more vigorous agreement. 'I expect she wishes I were with her' – great excitement – 'arranging the christening presents' – more nods – 'a purseful of money' – emphatic nods. Voice and piano come pounding up happily – 'sagt nur, ich käm' in zwei Tag' oder drei' (just tell her I'll be back in two or three days). But they both drop back in awful suspicion. A hesitant enquiry – ' why are there *two* of you?' – ominously encouraging nods. The voice falters and stammers, reluctant to pronounce the dread word 'Zwillinge' (twins). The following effect is spectacular. The storks' confirmatory octaves climb up, unfold their wings, and, to the gayest of waltz tunes and a brilliant top note from the voice, fly off; wellnigh falling out of the sky with laughing.

NOTES. 1. There are two particularly apt examples of the use of typical thematic material:

    (*a*) At 'da stehen zwei Störche', etc., the mysterious motif 19.

    (*b*) At the piano solo immediately after 'rührt ihm den Brei', the uneasy motif 5.

  2. The main theme throughout has the 'singing' of motif 10.

  3. The text at bar 4 should read '*so'n* Nachtquartier', not '*sein*'.

61 (M 49). Zur Warnung: By way of warning

25th February 1888

One morning, after a convivial night, I woke feeling very queer. Thirst, irregular pulse and a sentimental mood made me feel – well, almost poetic. So I asked my Muse for a song. She made fun of me by presenting me with this odious doggerel:

        'A nightingale calls
        By the waterfalls

Another bird does the same –
Wryneck is its name.
It does a dance
Among the plants
By the aforesaid waterfalls.'

So it went on. I grew more and more alarmed. Eventually I pulled myself together, jumped up and had some more wine. That saved the situation. So let this be a lesson to all sentimental versifiers – don't mistake a hangover for inspiration.

This song is an example of a very intimate art, relying greatly on interpretation, and assuming foreknowledge and sympathy on the part of the listener. It is perhaps unsuitable for the concert platform; at any rate it is rarely heard there.

It was probably the song that Wolf had in mind when he confessed to a friend that he had written music so weird that it frightened him, and that he felt sorry for the unhappy people who might one day have to listen to it. Having become involved in a burlesque piece of writing intended as a good-humoured musical description of a hangover, Wolf found, no doubt, that his theme had possibilities as absolute music. The result sounds weird because bathos is being taken seriously. The first page and a half, with curious croaking and crawling figurations in the piano and bizarre interjections from the voice, are like nothing else in Wolf's writing. Normality creeps in at 'Ja, ich bat die Muse um ein Lied' (I besought my Muse for a song). Mocking acciaccature lead into the delightful middle section where the would-be poet delivers himself of his masterpiece. Here Mörike's parody is heavy-handed; it seems that he could take hangovers lightly, but not bad verse. Wolf's music is somewhat the other way round; his rendering of the shrill exaggeration of the poetaster is as adroit and apt as anything he wrote. The voice is allotted a banal melody. In the piano, lightly flicked falling fifths appear over a rigid and empty accompaniment, all in single notes. The impression of the feeble poet striking his tiny lute is irresistibly vivid. This texture is subtly blended into what follows; as Mörike says, 'so ging es fort; mir wurde immer bänger' (so it went on; I grew more and more alarmed). The accompaniment trills and leaps up with alacrity at 'Zum Wein!' (more wine!) and is pompous, maudlin and didactic by turns in the closing bars.

NOTES. I. Augmented fifths are used for bathos in the piano prelude, etc. (motif 23).

2. The acciaccature illustrating the Muse's mockery are motif 4.

3. In the 'masterpiece' section there is an echo of the falling fifths from the first movement of Beethoven's Ninth Symphony. This is surely not accidental.

4. There is a hint of self-parody in the passage marked 'Pompös' on the last page, owing to the use of motif 6, often used by Wolf in contexts suggesting manliness. It occurs good-humouredly in *Der Jäger* (52), written only two days earlier. In many of the Eichendorff songs (e.g. 66) this motif is used in all seriousness.

5. The semiquaver figures in bars 3, 6–8 and 10 are part of the evidence for suggesting that sliding chromatics meant 'deception' to Wolf (motif 20).

6. At the end of the song voice and piano join together in a burlesque Handelian recitative. This effect is put to more subtle use at the end of *Spottlied* (89).

62 (M 50). Auftrag: An appeal
24 February 1888

(Mörike writes a letter in verse to his cousin. It appears that their two sweethearts are close friends, and that the poet is in some difficulty with his. Can the cousin help?)

Dear cousin,

I'm desperate for news. Why don't you write? People in love are not to be trifled with, poets least of all – I claim to be at least half a poet, if only because I'm half-demented.

If your sweetheart's lips can tell me anything helpful, Cupid won't let them go unrewarded.

So go and see her and contrive to find out every single word my sweetheart has said to her. Write it all down instantly in a long letter to me, enclosing a treatise of advice on what I ought to do next.

The poem is offered as a piece of light-hearted entertainment for a casual moment. The setting matches and even outdoes the poem in light-heartedness, and the result is a gay little song, of no great musical value but of lasting appeal. A breathless piano prelude gives place to a series of bouncy little tunes and rhythms. These are basically all of the same design but are delightfully varied from verse to verse, in a vein reminiscent of Schubert's *Taubenpost* on a similar theme; they echo the voice part in a manner wholly Schubertian.

NOTE.—At the end of the piano postlude appears the typical phrase lifting to the tonic that is the Wolfian prototype of irrepressible gaiety (motif 7).

63 (M 51). Bei einer Trauung: At a wedding
1st March 1888

In the exclusive presence of exclusive people two of them are being united in holy matrimony. The organ's carillon peals out: but there won't be any bells ringing in Heaven, I fancy. She's weeping piteously, he's grimacing horribly; it's obviously not a love match!

This is a trifle, but by no means ineffective or negligible. The composer points Mörike's social criticism by providing music suitable for so unusually solemn an occasion – a funeral march. The dull, plodding organ accompaniment interspersed with wry commentary from both voice and piano forms one of the clearest examples of irony in music. It is hardly programme music in the ordinary sense, but more akin to a sort of musical journalism; a rendering of some such headline as

'No Love Lost at Society Wedding'.

NOTES. 1. The augmented fifth is so authentically Wolfian for pathos (motif 23) that its bathetic use here and elsewhere seems almost self-parody.

2. The dry cackling of the persistent little right-hand accompaniment figure is related to motif 4.

64 (M 52). Selbstgeständnis: A personal confession
17th March 1888

Being an only child, I was given enough affection and attention for a whole family.

I am grateful for that, but I sometimes think it might have done me good if I had been punished on the same scale.

This is pleasantly flat-footed music, well in keeping with the words. A bouncy little prelude leads into an agreeable vocal melody with orthodox accompaniment. The melody is then echoed in a piano interlude, with mock-serious repetition over a chromatically climbing chordal bass. The same vocal phrase is used again for the last words of the song. This time however it is decorated, in the accompaniment and in the postludes, with a little whip-like run up to the top note – with striking effect.

NOTES. 1. At 'ich hab' müssen die Liebe', etc., the vocal line corresponds, for no very obvious reason, with a melody found in *Fussreise* (22) and *Gebet* (40).

2. For the diverging melodic lines in the piano postlude, see motif 14.

65 (M 53). Abschied: A valediction
8th March 1888

A man burst into my room one evening – without knocking – and pompously announced that he had the honour to be my critic.

Then he got hold of my lamp, and surveyed my shadow on the wall. He examined it from all angles, and finally pronounced that my nose was much too big for my face. And – would you believe it? – he was quite right: I had no idea!

He made various other comments; for the life of me I can't remember them now. I think I was supposed to make a full confession or something. Anyhow, he eventually got up to go. When we came to the top of the stairs I bade him a friendly farewell by applying my boot to his backside – very gently of course. The effect was extraordinary; what a clatter, what a din! I've never seen anyone go downstairs so fast in all my life.

There is, as Mörike points out, a kind of personal, intrusive and irrelevant criticism of art. It is as common in our day as in his, and as unwarrantable. The gentle Mörike confined his protest to this one good-humoured poem. Wolf on the other hand had himself been a critic, often a remarkably trenchant one; his counter-attacks when his own work was in question show that he was not averse from replying in kind. Much of the simple pleasure of retaliation is packed into the ebullient music of this song. Both its title and its content made it an obvious choice for the last song in the volume.

It begins without introduction with voice and piano in unison to an angular carping theme notionally representative of critics – deliberately fashioned so as to be apparently incisive, but in fact insipid.

As the voice explains 'Ich habe die Ehr', Ihr Rezensent zu sein' (I have the honour to be your critic) the piano has a little figure of two sharply accented chords, four times repeated, suggesting a peremptory tone. This is in essence all the musical material of the song. It seems singularly unpromising. Yet Wolf produces from it a brilliantly inventive and witty work. The octaves in unison with the voice are resumed; as the criticism becomes more personal the angular theme is heard at double the first tempo (in quavers instead of crotchets) and completely dominates the music until at 'gewiss' (quite right) the victim admits the Cyranesque enormity of his nose. He duly broods on this fatal defect, to a mock solemn accompaniment from the piano. This is followed by an extended variant of the peremptory motif in the piano at 'Der Mann sprach noch Verschiedenes hin und her' (He made various other comments). Then the angular theme resumes, rhythmically altered so as to sound more ingenuous and unsuspecting, until we reach the touching little scene at the top of the stairs. The peremptory theme appears in a higher register in the piano part, in gleeful delight that the boot is now on the other foot. With a crash and hammering of alternating octaves the critic and his theme go down the stairs. Then suddenly the music becomes simple and diatonic and turns into a lilting Viennese waltz for voice and piano to the words 'I've never seen anyone go down the stairs so fast in all my life!' In the postlude, the hilarious waltz theme in quick time laughs and exults with a bewitching gaiety which suggests that Wolf would have made a fortune as a composer of salon music; a finale as delightful as it is unpredictable.

NOTE. A similar peremptory motif serves the same purposes (motif 4) in, e.g., *Rat einer Alten* (53) (for admonition) and in *Cophtisches Lied I* (99) (for something akin to laughter). Its extended use at 'Der Mann sprach', etc., is interestingly akin to the piano part at 'Gevattern stehn und schnattern' of *Der Schreckenberger* (74).

III. The Eichendorff songs

[Peters Edition 3147–8]

Joseph Freiherr von Eichendorff (1788–1857) is known to young students of German literature as a poet of blameless rusticity, whose theme is Nature and whose medium is folk-song.

Wolf discovers a new Eichendorff which may well come as a surprise to English readers. Few of the poems used in this song-book are typical; none is a well-known anthology piece. The selection is more a portrait-gallery of soldiers, sailors, students and minstrels, in verses of a refreshing zest and virility. This choice is interesting. Wolf may well have thought that no one could improve on Schumann's sensitive settings of 'typical' Eichendorff; or he may have felt the need for some relaxation after the Mörike outburst. Some of the songs are youthful efforts thrown in as makeweights; even among those dated 1888 there are a few that suggest early work revised by the mature craftsman. Nevertheless the Eichendorff volume is valuable both as an introduction to the lighter side of Wolf's work and in its own right. It hits off perfectly the swagger or the sentiment of the verses; it contains many attractive songs of the highest quality, and at least one acknowledged masterpiece.

66 (E 1). Der Freund: The friend

26th September 1888

Whoever sleeps at sea like a softly cradled child knows only his dreams and not the realities of life.

But whoever is called by tempest to wild revel, and leaves the world for the high dark seaways – he learns to bear himself bravely and steer surely through the night. He is a man tried and true, who puts his faith in God and the stars. Such a man shall be my comrade and my guide.

Critics have called this song 'Wolf at his worst'. But even at his worst he would repay attention. Here the reward is the delightful melody of the first verse set to a gently rocking accompaniment evocative of a quietly moving sea at night. It is clear that Wolf was taken by the first two lines of the poem:

'Wer auf den Wogen schliefe,
Ein sanftgewiegtes Kind.'

One suspects that he set them lovingly, as if in the process of reading them, only to discover that the idea of childlike sleeping at sea is one of which the poet strongly disapproves. This opening melodic mood is therefore hurriedly repudiated, as the text requires, in a series of grand gestures, rather histrionic but enjoyable to perform and to hear if not taken too seriously.

NOTES. 1. As in *Biterolf* (9) Wolf is attracted by the tender aspects of the poems and catches them to perfection; but in each case, the poet would have us believe, they are the 'wrong' aspects.

2. Three of Wolf's characteristic motifs are present:
   (*a*) the off-beat accompaniment of the opening bars is elsewhere associated with the idea of childishness or submissiveness (motif 2);
   (*b*) the left hand's rocking quavers in the opening bars are associated with night and sleep (motif 18);
   (*c*) the rising bass octaves (bars 12, 14, 16 and 27–30) are often used in contexts denoting manly vigour (motif 6).

It is interesting to compare the form in which these devices occur here with their more refined uses in greater songs, e.g. (*a*) in *An die Türen* (87), (*b*) in *Um Mitternacht* (31) and (*c*) in *Prometheus* (134).

3. The two preceding notes in conjunction might suggest that this song, like others of this songbook attributed to 1888, dates in conception from 1887 or earlier.

67 (E 2). Der Musikant: The minstrel

22nd September 1888

I like to wander through life, and live as best I can. Even if I wanted to work, it wouldn't suit me.

I sing my lute songs outside in the cold, never knowing where I'll sleep.

Many a girl smiles at me as if to say that I would suit her well if I learnt a trade and settled down.

May the good Lord provide you with a husband and a home, my dear; if we were together there might be no more singing for me.

There could hardly be a better introduction to Wolf's work than this gay and adorable song. Nothing about it is exacting for singer or pianist. Its charm is apparent at first hearing, and strikes fresh at every hearing. And it is not only a matter of charm. The use of the musical material is eloquent of the master craftsman. From an unsubtle little tune, and an uncompromisingly square rhythm ($\frac{2}{4}$ ♫ ♩) that persists with hardly a change throughout the left hand of the piano part, Wolf has fashioned a work of enduring delight. Some of this transmutation is effected by deft touches of conscious musicianship – the arpeggios of the piano prelude that reappear at the later mention of lute songs, and the sadly flattened sixth, again in the piano, introducing the phrase 'armer Lump' (poor vagabond) at the end of the third verse. But much of it lies in the intuitive recreative power of the great artist, for example the new piano interlude after 'weiss nicht, wo ich abends ruh' ' (I do not know where I shall rest at night). These same four bars in isolation would hardly be memorable, yet in their context they somehow convey the whole essence of the song, its easy-going good-humour together with a lingering wistfulness underlying the words and the music.

NOTE. The main vocal melody is of the kind associated by Wolf with singing (motif 10).

68 (E 3). Verschwiegene Liebe: Unspoken love

31st August 1888

Over the treetops and the standing corn the clouds go drifting by – who can guess their secrets? So my thoughts go flying free in the silence of the night.

If only she could guess who is staying awake to think of her when all else is asleep. My love for her is silent as the flying clouds, serene as the night.

A delightful poem, typical of Eichendorff. The composer's response was heartfelt and, according to tradition, instantaneous; this song is said to have been written down in one sudden flash of inspiration immediately following a reading of the poem.

This might seem an unlikely procedure for a composer whose normal practice was to work at the keyboard, and who had been familiar with the poems of Eichendorff since boyhood. But the song is so easy in its rhythmic and melodic flow that the story is understandable.

Like almost all the Eichendorff songs, this is not among Wolf's profounder conceptions. But the felicity with which the poet's picture is redrawn in floating melodies and lulling rhythms, and painted with all the dark and bright of the harmonic palette, makes of this little nocturne for voice and piano a memorable and moving experience.

The brief prelude sets the scene. A lulling theme in single notes covers a warm melody, a variant of which forms the opening vocal phrase. The rocking rhythm of the accompaniment shifts into slightly fuller chords and more recondite harmonies at the voice's parenthetical questions – 'wer mag sie erraten?' (who could guess their secrets?) etc. Then, over the background of the piano's murmurings, now warmer in a lower register, melodies come welling up in the voice part, the harmonies changing from subdued to poignant to bright at the word 'frei' (free). This is sustained in the voice as the accompaniment floats softly up to the higher register in which the song began. The music is repeated for the second verse, leading to a piano postlude in which the poignant discords are lingeringly resolved.

NOTES. I. The typical rhythm of Wolf's night-music (motif 18) is apparent throughout, e.g. at bars 6–8 and similarly later. This, together with the strophic form and the occasional semitonal clashes, is shared with *Um Mitternacht* (31).

2. This night-music is as it were passed through the harmonic prism of the motif associated by Wolf with the idea of mystery (motif 19).

3. The horn passages released by the word 'frei' (bar 12) are an example of the release of motif 8.

69 (E 4). Das Ständchen: The serenade

28th September 1888

The moon shines fitfully over the rooftops. In the street a lad is serenading his sweetheart. The springs plash and the trees rustle in the silent night; just as of old.

In my youth I too serenaded my love in the summer night.
But she died long ago; go on singing, happy lad, sing on, sing on.

It is generally acknowledged that this song is the masterpiece of the

Eichendorff volume. But it calls for a sensitive performance and a sympathetic hearing if its excellence is to be fully savoured. For example the opening bars of the piano part may sound rather odd at first. But given the situation latent in the poem – walking at night in well-remembered places, hearing the sounds of a serenade, being reminded of past singing and old sorrows, trying out mentally the accords of a half-forgotten instrument, achieving mastery, sketching a simple accompaniment figure – the piano prelude is a little masterpiece of depiction on its own, a musical equivalent of the emotion which the 'I' of the poem may be supposed to have felt even before the poem begins.

Similarly in the song that follows Wolf's interpretation of the poem must be taken into account. The singer seems to be imagined and presented as an old man. The matching texture and pulse of the music are both tenuous. The piano part is itself a lute song, with its thin strand of melody in the right hand accompanied by single notes in the left; and through this background vocal melodies go wandering, as wistfully and elusively as the memories they portray, with accents straying vaguely among the bar-lines. The result is a superb evocation of the sad echo of a remembered song from long ago mingling with a present serenade, the whole scene glimpsed through shifting moonlight. The whole essence of German romantic poetry is caught and held here.

NOTES. 1. The 'narrative-reflective' harmony (motif 21) at bars 9–11, 15–17 and 21–23, etc. is particularly useful as an indicator that the piano part is 'about' a remembered serenade from the past.

2. Interspersed in the text is the 'singing' of motif 10.

3. The mediant modulations may indicate that Wolf is thinking in terms of changing effects of light (motif 24).

70 (E 5). Der Soldat I: The soldier I
7th March 1887

Though my little horse is no beauty, he's no fool; he can find his way in the dark to a certain château.

And though the château isn't all that impressive, my sweetheart lives there; and she meets me at the gate every night.

And even if she's no beauty, it so happens that there's no girl I like better.

But when she talks of courting, I ride off. I'll keep my freedom, and she can keep her château.

This early work has all the dexterity of the mature songs in similar moods; the melodies and their treatment make an immediate and lasting appeal. Wolf is taken by the notion of the little horse; there is no mistaking the gay motifs that go cantering through this delightful song. The bouncing accompaniment announced in the piano prelude is also eloquent of the cavalier qualities of the singer. It takes on an unexpected lilting and even tender aspect at the thrice repeated 'die mir besser gefällt' (that I like better) in a way reminiscent of a passage in the well-known *Italian Serenade* for string quartet, of the same year; and develops an added jauntiness at the final words (also thrice repeated) 'und sie auf dem Schloss'. Just as in *Der Musikant* (67) there is inventiveness as well as surface charm. Note, for example, the way in which the prelude's melodies are teased apart into separate strands shared between voice and piano in the first part of the song; and the changing of the harmonies and texture to match the changing thoughts of the verse. Note also how decisively, in the piano postlude, Wolf returns to the home key of C major for the last phrases, as the little tune that has ended the vocal line of each verse goes briskly off into the distance.

NOTE. Acciaccature abound. They are in this case a Wolfian coinage for laughter tinged with malice (motif 4).

71 (E 6). Der Soldat II: The soldier II
14th December 1886

You must dare and do quickly. I can already hear footsteps behind us in the night. Mount behind me and kiss me as we ride off, my love: be quick! for Death travels fast.

This song is youthful, naïvely eager, solemnly excited; in striking contrast to the more worldly, relaxed and ironical humour of its counterpart. A driving hoof-beat rhythm is established at the outset. Bass octaves come rearing up, and harmonic resource and dynamic contrast abound, especially in the second page, with its repetitions of the final phrase – 'Geschwind! denn der Tod ist ein rascher Gesell' which dies away at the end to an ominous whisper.

Yet, despite its theatrical effectiveness, the song is clearly immature. At a later stage in Wolf's development he would hardly have countenanced this operatic convention in a solo song.

NOTE. The rising piano left hand at 'erbeuten' is a feature of the less successful Eichendorff songs (motif 6).

72 (E 7). Die Zigeunerin: The gypsy girl
19th March 1887

*When the stars and the campfires are burnt out I stand at the crossroads
listening for my true lover: singing la la!*
*'At dawn of day I saw a wild cat slinking through the wood: I fired and
knocked her spinning: ha ha!'*
*You won't get me! my love must be a true gypsy, swarthy and mustachio'd,
with a gay heart for the wandering life: la la!*

The poem begins well, but its three sections do not perhaps hang together well enough for a singable lyric. The general point of the allegori-
cal duologue is clear enough; but Wolf, understandably, always found
difficulty in translating allegory into musical terms. Instead the music
aims at, and excitingly achieves, a bravura effectiveness, with incisive
piano figures and warm melodies in the first and third verses, brilliant
piano writing in the second, and a profusion of 'la las' and 'ha has' and
local colour effects throughout.

NOTES. 1. The 'ad lib.' marking that accompanies the final chromatic downward rush of the vocal line is almost Wolf's only concession to the display of
vocal techniques as such.
2. At 'ein fröhliches Herze zum Wandern' is the cadence of Wolf's contented
open-air melodic line (motif 9). But, if the choice of key (A minor) is any guide,
the general mood of the song is not one of contentment. The tension and colouring of the music suggest rather the wry passion achieved in the Spanish songs.

73 (E 8). Nachtzauber: Night's magic spell
24th May 1887

*Listen; do you hear the streams in the distance running down to the quiet
woodland lakes where the marble statues stand in the lovely lonely silence?
Softly down from the mountains, waking age-old songs, comes the night; and
the valleys shine as in a dream.*
*Look; do you see the flower unfolding in the moonlit valley? Out of the
half-closed bud, white arms and red lips come blossoming: and the nightingales sing, and all around is a sound of lamentation as if Nature herself
were sighing for the lovely days lost long since. Come, oh come, to the silent
valley.*

This is typical Eichendorff. It has a hypnotic effect, lulling the mind
into an uncritical acceptance of its Romantic paraphernalia. Similarly,
Wolf's music is of a rich and somewhat confusing harmonic texture,

sustained and justified by its lulling movement and tranced melodies. The swaying accompaniment is repeated in the second section with little variation, while the vocal lines are inflected to suit the rhythmical nuances of the words. These long-flighted melodies, at times more characteristic of Brahms than of Wolf, are the secret of the magic of this song, which compels surrender from the opening bars to the final appeal, in which the voice is sustained while the opening melody floats up the piano and away in a last sigh. But all this richness and sweetness tends to cloy. Perhaps the formal structure of the song is not quite good enough. One feels that the music was inspired by the attractive first part of the poem rather than by the whole.

NOTES. 1. Only a year separates this song from the Mörike *Um Mitternacht* (31). This is also a strophic song, similar in poetic mood and in musical equivalents (motif 18 is in the piano prelude here and throughout the Mörike song), but on a higher level in both respects.

2. In the older Peters Edition No. 3147b a ♮ needs to be added at C on the word 'junge' p. 33, and a ♭ at B on the first sustained 'komm', p. 35.

74 (E 9). Der Schreckenberger: The adventurer
14th September 1888

Here's a toast to the goddess of Fortune! Her emblem is a weathervane, and her place is the soldiers' camp. Even if she leaves me I shall not care; for civilian life is so dull. Instead of the flash and rattle of cannon there are old wiseacres who prattle all pleasure from the world. And Fortune herself will weep with vexation – 'Where is my dare-devil soldier? He was a real man!'

She will offer me her arm, and the trumpets of Fame will sound the advance as we go up together to the Temple of Immortality.

'Schreckenberger' is untranslatable; a dare-devil knight-errant is the idea. The song begins without preamble in a burst of panache. Swift scale passages flash out like drawn swords as the toast to Fortune is proposed, with a veering tremolando interlude at 'Windfahn' (weathervane). The music falls into a more reflective mood at 'Und wendet sie sich' (and if she turns away). The piano has a strumming accompaniment which in turn is varied briefly at 'Gevattern' to illustrate the prattling of old wiseacres. The strumming resumes to a new and delightful vocal melody at 'Fortuna weint vor Ärger' (weeps with vexation). This gradually broadens into a swashbuckling climax in the piano interlude after 'Das war ein andrer Kerl' (he was a real man). The voice resumes quietly at 'Sie tut den Arm mir reichen' (She offers me her arm), only to build up to an even more resounding climax of mock-heroics at the extended accented melodic curve on the last word, 'Unster-blichkeit'. Then the piano postlude fairly thunders out its processional 'March to the Temple of Immortality', half-earnest, half-parody and wholly effective. The continuous creation in the music is remarkable. Within a limited framework a great fertility of musical wit and invention has been lavished on this song. Although for entertainment only, it is clearly the work of a master.

NOTES. 1. At 'Gevattern stehn und schnattern' is a prattling version of motif 4; the Mörike *Abschied* contains a similar passage (65, note).

2. The vocal line at 'Fortuna weint vor Ärger' is closely akin to Wolf's 'singing' motif 10, while the piano has the 'narrative' harmony of motif 21. Both recur as the opening of the Goethe *Cophtisches Lied I* (99).

3. Prodigality of invention is a noteworthy feature of Wolf's work, parti-cularly in songs which begin a new creative outburst after a period of infertility – e.g. the earliest in date of the Mörike songs, *Der Tambour* (17). One could almost guess (if there were no direct evidence of date) that this was among the first of the Eichendorff songs in this volume to be newly created in September 1888. Wolf may himself have felt the need for economy. Certainly the final processional theme is again used as the basis of the similar piano exeunt finale to the following song, dated two days later, giving musical as well as verbal unity to the pair.

75 (E 10). Der Glücksritter: The soldier of fortune
16th September 1888

When Fortune turns her back on me, I ignore her. If I just go on singing and drinking she always comes round, and sits with me.

Even then I am standoffish: I call for more beer and drink the health of other lasses – that makes her very cross.

And before long she comes closer – 'Have you finished?'

'Only three more tankards,' I explain; 'that won't take long.'

Then she smiles, and says 'You're a real man!' calls for wine, and drinks with me.

She pays: and I, my good humour quite restored, squire her out of the inn. Everyone doffs his hat as we go on our way.

The Viennese Schubert and Wolf seem to have had a penchant for military march themes, in a way quite foreign to Schumann or Brahms. One gets the impression that the streets of nineteenth-century Vienna must have resounded to military march music of high quality, which was heard, absorbed and recreated by these two composers. Each reacted in a typical way. The military music of Schubert is sweet and solemn and round-eyed, as if he had been rather impressed by it all. The more wordly Wolf on the other hand fashions bright little marches of great brilliance and verve, with a hint of ironical humour.

Just such a march forms the piano part of this song, to match the swagger of the words. All depends on the pianist; if he does not bring it off crisply in performance the effect is lost. Voice and piano begin in unison. At 'singe recht' (I go on singing) the march comes strutting out, discreetly at first, but bursting irrepressibly into a solo flourish as soon as the voice part is temporarily silent.

The form of Eichendorff's poem helps the composer to adhere to this schema. In each verse the march is ushered in by voice and piano; in the first and last two verses by fanfares, and in the middle verse, at 'Und bald rückt sie sacht zu mir' (and soon she comes gently closer) by an effectively contrasting tender variant with flutes instead of trumpets suggested in the piano part. In each verse the march itself undergoes slight but telling changes of harmony and texture, as Wolf adapts and re-orchestrates his basic theme to suit the melody and moods of the words, until in the piano postlude it goes strutting off into the distance (recalling for the purpose another version of the processional exeunt theme of the preceding companion-piece), finishing with a resounding comment from the piano.

NOTES. 1. The gay rising scale passage at the end of the march and of the piano postlude is a Wolfian equivalent for élan (motif 7).

2. Many other songs have similarly engaging march-tunes. In one of these, *Ihr jungen Leute* (202), there occurs a passage (bars 20, 22) that is reminiscent of the piano part here at 'echte Blum' und Perl' ' (bars 47–48) in a way that suggests that this was an actual effect that Wolf had heard in performance. Similarly the sustained crotchets of the descending tenor part in the postlude of this Eichendorff song sound like an authentic reminiscence.

76 (E 11). Lieber Alles: All three
29th September 1888

Soldiering is too dangerous, studying is too onerous; versifying is delightful, but the poet is a figure of fun in these barbarous times. I had best ride out into the world with sword and lute and a student's fighting spirit. Life is an untamed steed, its hoofs flash fire: but he who dares can tame it, and where it treads it resounds.

A pleasant genre piece in which much depends on the handling of the vocal line. The poem, though agreeable, is too slight to warrant dramatic or expressive treatment. The piano part helps with illustrations of the mood, but the words seem not to have made any profound impression on the composer. The musical responses are *réchauffés* from the Wolfian stock-pot, and the song as a whole in spite of its melodic appeal and occasional glimpses of true quality (in the prelude for example) does not figure among Wolf's major successes.

NOTE. At 'Zeiten' (bar 20) occurs the 'liberation' of motif 8, followed by the 'narrative' of motif 21 at 'ich möcht' am liebsten reiten' followed by the 'manly' octaves at 'Rechten' and later at 'leben' (motif 6). Each occurs in its most obvious form; and their juxtaposition in this short song seems to indicate that Wolf's inspiration is showing signs of temporary abatement.

77 (E 12). Heimweh: Longing for home
29th September 1888

The traveller in a far country should take his heart's desire with him or he will be for ever lonely. How far away over the mountain my homeland lies. But the stars shine here as when I last saw my love: the nightingale sings here too. And I love the morning when all is quiet and from the topmost peak I greet my homeland with all my heart.

This song has a quality found hardly anywhere else in Wolf's work: it is boring. The basic rhythm announced in the prelude is simply too dull to be used as an unvaried accompaniment figure without truly expressive melody in the voice part; but since this is for the most part insipid, there is little of interest in the result. A certain tenderness comes into the music at the thought of the far-away loved one and the ubiquitous nightingale. But the notion of saluting the fatherland from a handy mountain-top seems to have left the composer largely unmoved. The postlude's patriotism is singularly unconvincing.

NOTES. 1. In other songs, e.g. *Biterolf* (9), there is the same inadequacy of response for similar reasons.

2. The persistent rhythm ♪ ♩ ♩ ♪ is a feature of many songs in worshipful mood (motif 1).

3. Note the 'mysterious' harmonies (motif 19) at the passage marked 'heim-lich' (misterioso).

78 (E 13). Der Scholar: The scholar
22nd September 1888

When the sun shines, the birds sing: when it's raining, I can always sing to myself.

Even in storm and tempest the wandering life holds no terrors for a contented mind. I will traverse the whole field of knowledge, uncorrupted by Mammon, thinking deeply and drinking a little too.

When I tire of studying, when the moon goes softly up the sky, I shall sing serenades to my sweetheart.

Unassumingly modest, this song is none the less a masterpiece of its genre. There are grateful and memorable melodies for voice and right hand, and a pensive flow of scholarly quavers throughout the left hand; the whole being blended into a character sketch of extreme deftness and appeal. The quavers are played staccato, in the light piano prelude, and throughout the first verse (the first sentence above) and the piano interlude; then legato in the second verse (the second sentence). These treatments continue to alternate as the mood of the poem suggests: staccato for detachment and irony, legato for emotional involvement. There are the usual special felicities; the unexpected changes to the major chord at the end of the last two verses (at 'saft' and 'Tür') and in the last verse the delicious anticipatory serenade by the pianist at 'Wann der Mond', etc. (when the moon). The postlude summarizes the whole amusement and emotion (including a few lute chords) of the song.

NOTES. 1. The right hand has falling fifths in the first two bars, and at several other points in the song. These recur in the next, also a student's song.

2. The vocal phrase at 'singen alle Vögelein' has the melodic curve associated by Wolf with the idea of singing, mainly in this and the Mörike volume (motif 10).

3. The semiquavers running gaily upward to the tonic at the end of the first piano interlude are characteristic (motif 7).

4. The vocal phrase at 'ein zufriedenes Gemüt' is of a kind associated by Wolf with the idea of carefree enjoyment, often (as here) in connexion with walking and the open air (motif 9).

79 (E 14). Der verzweifelte Liebhaber: The despairing lover
23rd September 1888

A student's life is hopeless; my coat is out-at-elbows, my zither won't play, my sweetheart doesn't love me.

I wish the fairest of women were walking in the meadows; I'd be a dragon and carry her off. I wish I were a knight in armour; with my lance I'd

*chase all the Philistines away. But most of all I wish I could sleep in peace
and not bother much about anything.*

An unassuming trifle, pleasant but inconsiderable. The voice begins
unaccompanied and continues in recitative style punctuated by chords
from the piano. The romantic fantasy of the fair damsel at 'Ich wollt',
im Grün spazierte', etc. is treated as almost a parody of Schubert; and
much of what follows sounds like self-parody by Wolf. The music,
like the poem, is written with tongue in cheek.

NOTES. 1. The song resembles 76 above in general structure and also in consisting largely of material already used better in other songs.

2. The falling fifths of the preceding song appear again here in the recitative.

3. The 'mysterious' piano part (motif 19) at 'Ich wollt' ich jagt' ' finds much
apter use in other songs. Here it is mainly stereotype.

80 (E 15). Unfall: A mishap

25th September 1888

*One night when I was out walking I met a little boy with a gun. He aimed
it at me. This made me angry. I rushed at him, he fired, and I fell on my
nose. Then he laughed at me. His name was Cupid; he has added insult to
injury.*

Herrick could write charming lyrics in this genre. But Eichendorff's
verses are pedestrian, and Wolf's music matches them only too well.
The song is uninspired in themes and treatment, and the little illustrative touches, though no less dexterous than usual, serve only to
highlight the deficiencies of the verse. The first page is pleasant enough.
But the running motif, the firing, the detonation, the fall, the laughter,
the anger – all these attempts in the piano part to infuse life and character into the song fall as flat as its hero.

NOTES. 1. At 'ein Bürschlein traf ich *draussen*' – the contented open-air motif 9.

2. At 'Drückt das kecke Bürschlein *los*' – the release of motif 8.

3. This song is a forerunner of two other quasi-humorous disquisitions on
the pains of love – *Der Schäfer* (107) and *Ich liess mir sagen* (212), of which the
last is technically the most polished and the second surely the best. The three
songs have much in common, and a comparison is rewarding.

81 (E 16). Liebesglück: Happy in love

27th September 1888

I have a sweetheart with starbright eyes; where she looks the world shines.
Like a dark forest parting to reveal streams and tall trees in sunlight, so is
my heart. Like the sea from a mountain, like a falcon's flight, so is true
love.

There is excitement of a rather fussy kind in the springing prelude that
announces the song's persistent rhythm; and there is enjoyment to
be had from the sheer buoyancy of the impulse that drives the music
along. The effect, in good performance, is prodigious. But the song as
a whole is surely too clamorous and insistent for Eichendorff's poem.

NOTE. There is again a contrast with the Mörike volume (see also note on 73).
Jägerlied (16) has a similar mood, but Wolf's music fits the Mörike poem much
more sensitively.

82 (E 17). Seemanns Abschied: The sailor's farewell

21st September 1888

Farewell my love: you rejected me because I was too lowly. One night when
you walk in the moonlight you will hear the sweet sound of a mermaid's
song, in the warm night under the rolling clouds. Then think of me and my
mermaid wife and find another lover.

  Farewell to all landlubbers: we ride the bucking and prancing sea where
lightnings flash, sharks snap, gulls scream; that's the life for a man.

  Farewell all stay-at-homes, lolling idly by the fire. When God sends the
second Deluge all the soldiers will be drowned, while we sail off into Paradise.

The poem affords opportunities for spirited themes and humorous
illustration, and Wolf accepts them gratefully. The writing is easy and
relaxed, full of the boisterousness of the poem and the composer's
obvious enjoyment of his music-making. The story goes that Bruckner,
when Wolf showed this song to him, exclaimed in astonishment at the
very first bar of the prelude 'Teufel! woher haben Sie *den* Akkord?'
('Where the devil did you get *that* chord from?'). The chord in question

is not so startling nowadays but it still makes a rousing introduction.

The wind shakes the sails in these tremolandi. The waves soon come pounding up in the bass octaves, in a good-humoured parody, presenting a Flying Dutchman of comic opera. A broad vocal melody enters at 'Ade mein Schatz' over a rumbustious rhythm of alternating chords. The harmonies darken mysteriously for mermaids and moonlight and brighten again for the sweetheart's final casting off – 'nun such' dir einen andern' (find another lover). Here the last syllable of 'andern' falls on the first beat of the bar; but instead of the expected cadence the prelude figures come bursting out again, as if reminding the singer of more pressing matters claiming his attention. The second verse bristles with comic effects for lightnings, sharks and seagulls; and again the tonic cadence is avoided as the last syllable of 'das ist ein lustig Fechten' is cut off by the seascape piano theme. It is as if, while the singer is loyally extolling the grim but exciting struggle of the nautical life, he is suddenly soused in spray.

For the third verse the melodies broaden still further, the relentless rhythm abates, and massively strong bass octaves appear for the stern warning of judgment. Then the song resumes its original tempo and races along to a striking conclusion. The vocal line sails joyously up and away, and the huge exultation of the postlude sets the theme riding over a heave and swell of bass octaves until it in turn rides off to the predicted haven.

NOTES. 1. The 'mystery' of motif 19 appears at 'ein Meerweib singt' (bars 14–17) and again at 'Der Wassermann', etc. (bars 35–38).

2. The bass octaves of the piano prelude are (apart from their pictorial effect noted above) the 'manly' motif 6.

3. The whole of the final vocal phrase from 'derweil', with its brief echo in the piano's last bar, is an analogue of the open-air elation of motif 9.

4. Wolf's great personal enjoyment of his music is reflected in the harmonic effects, which are deployed with the utmost virtuosity. Among the more obvious felicities is the text-book comedy of the four different ways of considering the same chord in the first halves of bars 5, 6, 9 and 10.

83 (E 18). Erwartung: Waiting

26th January 1880

My heart's greeting to her bright eyes, her rose lips, her sunny dress. The nightingale laments, the trees rustle, all speak of her. Where can she be? When all was dark I saw a bright light. Now all is light and clear but my life is dark. Surely the sun was reluctant to rise. It looks sleepy; it is waiting all day for night to come again. Yet love's thoughts can fly and reach her far away: she will one day be mine.

Wolf was only 20 when he wrote this song, surely the most endearing of his youthful compositions. The poem has little to say; but the music is eloquent of tenderness. The falling thirds of the piano part make a gentle background for the heartfelt vocal line. The melody and harmonies are Brahmsian in manner, delicately inflected at every turn in a way that is wholly Wolfian. But when presented with a change of mood at the end of the poem, the young composer loses his grasp of the song. The last page wrenches the music from shy love to adolescent bragging. The opening themes are used again in voice and piano for a would-be triumphant conclusion: but they are clearly conceived in terms of the initial treatment and belong only with it. Dressed in a loud chordal cloak several sizes too large, they look and sound unconvincing.

One could wish that Wolf had revised this song before publication at the time of his real mastery of formal construction.

NOTES. I. A comparison with *Der Jäger* (52) is interesting. The new ideas at the end of each poem are parallel. In the Mörike song Wolf simply matches the new idea with new musical material, with admirable effect.

2. This song shares with *Biterolf* (9) and others, mainly early work, an inability to make convincing a change of mood from tenderness to determination.

84 (E 19). Die Nacht: Night

3rd February 1880

Night, like a quiet sea, lulls pleasure and sorrow in its waves. My wishes sail like clouds through the air: who can tell whether they are thoughts or dreams?

As I close my lips and heart from lamenting to the stars, I feel, in the depths of my heart, the soft waves still beating.

A very attractive song, clearly prophetic of the coming master. But there is something uneasy about the way in which the basically simple and appropriate melodies are made somewhat complex harmonically. The modulations look more recondite on the printed page than they really are; nevertheless the impression left is one of the conscious use of harmony for purely decorative purposes in a way not organically related to the particular poem being set.

NOTE. Night and dreams suggest to the young composer, in both the vocal and instrumental melodies, the germ of the rocking movement that later became almost an obsession with him in similar contexts (motif 18).

85 (E 20). Waldmädchen: The forest fairy
20th April 1887

Like a bright fire I go dancing with my lover, the sea-wind. Rising, falling, here and there: come not near me, or I'll burn you.

Where the streams flow among the tall trees, the deer step delicately as the hunters listen. Now I am a deer leaping on the snowy heights; do not follow, I am not to be caught.

And now I am a bird in the air flying over the sea where no arrow can touch me, high above the meadows and lonely woods left far behind over the sea. Ah, now I have flown myself away.

This song is no doubt intended as a brilliant *tour de force* for voice and piano. But even on that level it seems to fail; the vocal melodies and the bravura accompaniment are for the most part banal, and the two set-piece piano interludes seem absurdly rowdy. Of course there are fine moments, for example the effective postlude. But the fairy's arrival at the point of no return is by that time scarcely a matter for regret. It is hard to realize that this is the same Wolf who a year later produced (in the Mörike songs) fairy music of such sensitive delicacy and eerie sweetness.

IV. The Goethe songs

[Peters Edition 3156–9]

Johann Wolfgang von Goethe (1749–1832), poet, dramatist, novelist, critic, statesman and scientist, was the greatest and most universal genius of his time. His mind and work dominated two centuries of Europe. His poetry has Mörike's qualities of humour, fantasy and beauty of imagery, together with an intellectual vigour, a range of vision and depth of understanding with few parallels in the literature of the world.

The first ten poems in this songbook occur as occasional lyrics in Goethe's novel *The Apprenticeship of Wilhelm Meister*. This is especially memorable for the lyrics sung by the mysterious Harper and the child Mignon. Neither knows that Mignon is the Harper's child by his own sister. This is the sin that has sent him wandering crazed through the world, far from his native Italy. His songs are heavy with guilt and despair. Mignon's songs are full of secrecy, grief, and yearning for love and homeland. The sheer magnificence of Goethe's poetry gives all these emotions a universal quality that speaks for mankind.

Nos. 117–133 are taken from the *Westöstlicher Divan*. This late collection of poems, modelled on the work of the Persian poet Hafiz, is divided into books in praise of wine (Schenkenbuch), poetry (Buch des Sängers), and love (Buch Hatem, Buch Suleika). English readers may catch other echoes of Fitzgerald's rendering of Omar Khayyam (e.g. the cupbearer Saki). But the true home of these poems is nineteenth-century Germany and their inspiration is Goethe's rejuvenating love for Marianne von Willemer. The poet himself appears in the guise of 'Hatem', the lady is 'Suleika', and herself the authoress of some of the poems.

The last three songs of the songbook form another separate group; each is about one aspect of the relationship of man to God. In these songs and in the Wilhelm Meister lyrics Wolf for the first time seriously challenged comparison with his great predecessors, Schubert and Schumann; and it can safely be claimed that he equals their level of achievement. But unless he felt that he had something significant to add to previous settings, he avoided the poems that had already been definitively set by other masters. This consideration may have limited his choice of Goethe poems; the rest of the selection is not wholly representative of Germany's greatest poet, though productive enough of musical masterpieces.

86 (G 1). Harfenspieler I: The Harper I
27th October 1888

*He who surrenders to solitude is all too soon alone. Others live and love
and leave him to his pain. Then leave me too with my grief! And if I can
once know true solitude – still I am not alone.*

*For as a lover softly steals to see if his loved one is alone, so pain and
grief creep softly after me by night and day. But if I once find true solitude in the grave, there shall I be left alone.*

In Goethe's novel (Book II, chapter XIII) Wilhelm Meister visits the
Harper in his lonely room. They speak of solitude, and the old man
improvises this song.

The words 'einsam' – 'allein' – 'Pein' (lonely, alone, pain) toll
through the poem. Yet the feeling of the verses and of the song is not so
much agonized as pervaded with a gentle melancholy. It is suffused with
emotion, but not emotionally demonstrative; and this restraint heightens
the effect immeasurably. The song begins with a quiet prelude of falling harp-chords, like gestures of abnegation. These lingering phrases,
subtly varied, are the source of the whole first section of the song, down
to one of the most beautiful cadences that Wolf ever wrote, at 'nicht
allein' (not alone). Now comes a simile which sets the musician a difficult problem. Some change is clearly needed in the music; and yet the
simile serves to reinforce the same mood. Wolf's solution is masterful.
A certain wistfulness in the first section, a prolongation of its main
theme, the cadence already mentioned, all these prepare the mind for
the notion that grief and pain can cherish and be cherished. When
lulling triplet quavers take temporary charge of the accompaniment and
the voice is left to a gentle meditation, there is an impression of contrast but also of continuity. There is even fulfilment in the music as
voice and piano rise gently together to the word 'Pein' and fall again,
still with the same tender accompaniment figure. This now leads the
voice back to the first strain. The spread harp-chords resume; the voice
dies away in infinite regret, the postlude in wistful questioning.

NOTES. 1. The falling melody of the first five bars, which is also found in
augmentation in bars 6–7, resounds through this and the other Harper songs
and is frequently found elsewhere in similar contexts (motif 22).
   2. Some possible consequences of the interpretation suggested above are:
      (a) the phrase 'bin ich nicht allein' may be taken rallentando, pausing
         slightly before 'allein' and sustaining the last syllable.

(*b*) the middle section may be taken a shade faster than the governing tempo of the song.

(*c*) the resonance of the high F on the word 'Pein' in this passage should be perfectly controlled and if anything restrained.

3. Cf. Schubert, Op. 12 no. 1; Schumann, Op. 98a no. 6.

87 (G 2). Harfenspieler II: The Harper II
29th October 1888

I will beg from door to door, quiet and docile. Christian hands will give me food, and I shall go on my way.

Whoever sees me will count his blessings, and shed a tear for me, while I wonder why he weeps.

This fragment is described in *Wilhelm Meister* (Book V, chapter XIV) as a snatch of song that the Harper is overheard singing. It expresses the tragedy of an old man crazed with suffering and become docile and uncomprehending. The feeling is perhaps deeper here, both in words and music, than in the previous song. But again the keynote is restraint, and again the effect is immeasurably heightened by this means. The prelude has an imploring melody over creeping chromatic thirds. At the entry of the voice with its quiet but strongly-felt even crochet rhythm the accompaniment figure is shifted off the beat. The interlude is the prelude with this off-beat rhythm incorporated, as if affected by what has just been heard. In the second verse the voice reaches a restrained climax at 'eine Träne' (a tear) and hushes movingly into the last words 'was er weint'. The postlude dies away brokenly yet peacefully.

NOTES. 1. The off-beat rhythm in contexts suggesting childish submissiveness is motif 2.

2. The 'sorrow' of motif 22 resounds throughout.

3. The incorporation of the voice's first two bars into the accompaniment at bars 9–10 is characteristic of songs of intense inwardness in Wolf (e.g. *Verborgenheit* (24)) as in Schubert (e.g. the last page of *Ganymed*).

4. Interpretation is a subjective matter. But it seems advisable to sing this song without overt expressiveness. The music provides all that is needed and, fine though it is, it will not stand up to misjudged histrionics.

5. Cf. Schubert, Op. 12 no. 3; Schumann, Op. 98a no. 8.

88 (G 3). Harfenspieler III: The Harper III

30th October 1888

The man who has never eaten his daily bread with tears, nor spent the sorrowful nights weeping on his bed – he knows you not, you heavenly powers!

You lead us into life, you let the poor man become guilty, then you abandon him to torment; for all guilt is punished here on earth.

This extraordinary work is perhaps the most deeply felt of these songs; and perhaps also the least satisfactory. Wolf follows Goethe's description of the Harper's rendering as part singing, part recitative (Book II, chapter XIII). The tragic phrases serving as prelude, interlude and postlude are beautifully conceived and finely wrought. They are in a way an amalgam of the moods of the first two Harper songs – resignation and pleading – together with a new element of anguish. Already in the first verse the disturbed harmonies sound a quasi-pathological note, and towards the end the restraint of the earlier songs is thrown aside. A crescendo of great nervous intensity leads to a shattering final outburst which is practically without parallel in Wolf's music. No sooner is this over than the postlude quietens, despairs and dies.

NOTES. I. The 'sorrow' motif 22 occurs throughout.

2. It is true that the Harper is guilt-stricken. But Wolf seems to outdo Goethe in the last phrase. However this may be, the effect of the vocal climax is so central to the song that one feels that an emphatic pause on 'Schuld' is desirable.

3. Cf. Schubert (three settings, of which the well-known Op. 12 no. 2 is no doubt the best); Schumann, Op. 98a no. 4.

89 (G 4). Spottlied aus 'Wilhelm Meister': Lampoon from 'Wilhelm Meister'

2nd November 1888

I, my Lord Baron, am just a poor devil that envies you your rank, your position, your wealth, your ancestral castle and your lands.

But it seems, my Lord Baron, that you in turn envy me my natural endowments; though I am poor, I still have gifts.

Well now, my dear Lord Baron, shall we not call a truce? You can have your father's inheritance, and I my natural inheritance. So let us set aside envy of each other's titles. You have no place in Art; I have none in Society.

The Baron in Goethe's novel has artistic pretensions. This satirical poem is circulated anonymously among the troupe of itinerant actors with whom Wilhelm is associated (Book III, chapter IX). The musical interest of Wolf's setting is rather slight. The piano introduction, which also serves for two interludes and a postlude, is a delightful piece of high-spirited mockery. But the music has to depend for its general effect on the melody, which is not one of Wolf's most attractive. Only in the impudence of the last two lines does the voice part develop the charm and lightness of touch which alone could save this song; and by that time it is probably too late. Skilled interpretation is needed to make the most of the voice part. We can then enjoy the song for its telling vocal climax and the witty passages for piano solo.

NOTES. 1. If the song is to be sung for interpretative effect, the indicated tempo (moderato) is too slow.

2. The rising phrase that ends the prelude wherever it occurs is a Wolfian coinage for high spirits (motif 7).

3. Motif 8 occurs in the horn passages released at the word 'Titel'.

4. The last two lines look forward to the equally impudent climax of *Ich hab'* *in Penna* (232)—and share the same harmony, in the same key.

90 (G 5). Mignon I
19th December 1888

Bid me not speak, bid me be silent, for I am sworn to secrecy. I should willingly show you my whole heart, but Fate has willed it otherwise. In its due time the sun disperses the dark night, the solid rock cleaves to release its hidden springs.

We all seek a friend's embrace to sob out our grief, but my lips are closed by a vow; only a god can unlock them.

Unlike most of the other *Wilhelm Meister* lyrics, this is not set in any particular scene; it is appended to Book V, chapter XVI as a poem that Mignon had recited once or twice. The intense inward secrecy of these lines makes them perhaps unsuitable for musical treatment. At any rate it was mainly the metaphors of imparting the secret that inspired Wolf. In this passage, beginning 'Zur rechten Zeit' (In due time), the majestically rising octaves are a fine imagining, and the subtle shifts of stress in the corresponding voice part are beautifully sensitive. But this is to some extent cancelled by infelicity, even banality, in the rest of the musical material.

NOTES. 1. Perhaps this song's opening bars for voice and piano were in Wolf's mind when he wrote the masterly *Dass doch gemalt* (195). The key is the same and the progressions similar.

2. Cf. Schubert, Op. 62 (and earlier); Schumann, Op. 98a no. 5.

91 (G 6). Mignon II
18th December 1888

Only those who have known hopeless love can fathom grief like mine. Alone and sundered from all joy I scan the skies to the south, for he who loves and knows me is far away. My senses reel, my whole being burns.

Only those who have known hopeless love can fathom grief like mine.

This world-famous poem is described by Goethe as being sung by Mignon and the Harper as an irregular duet (Book IV, chapter XI). But most of the great composers who have been moved to set it to music have done so as a solo song for a woman's voice. We are also told that the song corresponded to the dreamy and yearning mood of Wilhelm Meister at the time he heard it. From this point of view Tschaikowsky's Opus 6 no. 6, universally popular under the title *None but the lonely heart*, is the prize-winning setting. But the usual conception is that the mood is one of heartfelt sorrow.

Wolf's music both dreams and grieves. There is little melodic interest in the ordinary sense, but much excitement. His Mignon experiences the words as she sings them, lives them in every line. Even in the piano prelude, whose lightly drooping treble octaves sing and pulsate over throbbing chords throughout, the tempo is changed from bar to bar as if under some great emotional stress. The voice enters in unison with the piano melody at first, then soars up more intensely at 'aller Freude' (all joy). Similarly throughout the song the vocal line rises or falls, the tempo slackens or quickens, incessantly. At the same time there is little or no change in the texture of the music; the composer relies to a most unusual extent on interpretation, and it is necessary to hear this song finely sung before it can be properly appreciated. What looks rather thin on the printed stave is almost unbearably effective in virtuoso performance. Wolf seems deliberately to have restrained his music so that the quality of a soprano voice should be allowed to make the point of the song unhampered. So the whole song thus becomes as it were an accompaniment to vocal timbre and expression, and to the depth of feeling latent in the German words – which are perhaps beyond the power of music to convey in the short compass imposed by a song.

NOTES. 1. The 'sorrow' motif 22 is heard throughout.

2. Cf. the best-known of Schubert's six (!) settings, Op. 62 no. 4; also Beethoven; Schumann, Op. 98a no. 3; Loewe, and a host of others.

92 (G 7). Mignon III
22nd December 1888

Let me seem to be an angel till I become one. Let me go on wearing my white dress. I am passing from this fair earth down to my long home.

There I shall rest a while until my eyes open renewed. Then I shall leave behind this pure raiment, girdle and garland. For in Heaven they make no question of man or woman, and no clothes trammel the body risen.

True, I lived without worldly cares; but I knew deep sorrow. I grew old with grief before my time; now let me be made for ever young.

The child Mignon was dressed as an angel, white-robed and golden-winged, for her part in a children's charade. The younger children were a little frightened at first, believing the apparition to be a real angel; and even when they recognized her they were still unsure. When their excitement had subsided and their questions had been answered, the time came for Mignon to change her costume. Then she sang this little song, to a zither accompaniment. In the lyric and in its whole context there is deep tragic feeling; Mignon is to die young.

Wolf clearly had the scene from *Wilhelm Meister* (Book VIII, chapter II) in mind in writing this fine song. The piano left hand indicates a zither accompaniment. The slow high chords of melody in the right hand tinkle in tinsel finery and are at the same time a truly angelic pavane. The slender voice part is, so to speak, the form under the piano's dress. Grace and grief and childlike gravity sing together in this matchless music. Particularly memorable is the last vocal line, where long octaves fall and then rise again bright with A major harmony on the final word 'jung'.

NOTES. 1. The 'sorrow' of motif 22 is most evident at the moment of the song's greatest grief – in the piano part at 'hinab in jenes feste Haus'.

2. Wolf seems to have associated the key of A minor with a woman's mood of grief or distress. The brightening effect of the major form of the tonic minor towards the end of a song is also a feature of his work.

3. Cf. Schubert, Op. 62 (and earlier); Schumann, Op. 98a no. 9.

93 (G 8). Philine
30th October 1888

Why sing so mournfully of the loneliness of night? For night is made for good fellowship.

As woman is man's better half, so night is the better half of day. How can we like the daytime, that interrupter of joys; it may be useful as a distraction but for nothing else.

At night, in the sweet uncertain lamplight there is intimate exchange of love and jest from mouth to mouth, the fleet-footed Cupid will often tarry awhile, the nightingale sings its song that gladdens those free and in love and saddens others; and the pompous chimes of midnight announcing peace and security bring a delicious tremor to the heart.

So remember during the long daytime – each day brings its worries, each night its pleasures.

Philine is the soubrette of the company of itinerant actors that Wilhelm Meister meets and joins on his travels. She is light-hearted, shallow and charming; so is her music here. In the novel (Book V, chapter X) the poem is prefaced with 'There was a lull in the conversation . . . it was already late; the company seemed to be on the point of dispersing. As they stood there undecided, Philine began to sing a little ditty with a very graceful and pleasing melody.' This is exactly what Wolf provides, and his music in its playful delicacy adds a hint of the playful indelicacy that is Philine herself. The prelude and the recurring main melody with its graceful accompaniment are delightful. The alternating strains are less attractive, and rely perhaps overmuch on piano commentary. The lightly skipping semiquavers that announce the arrival of Cupid are not only unsubtle but seem to miss the real point of the verses. The nightingale's trilling triplets are perhaps over-elaborate. But all this is forgiven for the sake of the delightful main theme. As this returns for the last time, it is followed by a reflective moment at 'Darum an dem langen Tage' (in the long daytime), which emerges, by means of one of Wolf's favourite progressions, in sudden brightness at the word 'Nacht'.

NOTES. 1. The grace-notes in the piano part (bar 9 et seq.) and later in the voice are indications of the suppressed laughter underlying the words (motif 4).

2. In the last four bars of the voice part the essence of the poem is stated epigrammatically. Wolf indulges in a musical epigram of his own. He takes the first three notes of the voice part in this passage, lets them make their own way sequentially to the last three, adds a bass part, and so fashions a light lilting

piano solo that can rightly serve as prelude, interludes, and postlude to convey the essence of the music and the poem at once.

3. In this setting Wolf challenges Schumann – and arguably loses in the comparison. The latter's setting of this poem (Op. 98a no. 7), though not often heard, is surely a masterpiece of the 'graceful and pleasing melody' called for. A comparison of the two songs is interesting.

94 (G 9). Mignon
17th December 1888

Do you know that land where lemon trees blossom, where oranges glow golden among dark leaves? A soft wind breathes from the blue sky; the quiet myrtle grows there and the tall laurel. Do you know that land? Would that I might go there with you, my love.

Do you know the pillared house? Its rooms shine and gleam. Its marble statues seem to say 'What have they done to you, you poor child?' Do you know that house? Would that I could dwell there with you, my protector.

Do you know the mountain and its cloud-wrapped paths, where the mules stumble in mist, where dragons still dwell in the caves, where the rock falls sheer and over it the river? Do you know that mountain? There lies our path. Let us go there, my father; let us go.

The evocative 'Kennst du das Land wo die Zitronen blühn?' is perhaps the best-known single line of German poetry. But the rest of the poem is less well known and indeed can hardly be understood without some knowledge of its background in *Wilhelm Meister*.

The child Mignon had been born in Italy and had been abducted by vagabonds and brought into Germany, a beaten and half-starved waif who was forced to dance and sing in a troupe of entertainers. In this song she is portrayed remembering as if in a dream the beauty of a southern homeland, the splendour of her home and the mountain paths over which she was brought by her captors. She sings the song to her protector Wilhelm with zither accompaniment. Goethe says of her that she began each verse with great solemnity and stateliness, as if she wished to draw attention to something remarkable, as if she had something important to convey. At the third line the singing became duller and gloomier, 'do you know it?' mysterious and discreet, 'there' with irresistible yearning and 'let us go' was contrived to change subtly with each repetition, now pleading, now compelling (Book III, chapter I).

Wolf follows this pattern faithfully with a setting which in spite of its apparent complexity is basically in simple strophic form. A piano prelude of haunting melodic beauty introduces each verse. Each begins with expressive solemnity, with a darkening harmonic change at each third line. The voice sings out hushed amid passionate piano interludes for the repeated 'Kennst du es wohl?' and voice and piano combine in a thrilling effect at each 'dahin'. The vocal line at the end of each verse is changed subtly to reflect the changing appeal to Wilhelm as loved one, protector and father. To this pattern Wolf adds his own interpretation of the poem. The excitement and tension are made to increase from verse to verse, as the music becomes steadily more ecstatic and exalted. The first verse is simple and beautiful to match the words. The second is heightened by added rhythmic interest in the piano part. The third is treated dramatically to conform with what Wolf knew of the fate of Mignon. Her imagination is running wild, the music suggests; she will never go there, there is no such place, it is a dream, she will die. The music is superbly overwrought here, depicting a mad confidence in the reality of a dream, and heightening the contrast between dream and sad truth. This is a splendid conception, beyond anything attempted by any other of the composers who had set this poem to music. It is doubtful whether it quite succeeds: but even so it outstrips all ordinary successes. It is one of the world's most memorable songs.

NOTES. I. The piano counterpoint in small notes on the first page comes from the composer's orchestral version; it is perhaps best omitted by pianists.

2. In the prelude occurs the adoration of motif 11.

3. For a similar harmonic scheme in the same keys with the same G flat minor again written enharmonically as F sharp minor see *Der Mond hat eine schwere Klag' erhoben* (193).

4. There may be a further element in Wolf's interpretation of this situation – see *Geh' Geliebter* (180, note 3).

5. Cf. Beethoven, Op. 75; Schubert; Schumann, Op. 98a no. 1; Liszt.

95 (G 10). Der Sänger: The minstrel

14th December 1888

'Who is that singing outside my gate? Let him be brought to sing before us here!' So spoke the king; and the page ran and brought in the old minstrel.

'Greetings, lords and ladies,' he said, 'as many and as shining as the stars.' Then he closed his eyes and sang full-throated. The knights looked on boldly, the ladies looked down demurely. The king, pleased with the song, commanded a chain of gold to be brought.

'Give this not to me but to your victorious knights; or to your chancellor to add a golden burden to his other burdens. I sing as the birds sing in the

trees, and such song is its own great reward. But if I may ask for a boon, I ask for a beaker of your purest golden wine.'

He drained it, and said 'A blessed house indeed where this is a small gift. In your good fortune think of me and thank God for your blessings, as I thank you for this wine.'

This is the Harper's first, and least characteristic, song in *Wilhelm Meister* (Book II, chapter XI). It had been set, but not particularly memorably, by both Schubert and Schumann. Wolf has no better luck. A poem thought worthy of musical treatment by three great composers cannot be without interest, although it is at first sight not apparent what attraction this long and rather dull ballad held for them. No doubt they sincerely responded to some truth in Goethe's allegory of the artist in society, and in its central idea that song is its own reward. Each treats the text deferentially, especially Wolf.

The piano has a soft prelude of melody with harp-like accompaniment to give background to the opening words. The king's commands are powerfully accompanied by falling fifths in octaves in the piano bass; the page's excursion is illustrated by scampering semiquavers; harp-notes resound. The song is finely effective for a good bass-baritone. But its construction is diffuse, and the central ideas and their musical equivalents become tedious when extended through well over a hundred bars of moderate time.

NOTES. 1. The falling fifths are also used in bars 7–11 of *Gesegnet sei* (190) in a musical context similar to bars 9–12 etc. here, and a verbal context suggesting not power but omnipotence.

2. At 'die goldene Kette gib mir nicht' the piano part has some of the 'loneliness' of motif 15; detachment from society is the idea of the words.

3. The piano postlude in praise of wine is remembered in the frankly bibulous songs of the *Westöstlicher Divan*, e.g. *Ob der Koran* (119).

4. Cf. Schumann, Op. 98a no. 2; Schubert.

96 (G 11). Der Rattenfänger: The ratcatcher
6th November 1888

I am the well-known minstrel, the much-travelled ratcatcher. It looks as if this famous old city needs my services; I can get rid of rats or any other vermin.

I am among other things a child-catcher, and can tame even the most unbiddable brats with my golden fairy-tales; boys and girls must all come dancing after me.

On occasion of course I use my powers to catch women. I win their hearts wherever I go; they all fall under the magic spell of my playing and singing.

I am the well-known minstrel, the much-travelled ratcatcher. I can rid your city of rats or any other vermin.

The Pied Piper of Hamelin is familiar to English readers from Browning's version of the legend. In any language he is a fairy-tale figure with magic powers that make rats, and children, follow his music. Goethe, with his penchant for making legendary figures human, presents us with his own reflections on the character. His ratcatcher is a boastful rather worldly spellbinder with powers over women; and, as befits a Don Juan, he is a lutanist rather than a piper, a serenader as well as an enchanter.

This presents a tremendous challenge to the musician. To match the poem a musical formula had to be found to suggest in its rhythm a compelling force, in its melody an irresistible gaiety and magic, turning at times to tenderness; a strain to bring everyone trooping after it. The result in Wolf's song is a dazzling *tour de force*.

The piano part, which compels our attention from the very first notes of the first bar, has the rhythmical strength and urgency of Schubert's *Erlkönig* or *An Schwager Kronos* combined with a brilliance that is pure Wolf. The prelude falls in volume and pitch to a soft strumming accompaniment; the voice enters, and all is lilt and fire. During each verse the piano leaves its neutral figurations from time to time to vie with the voice whether in Mephistophelean swagger and abandon, or in delicacy and tenderness; after each verse the brilliant prelude reappears. The song abounds in specially illuminating moments. Thus, at the words 'wenn er die goldnen Märchen singt' (when I sing my golden fairy-tales) in the second verse, the vocal melody is hushed and drawn out lovingly. The third verse is the climax of the poem and the song. Here, after the sighing and swooning of voice and piano at 'allen wird so liebebang' (they all feel the pangs of love) the 'magic strings and song' suddenly emerge with a new brightness in A major.

To round off the song the first verse is repeated. In the postlude the accompaniment themes are heard again in the original mode, prolonged and extended, in ecstatic figurations. This is extremely difficult for the pianist, who must make them sound like brilliant string-playing. Having pointed the worldly moral Wolf, if not Goethe, is content to let the ratcatcher return to fairyland. The theme rises and vanishes into thin air like the fairy music of *Nixe Binsefuss* (57).

NOTES. 1. The rising lilt at the end of the piano prelude is motif 7.

2. See 166, note 1.

97 (G 12). Ritter Kurts Brautfahrt: The knight's wedding-ride
9th December 1888

The valiant Sir Kurt mounts his trusty steed. He is off to his wedding at the castle of his fair lady. He meets on the way a menacing foe. Without a word spoken they begin to fight.

The issue is long in doubt, but at last he wins. He resumes his journey, bruised.

But then he sees a young mother with a baby. She beckons to him – 'Why the hurry, sir? Have you no word for your sweetheart, no gift for your child?' He feels greatly inclined to stay a while, finding the mother as charming as he found the maiden.

But the trumpets sound in the distance and he remembers his high-born bride. He sets off again but stops at a market and a fair to buy tokens of love. Then moneylenders suddenly appear, waving I.O.U.s.

So judicial proceedings hold up his career, an unseemly fate for our hero. It really is very tiresome and perplexing that a knight can never get free of enemies, women and debts; he just never gets free of them.

This is a brilliantly effective and original song which might have made many a lesser man's reputation. It contains dozens of themes and accompaniment figures, as if the poem had inspired fresh invention on a lavish scale. But many of them seem to be echoes of previous work. This song and the next (to which much of this comment also applies) were written at a time when the Goethe inspiration was showing some signs of flagging. Technically the music is deft and effective, but the musical devices which illustrate and comment on the text seem contrived.

NOTES. 1. The main sources of the materia lare *Feuerreiter* (56) and *Seemanns Abschied* (82). The defiant phrases heard in the piano at 'als am öden Felsenorte' anticipate *Prometheus* (134) and the main march themes *Epiphanias* (104) – if those two fine songs, dated somewhat later, were in fact later in conception.

2. The 'gaiety' motif 7 at bar 12 suggests mock-heroics.

3. The piano right-hand theme at 'aber ach!' et seq. is used again in a context descriptive of a crowd scene in *Was in der Schenke* (123).

4. We learn from Decsey's biography the sources of the musical description of moneylenders. The left-hand melody at 'aber ach', etc. is in debt to a motif in the introduction to Goldmark's Queen of Sheba; the right-hand countermelody at 'da kommen Juden' is on loan from A. von Goldschmidt.

5. One would have expected the major triad (B♮, not B♭) in the right-hand chord at the word 'freut' in bar 44; a natural is marked in the corresponding chords of bars 43 and 45.

98 (G 13). Gutmann und Gutweib: Goodman and goodwife
28th November 1888

It is the eve of St Martin. Goodwife, who loves her husband, has been making puddings for the feast day.

Now they are both lying in bed, and the door starts to bang in the wind. So goodman says to his wife, 'Get up and bar the door.'

'I'm only just in bed,' says she, 'and not properly warm; I'm not getting up.'

So they made a bet – the one that spoke first was to get up and bar the door.

At midnight two travellers arrive, thinking it must be an inn. Although the door is open, there is no light, not a sound. 'What sort of place is this? We can't make it out.' But there was not a word of reply – because of the door. They found the puddings and ate them; and goodwife said quite a lot to herself, but nothing out loud.

Soon they were complaining of thirst – 'here's a cupboard open,' says one, 'that'll be where they keep it! Ah, Schnapps! This'll warm us up.' At this, goodman couldn't contain himself. He came roaring out of bed, bellowing, 'Whoever's drunk my Schnapps will have to pay for it, in cash!' And good-wife jumped up and skipped about delightedly – 'You've spoken first; you bar the door!'

The source of Goethe's poem is a ballad in English, quite well known. As in the preceding song, Wolf lavishes a mint of music on a lyric that is unproductive from the song-writer's point of view. The composer has imagined the scene vividly in descriptive terms without real evocation of mood or character. Though the song is full of verve and brilliance and interprets the changing scene with sustained inventiveness of a high order, the result is stage scenery and stage effects.

NOTES. 1. Wolf in this detached ironic vein often uses characteristic themes to match verbal contests. Three among many are:

(a) The 'gaiety' motif 7 in the rising piano phrase at bar 12 shows, as in the preceding song, that the music is not to be taken too seriously.

(b) For the piano part at 'Im Bette liegen beide nun', which recurs after 'ich riegelte sie nicht zu', see motif 17.

(c) The exultant piano postlude has the laughter of motif 4.

2. See 117, note 2.

99 (G 14). Cophtisches Lied I: Coptic song I
28th December 1888

Leave pedants to quarrel and argue; let scholars be austere. All the wisest men of all time are in agreement on one point: – it is foolish to wait for fools to become enlightened; the wise man will deal with the fool according to his folly, as is right and proper.

Old Merlin from his shining grave where I consulted him in my youth gave me the same instructive advice: – it is foolish to wait for fools to become enlightened; the wise man will deal with the fool according to his folly, as is right and proper.

Whether on the windy peaks of India or in the depths of Egyptian tombs, all oracles gave the same answer: – it is foolish to wait for fools to become enlightened; the wise man will deal with the fool according to his folly, as is right and proper.

This and the following poem are taken from an early play of Goethe's, *Der Grosskophta*. Coptic, as the language of the Christian descendants of the ancient Egyptians, is clearly a suitable tongue for oracular utterance. The striking and attractive song has a measured chordal rhythm ♩ ♫ ♩ ♫ in piano and voice. This gives it a certain solemnity, to which the vocal melodies add grace and the harmonies wit. For example the last words of the refrain 'wie sichs gehört' (as is right and proper) are accompanied each time by a deliberately orthodox and academically correct progression. The piano interlude at the end of each verse serves as a synopsis. It is derived from the piano part at 'Töricht auf Bessrung der Toren zu harren!' (it is foolish to wait for fools to become enlightened) and in addition hammers the point home with accents suggesting the wagging of an admonitory forefinger and grace-notes suggesting ironic amusement. The treatment of each verse is similar, but with refined variations of harmony and melody. In the last verse there is also a variation of texture; the refrain has widely spaced chords giving an impressive effect of the voice from the oracle, as if the advice came from some great empty echoing vault.

NOTES. 1. This song is a useful example of the way in which Wolf blends prototypes into something absolutely new and original. Practically every bar has been heard before somewhere in Wolf's work. Even the singing of the opening melody (motif 10) looks back to *Der Schreckenberger* (74) at the words 'Fortuna weint vor Ärger'. There is the 'mystery' of motif 19 at bars 9 and 10, etc., the narrative of motif 21 at bars 1 and 2, etc., and the ironic acciaccature of motif 4; all these have been noted in the Mörike-Lieder. Even the piano's empty echoing effect described above is borrowed from the last page of *Feuer-reiter*. Yet the total effect is novel, not derivative.

2. In the absence of a prelude the first two lines of the song are essentially introductory, and it seems permissible to make a pause at the C major chord on 'sein' in bar 4.

100 (G 15). Cophtisches Lied II: Coptic song II

28th December 1888

Take my advice; spend your youth profitably; be wise in time. The pointer on the scales of Fortune is seldom at rest.

You must rise or fall; win, and be a master, or lose, and be a slave. You must suffer or triumph, be the anvil or the hammer.

The poem has the savour of a text from a secularized Book of Proverbs. The two halves of the song – the first solemn and pensive, the second strong and decisive – are in marked contrast both in key and in texture. They are linked by a passage that vividly suggests the swinging movement of a balance before a definite tilt is established. A piano interlude extends this image, borrowing for the purpose the melodic figure previously heard in the voice at the mention of the 'scales of Fortune'. In this way Wolf is perhaps suggesting his own view – there isn't much in it either way, and the merest touch might decide. But he has no doubt as to the choice between anvil and hammer. The last nine bars of piano postlude are unequivocally hammered out with great force.

NOTES. I. Both halves of the song begin in the minor and end on the *dominant* of the relative major; which is one way of making the unspoken point of the poem, as well as providing harmonic unity (beginning on D minor and ending on D major).

2. The exultant climax of the voice part (at 'Hammer') foreshadows the more exalted conclusion of *Wohl denk ich oft* (240) at 'alle Leute'. The anvil is also heard clanging at the end of *Prometheus* (134).

3. The 'mystery' motif 19 occurs at 'auf des Glückes grosser Wage', etc.

101 (G 16). Frech und Froh I: Uninhibited I

14th November 1888

Getting on well with girls, knocking about with men, and more credit than cash; that's how to get through life. Pleasure is the thing. If it won't come, take it. Get rid of people that stand in your way, never bother about sour grapes, and be truly carefree; that's the beginning and end of wisdom.

Don't forget to write verses; be a conformist, and always remember in good times and bad this golden ABC.

102 (G 17). Frech und Froh II: Uninhibited II

2nd February 1889

I scorn the pains of love, the gentle moan, the sweet distress. I am only interested in getting down to business; passionate glances, rough kisses.

Pleasure mingled with pain is for invalids. What a healthy man wants from love is no pain, all pleasure.

The two songs, related in words and music, are of no great account; but each is lively and effective and would make a welcome addition to the standard concert repertoire. Continuous quick bouncing scale passages and repeated chords in the piano part set the tone of the first song. It is the precise counterpart in music of the ironic detachment advocated by Goethe. As the accompaniment proceeds gaily on its way the voice interjects its pithy phrases. The song is not without its melodic appeal; but one cannot help feeling here, as elsewhere in the Goethe volume (e.g. 89 and 118), that much of the wit of the writing is more apparent in study than in performance. There is one obvious point (perhaps too obvious); at the end of the song the letters ABC are sung by the voice in unison with piano octaves in both hands, to these same notes (the German B = B flat).

The second song begins with a burlesque of the 'pains of love'. Then, in an effective contrast, the piano part announces a very decided version of the *Frech und Froh* theme already heard in the first song. The voice proclaims the poet's real view of the question, to melodic phrases, now rather more grateful than before, that lead to a ringing climax at 'alle Lust' (all pleasure).

NOTES. 1. The first song bristles with stereotypes. The whole accompaniment is a rendering of the 'gaiety' motif 7. The horn passages at bar 4, etc. are also characteristic (motif 8). The accompaniment at 'das wenig vieles sei' and elsewhere is a well-known formula (see motif 19).

2. In the second song there is a suggestion of self-parody. The first six bars resound to the 'sorrow' theme so characteristic of other Goethe songs in a serious vein (motif 22). In the unison octaves at 'sei ein armer Hund' there is more than a hint of the refrain of the first *Cophtisches Lied* (99).

3. The words of the second song form a telling rejoinder to those of *Nimmersatte Liebe* (21).

103 (G 18). Beherzigung: A lesson learned
30th December 1888

What should a man desire? Should he live quietly and clingingly, or should he be up and doing?

Should he build a house? Live in tents? Can he trust the rocks? Even the solid rock shakes.

There is no one answer. Let each man look to himself, what he does, where he dwells; and if he is on his feet, let him see to it that he does not fall!

This is a song full of latent strength. The idea that Wolf seeks to convey is shown by the odd direction 'Quite moderate tempo but with great inward excitement'. This seems to imply that the singer's mind is as it were already made up before the song begins. The piano's introductory motif

suggests discontent rather than indecision. The questioning phrases are set to a falling inflection, as if they were being interpreted as quasi-rhetorical. The result is that when, in the interlude after 'Felsen beben' (rocks shake) the introductory phrase already quoted is transformed to usher in the final section in A major

it has the effect less of a clarion call than of a political manifesto. The music of the last page is sententious; indeed the whole song gives an impression of contrivance in the way in which it is all built up from one single phrase. But this procedure is Wolf's way of saying that in his view the poem is all on the same theme, and that Goethe's message is never in doubt. The resulting unity and power of the music can make a thrilling impression in performance.

NOTE. For the word 'treiben', and in the two following bars, the piano has an analogue of the 'unrest' motif 5 which is used in a simpler and strengthened form in the great *Prometheus* (134) dated only three days later, e.g. at bars 18-19.

104 (G 19). Epiphanias: The three wise kings

27th December 1888

Here come the Three Kings with their star. They like eating and drinking, but they don't like paying. There are three of them, not four; and if a fourth were added, that would be one more Three-King.

(The first King:) I'm the handsome white one, best seen by day; but unloved in spite of my spices.

(The second:) I'm the tall swarthy one, popular with the ladies. I bring gold, not spices, so everyone likes me.

(The third:) I'm the little black one; I could be quite happy just eating and drinking, and saying thank you.

(Together:) The Three Kings are in good humour. They are looking for a stable, a Mother and a Child, for Joseph and the ox and the ass. We bring myrrh and gold, and given good wine we three will drink like six. As there are only fine ladies and gentlemen here, and no asses, as far as we can see, it is clear that we have come to the wrong place and must proceed on our way.

Wolf spent the Christmas of 1888 with his friends the Köcherts. This song was written for the three children of the house to sing and act at Epiphany. One hopes that the family was as pleased with it as posterity has been. The pawky humour of the poem is still not unamusing. At one level it evidently relates to the old traditional house-to-house visits of waits in costume, with a cardboard star on a pole. But, as often in Goethe, there is deep earnestness underlying the broad effect. Similarly, Wolf's setting, though high-spirited burlesque, also gives the impression of a certain underlying seriousness.

The broad swinging melodies of this song make it a universal favourite. In addition, Wolf takes full advantage of the opportunities for graphic illustration. The opening theme of the three local worthies, alias the Three Wise Kings, is sedately processional, with a hint of suppressed hilarity in the piano at 'kommen allhier', anticipating the forthright jollity of the voice in the following playful lines about the number of kings (no doubt there was no lack of volunteers to make the number up). The following three episodes are sharply characterized, with new and distinctive music for each.

The first 'solo' is tuneful and charmingly diffident, apart from a brief boast at 'best seen by day'. In the second, the strength and crispness of the accompaniment is a delight for pianists – though the graphically tall vocal phrase climbing to a high B flat at the word 'lang' is the despair of baritones. In the third, the piano part sparkles and twinkles its way back to the original joint march theme. An ironic bewilderment comes into the music at 'Da wir nun hier schöne Herrn und Fraun', when the kings remark that there seem to be no asses present. (The story goes that on one occasion when the composer was accompanying this song at a public performance he was seen to look quizzically at the audience at this point.) In the long postlude we are to imagine each king making a separate exit, each to his characteristic rhythm. They then reassemble and their joint theme is heard fading into the distance.

NOTES. I. The 'Three-King' theme divides neatly enough into three parts, (*a*) a rising fourth, (*b*) a group of quavers, (*c*) three strong crotchet chords incorporating an 'Amen' cadence. Each king is allotted, in addition to his new distinctive rhythm, a portion of this material, e.g. the first king has (*a*) in bars 18–19, the second has (*c*) in bars 26 and 28, the third (*b*) in bars 38–41.

2. The effect of irresolution at 'Da wir nun hier', etc., is achieved by unresolved chords. Their resolution comes at 'so sind wir nicht am rechten Ort', with their realization that they must be in the wrong place, which is after all a conclusion of sorts.

3. The piano part of the third king's episode ('Ich endlich', etc.) qualifies for motif 3 (at 'sein') and motif 4 *passim*, since this king is described as being small and (at least potentially) merry.

105 (G 20). St Nepomuks Vorabend: The eve of St Nepomuk
15th November 1888

Lights are gleaming on the river; children are singing. The cathedral carillon enhances our reverence and delight.

Then the lights fade, the stars fade. So our saint died rather than betray a trust.

Float again, lights; play, children; children's voices sing, sing! He is with the stars in heaven.

St Nepomuk was martyred by drowning for refusing to divulge information learnt through the confessional. Tradition has it that stars shone round his body as it floated down the river Moldau. A similar effect was arranged each year on the eve of the Saint's name-day in pious memory of the miracle.

Wolf's song is a great joy. A radiance plays about it. Despite the recondite look of some of the harmony, all is concord and sweetness. A gently rocking accompaniment, with thirds and sixths high on the keyboard, suggests the quietude and reverence of the night. Into this the voice weaves its tender phrases, never rising above mezzo-forte, while the changing piano harmonies gleam and fade. The composer directs 'slowly and with the utmost delicacy throughout' and only strict observance of this direction can bring out all the beauties of the music. A tenor who can take a long high A flat from a low E flat pianissimo, yet with full resonance, can achieve one of the loveliest moments in all song. The simple words 'sing, sing' are transfigured by this ecstatic leaping phrase.

NOTES. 1. Wolf can have had no qualms about the time-signature of this song, since he has taken the trouble to write out the last two bars quite deliberately in $\frac{6}{4}$. But though this is well enough for the piano part, much of the vocal melody is nonsensical unless scanned in $\frac{3}{2}$. The effect to be achieved is no doubt a virtual absence of stress. The lightest of touches on the first crotchet of each bar will carry the voice along following the verbal stress; the slightest of accents on the first and fourth crotchets will suffice for the piano part.

2. There is a possible explanation of this mild eccentricity of barring. The characteristic rocking movement of the piano part is a good example of the musical equivalent used by Wolf in contexts where night is mentioned (motif 18). The essence of this motif is adjacent or close notes in a rocking cross-rhythm, which is not achieved unless the time here is $\frac{6}{4}$. So the motif dictates the basic time, although the vocal inflections demand $\frac{3}{2}$.

3. It is worth noting how Wolf goes to immense pains to remove any asperities that might trouble the sweetness of the music. A good example is the difference between the piano's four-quaver group at the words 'Strome' and the analogous group at the words 'spielt, ihr' where the first two quaver chords are altered to avoid a clash with the vocal line.

106 (G 21). Genialisch Treiben: Creative activity
10th February 1889

I trundle my tub about from place to place, like the saintly Diogenes.

Sometimes in earnest, sometimes in jest; now loving, now hating; now this, now that; achieving nothing, and yet achieving something.

I just trundle my tub from place to place, like Diogenes.

The Cynic philosopher Diogenes was reputed to live in a tub. Goethe's half-humorous, half-wry use of this garbled tradition as a description of the poet's way of life compresses the relevant ideas into a few lines; austerity, energy, curiosity, changeability and occasional achievement.

The extended piano scherzo that Wolf provides as musical equivalent is similarly bursting with zest and invention (in treatment not unlike the work of Chopin in his sombre and virile vein). It is clearly the wry and austere aspects of the poem that Wolf wishes to emphasize: his own creative life was much more arduous than joyous. So there is nothing winning about the piano part except its drive and energy, which

136

are exceptional even for Wolf. The voice part is as it were caught up and carried away by this surge of energy, but is yet buoyed up and sustained by it, never submerged. A moment of relieving brightness occurs at 'Was' – the notion of something achieved – where the piano accompaniment changes from its chromatics into a short outburst of diatonic rollicking, so that the relentless quavers are momentarily halted before plunging down into the main theme which ends the song as it began.

NOTES. 1. The basic theme that begins and dominates the accompaniment is a Wolfian coinage for the idea of restless activity, and occurs often in analogous contexts (motif 5).

2. The song appears to allude to the Phrygian mode: the only example in Wolf's work. It is tempting (though no doubt fanciful) to interpret this as a tribute to the birthplace in Asia Minor of Diogenes himself. Gabriel Fauré had already set a precedent in alluding, in his song *Lydia*, to the Lydian mode.

107 (G 22). Der Schäfer: The shepherd
4th November 1888

Once upon a time there was a lazy shepherd, who could never be bothered about his sheep.

But a girl took his fancy; it was goodbye to appetite and sleep.

He took to aimless roaming, counting the stars at night, moaning and complaining.

But now that she's accepted him, he's quite himself again. He's got them all back – thirst, appetite and sleep.

A refreshingly simple and pleasant song, tailored to the verses in attractive musical material. The piano begins with a kind of yawn

Voice and piano are in unison, a not uncommon device of Wolf's for rendering simple statements or questions, in droopingly idle phrases. The music perks up and takes a livelier interest when the girl is mentioned. The octaves reappear, appropriately broken, to describe the shepherd's distracted wanderings. Then to a more formal accompaniment comes the happy ending, 'Durst, Appetit, und Schlaf'. The tiny postlude gives a final yawn and goes to sleep again.

NOTES. 1. This song, like some others in the Goethe volume, foreshadows the later refinements of Wolf's style in this kind of short genre-piece. Here there is kinship with *Ich liess mir sagen* (212) in the same key and on the same theme.

2. Older Peters Editions have B flat at the last treble note of the first complete bar of the song; it should be G.

108 (G 23). Der neue Amadis: The latter-day Amadis
5th February 1889

In my sheltered childhood I spent many years brooding on my own.

Day-dreaming was my pastime, and in my imagination I became a romantic hero and roamed the world. I built, and shattered, castles in Spain, and slew dragons with my shining spear. I was a real man.

As a knight-errant, I rescued the Fish Princess. She was so kind and hospitable; and I was gallantry itself.

Her kisses were ambrosial, glowing like wine. I almost died of love. She was all spangled with sunshine.

What has sundered me from her? Is there no magic wand to stay her swift flight? Where is her country now, where the road that leads there?

The title refers to Amadis de Gaul, a pseudo-historical chivalric hero of fourteenth-century Spanish romance. Goethe's verses are warm and imaginative, and full of pathos in the last lines. Needless to say Wolf's music recreates them, with typical added touches of picturesque detail. It is surprising that this splendid song is not heard more often. The melodies are charming throughout, and the piano part full of wit. The accompaniment is noteworthy for a crisp hobby-horse rhythm announced in the tiny prelude – ♩♩ – the knightly steed of childhood fantasy. At 'und ich war galant' the vocal line and the piano part combine hilariously in a splendid piece of comic invention. The last page is full of deep feeling which explores to the full Goethe's change of mood, while avoiding all trace of sentimentality.

NOTES. 1. Much of the song, and in particular the final note of the voice sustained over a characteristic rhythm, is akin to *Der Tambour* (17) which is also about wishful and wistful thinking. Each has the élan of motif 7, here at the words 'durchzog die Welt'.

2. See 120, note 2.

109 (G 24). Blumengruss: Flower greeting

31st December 1888

May this garland I have gathered bring you a thousandfold greeting. I have stooped down, surely a thousand times, and pressed it to my heart, how many hundred thousand times; how many, many times.

This is a perfect page. The persistent accompaniment figure

somehow epitomizes the whole essence of the poem. The continuing drooping tenderness of this phrase with its subtle changes in pitch and harmony, and the wistful cadences of the vocal melody, combine to recreate most movingly the love and sorrow behind these simple words.

NOTES. 1. The song is a perfect example of one aspect of Wolf's harmonic procedures. The tonality is clearly based on F major, but the stress of emotion leads it away from this key through poignant harmonies, and gently back again, to match the simplicity of the closing words.

2. This song and the next in their great achievement within a limited compass look forward to the refinements of the Italian Songbook.

3. The opening of the vocal melody seems to have made a deep impression on Wolf. It is found again in the same key and similar harmonies in similar contexts of self-surrender in *Nicht Gelegenheit* (124) and *Ach des Knaben Augen* (142).

110 (G 25). Gleich und Gleich: Like with like

6th November 1888

A flower had bloomed early; up came a bee and sipped daintily. The two must surely have been made for each other.

A miniature masterpiece. The spacing and placing of the accompaniment, the shapely grace and sensitivity of the vocal line, combine to make a radiantly perfect little summer idyll, troubled only at the last few words by a hint of doubt before ending brightly in the piano postlude.

NOTES. 1. Since it is clear that the poem's symbolism of human love had not escaped the composer, it is amusing to note that the bee-and-flower relationship is presented in musical terms akin to those used in *Mausfallen-Sprüchlein* (6) for a mouse-and-mousetrap relationship.

2. Like other Goethe songs (e.g. 107, 109) this is an interesting blend of earlier and later styles. In recapturing the charm of *Mausfallen-Sprüchlein* it

anticipates the technical perfection and deep emotion of *Heut' Nacht erhob ich mich* (227).

3. Note how the expected rhythm ♫ ♩ in the piano is simplified at 'naschte fein' – because that rhythm is needed in the voice part and its duplication would damage the delicacy of the texture.

111 (G 26). Die Spröde: The coy shepherdess
21st October 1889

On a spring morning a young shepherdess went singing through the fields: fa la la!

Thyrsis offered her three lambs for a kiss, but she went on singing: fa la la!

And another offered her ribbons, and a third his heart, but they too were answered by: fa la la!

Goethe's gay poem and its sadder sequel (112), written in the mock-pastoral convention, are full of life and warmth. This sort of verse was perfectly suited to Wolf's own genius for infusing melodic and harmonic grace and fire into formal thematic constructions.

This first song is a blend of beauty and brilliance: its lilting melodies linger in the memory. The flouncing piano figure heard in the short prelude coquettes through the song. It changes in rhythm and texture to accompany the singing, 'so la la lerallala!' and finishes the first and last verses with a little gay strumming. In the middle verse, Thyrsis makes a brief appearance to a new serenading strain. After his proposed exchange the flouncing rhythm returns; and at the words 'schalk-haft blickte sie ein Weilchen' (she looked at him roguishly for a moment) it hesitates delightfully before going on triumphantly and bursting into song as before. But the singing now ends on a pensive sustained top note, diminuendo. Evidently she is not wholly unaffected or unpleased by Thyrsis' proposal. Indeed all the music has, underlying its surface gaiety, a certain wistful unease that prepares us for *Die Bekehrte*.

NOTES. 1. The minor seconds of the piano prelude, etc., may suggest that Wolf has pictured a little Dresden shepherdess (motif 3).

2. The appealing serenade accompaniment devised for Thyrsis is used in a more extended form in *Ein Ständchen euch zu bringen* (208).

3. The vocal melody at 'so wie mit den Lämmern Scherz' is often found in contexts suggesting contentment, often, as here, associated with the open air (motif 9); it also has Wolf's rollicking F♯ major tonality.

4. The gay grace-notes in voice and piano stand for mocking laughter (motif 4).

5. The thematic relationships between this song and its sequel make a

fascinating study. It seems difficult to resist the conclusion that both were sketched at the same time (early 1889). This one may have proved less tractable to work out technically, as its occasional hints of artifice suggest; at any rate it was not completed until October 1889. This was eight months after all the other Goethe songs, but only a week before the outburst of the Spanish Songbook; and the song has certain characteristics, such as the uncertainty of accentuation at the half-bar, which suggest that the piano part is the basic concept – a noticeable feature of the Spanish volume.

112 (G 27). Die Bekehrte: The sad shepherdess
12th February 1889

At sunset I walked through the wood. Damon sat playing the flute and the rocks resounded: fa la la!

And he drew me down to him and kissed me so sweetly; and I said 'play again!' and he played again: fa la la!

And now I know no peace or joy any more, and I can hear nothing but that sweet fluting: fa la la!

We are to imagine the song as being sung by the shepherdess described in the previous song. The German title means that she has been 'converted'. Wolf's music mirrors the poet's change from the third person to the first; in this beautifully intimate and personal song all is direct simplicity and tenderness. Once again it is the piano prelude that gives a basic shape and rhythm to the whole accompaniment. A gentle rise and fall in the piano's melodic figures convey both the emotional state of the singer, and the symbol of its cause – the sound of the flute.

In the second verse the surface of the music is still unbrokenly tranquil, but there is more than a hint of passion and regret in the restrained crescendo at the word 'süss' (sweetly). After the sad singing the tiny piano interlude slows down and tails off sadly, with an effect not unlike that of the famous passage in Schubert's *Gretchen am Spinnrade* in which the spinning-wheel accompaniment is made to falter before the reappearance of the first theme. Indeed, the melodic flow of the voice part and the grace of the accompaniment make the song not unworthy of comparison with Schubert, while remaining wholly Wolfian in such subtle touches as the way in which the 'so la la' burden becomes progressively more restrained in its melodic range at each repetition.

NOTES. 1. A sentimental interpretation is perilous. Wolf's direction is 'with a light movement, not dragging'.

2. An analogue of motif 5, elsewhere associated with unrest or unease, is found in this song, appropriately in the soprano register (piano treble bar 5, etc.).

3. Wolf was fond of using the key of A minor in songs for a woman's voice in wistful mood.

113 (G 28). Frühling übers Jahr: Spring all the year
21st December 1888

The garden is budding snow-white, saffron-gold, emerald green, blood-red;
pert primroses, hidden violets, all the new life of Spring.

Yet no flower in all the garden blooms as sweet as my darling, smiling at
me, singing; sweet of voice, fair of face and pure of heart like a flower,
friendly and demure.

Even the lilies and roses that summer brings would vie with her in vain.

Goethe's radiant poem here paraphrased is a spring song and a love-song
at once. Wolf's music captures both aspects most beautifully; it is a great
enchantment from the first note to the final chord. The delicate chiming
and pealing of the short prelude dominate the song. Was it, one wonders,
that Wolf's imagination had been especially taken by the second line
of the poem, 'da wanken Glöckchen so weiss wie Schnee'? (literally –
there sway little bells as white as snow).

With the entry of the voice part we are in Spring. The staccato
chiming and flowering of the piano part sets the scene, the harmony
paints it, the contours of the vocal melody fill it with life and character.
Soon the first climax of the song is reached with a high A fortissimo:
'The new life of Spring!' The piano exults but soon quietens and
subsides. The accompaniment becomes more reflective and legato, the
voice part more restrained. The composer here has been at pains to give
separate directions: 'innig' (rapt) for the singer, 'weich' (tender) for the
pianist. With the same music and in the same breath the loved one
appears; herself a fairer flower. There is another exquisite moment in
the high vocal phrase, hushed and a little slower, at 'Ein immer offen,
ein Blütenherz' (an ever-open flower-heart). After the piano interlude
the song resumes its first strain. But, for the new thought that 'Summer's
flowers too would vie with her in vain', the voice has a new and charming
melody; and at 'vergebens' (in vain) a little jet of irrepressible delight
bubbles up from the piano, as amid more chiming and swaying the
song ends.

NOTES. 1. The chimes appropriate to a 'Schneeglöcklein' (snowdrop: literally, and pleasantly, 'little snow bell') are treated not dissimilarly in the Schubert
song *Viola*.

2. There are all kinds of felicities in the melodic line, such as its becoming
bold for the preening primrose, and then unobtrusive for the violet in the next
phrase. The first of these examples is not unlike the opening phrase of that bold
Spring song *Er ist's* (18).

3. In places, the vocal phrases sing through the bar lines. Thus the scansion of the first four bars for the voice is 3 + 3 + 2 crotchets, and similarly in bars 13–16.

114 (G 29). Anakreons Grab: The tomb of Anacreon
4th November 1888

Here roses bloom, vine and laurel entwine, turtle-doves coo, and the cricket sings for joy. Whose grave can this be, so lovingly endowed with life by all the gods? It is Anacreon's resting-place.

He delighted in spring, summer, and autumn; and now he is sheltered from the winter.

The Greek poet Anacreon is thought of as the laureate of nature, love and wine. Goethe's beautiful lines are replete with insight, reverence and love, and are rounded by their elegiac metre into a classical object of shapely perfection. Wolf's music has an atmosphere of tenderness and beatitude with hardly a parallel in song. His setting seems to re-create not only the poem itself, but the actual experience that he imagines as having inspired it.

The two bars of introduction are tranquil and meditative. At the entry of the voice the piano has evocatively entwined phrases, softly falling and swaying. All is warmth and peace. The tonality darkens for a moment at the word 'Grab'; and now the music both illustrates and meditates upon the contrast of rich exuberant life that makes this grave beautiful. The harmony is richer and more complex; tendrils of rhythm and melody stray across the bar-lines; the word 'Leben' is lingered out in the voice part. Then once more we hear the rising semitones of the first two chords of the piano prelude repeated with a quiet insistence. Their harmonic tensions add a wistful questioning which resolve into simple harmony as the voice sings, most memorably, 'Es ist Anakreons Ruh'. Everything that has gone before combines to charge this magical phrase with emotive effect. The voice seems to read the inscription. 'It is' – then a slight pause – then, savouring the beloved name, 'Anacreon's resting-place'. On this last word 'Ruh' the piano's gradually relaxing harmonies come finally to rest.

The music resumes with a variant of the piano prelude. The emotional tensions are relaxed. The music is warm and peaceful as before, but now the singer's art can make it new-radiant with the spirit of Anacreon. The postlude meditates on themes of release and sleep.

NOTES. 1. Slow rising semitones are heard elsewhere in moods of mystic comfort and joy; see 32, note 1. The whole feeling of the words and of Wolf's D major music alike is worlds apart from tragedy; nothing could be more mistaken than to sing this song lugubriously.

2. The postlude's horn passage after the last word 'geschüzt' may be thematic here in the context of 'release' (motif 8).

3. The rocking quaver triplets in the postlude are cousins to the music of night and sleep in, e.g., *Um Mitternacht* (31) (motif 18).

115 (G 30). Dank des Paria: The prayer of the outcast
9th November 1888

Great Brahma! now I know you as the creator of all worlds, and name you as my Lord; for all are equal in your eyes. You hear the prayers of the humblest; even we, the most lowly of all, are reborn in you.

Turn to this woman, who is made Goddess through pain. Now I await the vision of Him who alone can act and move.

The poem is one of a group central to Goethe's thought, and very productive of literary footnotes. But the song is curiously unattractive and laboured. The influence of Wagner, here as elsewhere, proves fatal to Wolf's true genius. As an operatic fragment, with the piano part orchestrated, this work might be effective. As a song depending for its effect on immediacy and intimacy of appeal it must regretfully be counted among Wolf's few failures.

NOTE. There are interesting affinities with *Wie glänzt der helle Mond* (186). The situations are analogous. Each deals with a humble vision of God. In this song bars 13–16 and bars 22–25 correspond to the two main themes of the later, and greater, work. This in turn seems to have a subconscious echo in *Geselle, woll'n wir uns* (200, note 1).

116 (G 31). Königlich Gebet: A king's prayer
7th January 1889

I am the master of the world. The nobles whom I command love me and I them.

God grant that I always deserve this power and this love.

There is perhaps more lording than loving in the music, and more pride than prayer. But the song is effective and by no means negligible. There is nobility in the vocal line and great strength in the piano part, particularly in the striding octaves of the bass.

NOTES. I. The strong themes of the piano part find a truer use, shorn of any suspicion of bombast, in the middle section of *Grenzen der Menschheit* (136) written only two days later.

2. One may compare the early Mörike song *Der König bei der Krönung* (8) on a similar theme.

117 (G 32). Phänomen: Phenomenon
19th January 1889

When the Sun weds the falling rain a rainbow springs up.
   Sometimes in mist or cloud it seems white; yet it is there in the heavens.
   So let old men be blithe; though they be white-haired, they shall still find love.

Goethe had a lasting interest in physics as well as metaphysics; particularly in the science of optics, a field in which he made some original discoveries in his day.

Wolf achieves a particularly interesting unity between music and words. Nothing could be more chromatic than the rainbow, and practically every known key is referred to during the course of this short song. The key-signature is A major, but only the first half of the first bar is unquestionably 'in' this key. The music, before ending in (if anything) its dominant, E major, uses a whole palette of tonal colouring. Each phrase is harmonically self-contained, with an effect of colours changing in a rainbow of progression. And with all this the song has great strength and charm; the more it is heard the more highly prized it becomes. The vocal melodic flow is continuous and beautiful, and the piano postlude tremulous with promise.

NOTES. I. In the first two bars the piano has the 'narrative' harmony of motif 21. This and the corresponding vocal melody are related to that in the passages mentioned in 74, note 2.

2. There are cramped chromatics in four-part harmony in the piano part at, e.g., bar 11. This sort of writing is rare in Wolf; indeed, only one other such passage comes readily to mind, at bars 3–4 of *Gutmann und Gutweib* (98). In each case the words are – no doubt by coincidence – about happiness in old age.

118 (G 33). Erschaffen und Beleben: Genesis and Exodus
21st January 1889

God made Adam into a man. From Mother Earth he emerged, a clod. Then Jehovah breathed life into his nostrils. At once he gave signs of being able to rise above his background; he began to sneeze.
   Yet even with limbs and a head there was much of the clod about him, until at last Noah found just the right thing for him – Wine!

*That leavened the lump at the very first sip. So let us all (following the
sacred example of Hafiz, poet and wine-bibber) proceed on our way to
rejoin our Creator, to the sound of clinking glasses.*

The poem is racy and clever; and as usual with Goethe there is also a
tinge of reverence, even of philosophic reflection. Wolf has an uncanny
knack of finding music for all the aspects of a piece of verse, and the
result here is a rather odd mélange. The song begins with splendidly
thumping crotchet octaves, and one expects broad diatonic harmonies
and melodies. Instead there is melodic refinement and a strong hint of
tonal complexity. There are the usual felicities – e.g. a fit of sneezing by
the piano and a hilarious outburst at the mention of wine at 'Humpen'
(wine bowl). But it is not until the last verse that constraint is thrown
off. Piano and voice peal out exultantly, and the postlude is uninhi-
bitedly diatonic. No doubt this climax is made more effective by contrast with the preceding chromaticism. Given a rich voice and capable
pianist the song cannot fail to be impressive. But only the Wolf en-
thusiast, one feels, will enjoy it to the full.

NOTES. I. Processional exit is a favourite device of Wolf's; cf. *Der Schreckenberger* (74) and *Epiphanias* (104) among many others.

2. Motif 19 occurs at 'Die Elohim zur Nas' hinein' for the mystery of creation.

3. A rollicking mood often suggested the tonality of F sharp major to Wolf.
The music arrives in this key with éclat at 'Humpen'.

4. In older Peters Editions a sharp needs to be added to the first bass octave
in the fifth bar on p. 48.

119 (G 34). 'Ob der Koran von Ewigkeit sei? . . .'
17th January 1889

*Did the Koran exist from all eternity? I don't ask. Was it created? I don't
know. Of course I believe it to be the Book of Books, as a good Moslem
must. But it is at least certain that wine was created by Allah. Before the
angels, some say; and that seems not unlikely. Be that as it may, the wine-
drinker sees the face of Allah more clearly.*

The task of setting a poem which begins in the guise of a theological
meditation and turns out to be devoted to the praise of wine, presents
its own special difficulties. Wolf's achievement here is that one is not
conscious of them; the song is a perfect treatment of words.

With a fine sweep of rising octaves for piano with the voice in unison,
the music announces a solemn theological question. The piano echoes
the last part of the phrase softly, as if in reflection; then come the words

'darnach frag' ich nicht' (I don't ask about that) implying that it is not only a difficult question, but a boring one. 'Ob der Koran geschaffen sei?' – or was it created? Again a pause for reflection. 'Das weiss ich nicht' – I don't know; and, as the piano part now hints by borrowing the vocal phrase of 'darnach frag' ich nicht', I don't much care. 'But, of course', the voice part adds hastily, but without much conviction, 'I believe it to be the Book of Books.' Turning to a more congenial topic, the voice announces, this time with complete conviction, its considered view on the genesis of wine, with a spirited 'hear, hear!' from the piano.

A rhythmic excitement now begins to take charge of the piano part. The music becomes steadily more lively and assured. It bursts out suddenly into a bright A major (the first time this chord has been heard in the song so far) at the last words 'blickt Gott frischer ins Angesicht', and continues in a gay postlude which is first syncopated, then rollicking, then triumphant, conveying in eight bars a potted idealized history of the effects of wine-bibbing.

NOTE. The note of mellow elation in the piano postlude is heard in many of the love songs of the *Westöstlicher Divan* (see 129). The syncopations here may derive from the postlude to *Der Sänger* (95) which also follows a passage in praise of wine.

120 (G 35). 'Trunken müssen wir alle sein! . . .'
18th January, 1889

Let us all get drunk! Young men are drunk whether they drink or not, but old men must drink themselves young again; the grape is a great dispeller of troubles.

No more questions; wine is forbidden and, if you are going to get drunk, you might as well drink the best; you are a heretic twice over if you go to hell for drinking cheap wine.

So let us all get drunk! drunk!! drunk!!!

One of Wolf's best bravura display pieces for voice and piano. The purely musical interest is here deliberately subordinated to dramatic effect; and the riotous result in this Bacchanale is of shattering intensity, given adequate performance.

The piano part in the first section is boisterously robust. With bunched chords in both hands and insistent $\frac{6}{8}$ rhythms, it is a fitting vehicle for the vocal line; a chariot for the god of wine himself. A slightly more solemn (though no more sober) note is heard at the mention of old age ('Trinkt sich das Alter wieder zu Jugend'), etc., but the revelry breaks out again even more elatedly at 'Reben' (grapes). A bar or two later the time-signature changes to $\frac{2}{4}$ and the tempo quickens, as if to distract attention from the logical deficiencies of the text and to increase its persuasive powers. At the word 'Frätzer' (cheap wine) the piano part comes thundering up in octaves in both hands to the final outburst of drunken revelry that ends the song.

NOTES. 1. The gaily rising piano part after 'Reben' is motif 7.

2. The piano part of the middle section seems to have been the unconscious source for some of the characteristic phrases of *Der neue Amadis* (108).

3. The contented vocal melody at 'Trinke nur vom besten Wein' is a variant of motif 9.

4. Although this is a bravura song the first section should not be taken too fast; otherwise there is not enough contrast left with the middle section. A normal allegro is ample.

121 (G 36). 'So lang man nüchtern ist . . .'
16th January 1889

When sober, a man is bound to go wrong; he must drink to know what is right. But there is also the danger of excess. I wonder how Hafiz dealt with that difficulty?

What I think is that if a man cannot drink he should not love. But wait a minute, you drinkers – if a man cannot love, he should not drink.

The words may seem unpromising material for a lyric. But Wolf finds sweetness and serenity in them. It is an adorable song, with ingratiating vocal melodies.

The piano part is mock solemn with a dignity that remains unruffled in spite of occasional demisemiquaver hiccoughs. At the words 'das Rechte' (what is right) it becomes rectitude itself. It is orotund at 'nur ist das Übermass' (excess), and tender at the mention of the poet Hafiz. The interlude has a quiet pensive satisfaction; a problem is posed, and a conclusion reached. The resuming voice announces this conclusion, at 'Denn meine Meinung' (What I think). The music of the first verse is then repeated with only slight variations. The piano concludes the song with its interlude theme, a question asked and answered, this time with the complete conviction of a final sforzando chord.

It must be admitted that the strophic form is not wholly satisfactory as a treatment of the words, the phrases used for both verses not being equally appropriate to each context (see notes below). But the poem is so slight and the music so delightful that the composer seems justified in sacrificing verbal effects to musical impulse whenever a choice has to be made.

NOTES. 1. The 'mystery' motif 19 occurs at the phrase 'Nur ist das Übermass' which announces an unresolved problem; but the same music in the second verse is unthematic.

2. Conversely, the 'contentment' of motif 9 in the second verse at 'wenn man nicht lieben kann', etc., is delightfully suited to these words; but is unthematic in the first verse.

122 (G 37). 'Sie haben wegen der Trunkenheit . . .'
18th January, 1889

They accuse me of drunkenness; they chatter about it endlessly. Lying in a stupor all night is the usual effect; but I am harried around all night by my drunkenness. Being drunk with love is my trouble. Night and day, day and night, it quakes in my heart. My heart so swells with poetic drunkenness that there is no room for sober drunkenness. Night and day I am drunk with love, poetry, and wine; tormented and overjoyed by this divine drunkenness.

The title leads us to expect another of Wolf's Bacchantic outbursts. But he has rightly gone deeper. The idea of 'Trunkenheit' resounds through the music as it does through the poem; and Wolf follows Goethe in giving this idea a changing interpretation.

The first page is devoted to mundane drunkenness. $^{12}_{8}$ time, which is a great rarity in Wolf, is called on for this purpose. The crotchet-quaver movement slides and sways quietly, with uncertain harmonies and slurred vocal line, until the voice explains the real trouble – 'Liebestrunkenheit'. From this point on rhythm, harmony and melody alike become more coherent and compelling. In the last page the original falling swaying themes are set to work again as the emphatic bass of the piano part, as if to illustrate the point that the two kinds of drunkenness are similar in their effects if not indeed in their causes. All this is admirably done; one only wishes that the song had been made more attractive melodically.

NOTE. The right-hand piano part at 'Es ist die Liebestrunkenheit' recalls *Lied eines Verliebten* (55) and is itself the forerunner of similar passionate love-motifs fashioned from melodic lines based on intervals of a minor third in 131 and 132 below and in many of the love-songs of the Spanish Songbook (e.g. 164, 176).

123 (G 38). 'Was in der Schenke waren heute . . .'
16th January 1889

What a scene at the inn at dawn this morning! Girls, torches, crowds,
haggling, insults, flutes, drums; it was like Bedlam, but I revelled in every
minute of it.

They criticize me for not learning how to behave; but a wise man prefers
the jostling of the mob to the bickering of pedants.

The scene at the inn must have presented itself very vividly to Wolf's
imagination. 'Extremely fast and whirling' is his direction. The song
begins with an insistent quaver figure in octaves in the piano. The voice
enters, and is whirled away in a tumult of quaver chords. The impetus
slackens briefly for the poet's enjoyment of the scene, but resumes with
scarcely a pause in a piano interlude. This changes into slower portentous octaves that set the scene for the final verse – a weighty moral
pronouncement, to new musical material. But there is no slackening of
the tempo, and the running quavers in the bass are slightly syncopated
from time to time, as if to hint that wine is among the sources of inspiration of this philosophy. When the voice ends the piano returns in full
strength to the opening theme with a splendid bravura passage that
relives and relishes the tumultuous scene at the inn.

NOTES. 1. The genesis of the 'tumult' theme of this song is found in *Ritter*
Kurts Brautfahrt (97), dated two months earlier, at the point where the music
depicts a crowd scene.

2. It is perhaps far-fetched to claim the bass part in the second section at
'Dass ich von Sitte', etc. as an example of motif 15, yet it is characteristic in
appearance, and the text speaks of estrangement.

3. There is an idefinable kinship between this music and that of *Das Köhler-*
weib ist trunken (185) also in D minor.

4. The portentous octaves with their augmented intervals at the direction
'sehr markiert' are not unlike the theme associated with the Corregidor in Wolf's
opera of that name, composed six years later.

124 (G 39). 'Nicht Gelegenheit macht Diebe. . .'
21st January 1889

(Hatem:) They say that opportunity makes thieves, but I think it is itself a
thief. For it stole and gave away to you all my love, and left me begging for
your mercy. But I see compassion in your tender sapphire glances; and in
your embrace I am born anew.

125 (G 40). 'Hoch beglückt in deiner Liebe . . .'
23rd January 1889

(Suleika:) Rejoicing in your love, I do not chide opportunity; that theft delighted me. But why speak of stealing? Give yourself freely to me. Whatever you give willingly shall be well rewarded. Gladly I give you my peace and my life. And no more talk of begging; does not love make us rich? In your embrace is the greatest happiness I have ever known.

These two songs are considered together because a close inter-relationship is evident in both words and music; they even share the same melody. Yet the effect of each is quite different. The first song violates practically every known canon of song-writing. The two bars of piano prelude are a piece of banal strumming sheerly unbelievable in a Wolf song. The rest gives the impression of having been compiled from scraps of previous songs with scissors and paste. Before long we are wondering where we have heard it before. The construction is diffuse throughout, and the accentuation is awry, with confusion at the half bar. Yet somehow, mysteriously, there are passages of such intense beauty that we should be poorer without this song. The vocal melody does much to redeem it, irradiating the music in the middle verse and heightening the closing words with a tenderness that transcends criticism.

In the piano part of Suleika's reply, variations are worked out with great inventiveness. The zest and vitality of the music are impressive. In virtuoso performance, it is thrilling. Yet this song, though more original and less trite than its companion piece, is felt to be less moving. This, it may be argued, is precisely the relationship of the two poems; the first laboured but real, the second ingenious but unconvincing. Perhaps it is Wolf's instinctive feeling for his poetic material that has produced this very odd result in these two songs. If the emotion of the one and the invention of the other could have been combined, the world would be richer by a very great masterpiece.

NOTES. 1. It is just possible (though unlikely) that Wolf may actually have been striving to match the sententiousness of the first poem by the deliberate use of occasional triviality and almost continual reminiscence of his own previous work. For what it is worth, the echoes are:

> (a) bars 7–10 in their chromaticism are akin to the first page of *Frage und Antwort* (47) and of *Nimmersatte Liebe* (21).
>
> (b) bars 13–16, voice, cf. opening vocal line of *Blumengruss* (109).
>
> (c) bars 13–16, piano, cf. *Ganymed* (135), piano at 'Ach, an deinem Busen', etc.

(*d*) bars 17–21, piano, are reminiscent of *Mignon III* (92), piano part at 'Dort ruh' ich', etc.

2. The postlude of the first song, and the prelude of the second, has the converging melodic lines of the love-motif 13.

3. The second song strongly suggests the techniques of the Spanish Song-book, and in particular *Bitt' ihn o Mutter* (162).

126 (G 41). 'Als ich auf dem Euphrat schiffte . . .'
24th January 1889

(*Suleika:*) *I dreamed that as I sailed on the Euphrates the gold ring you gave me slipped from my finger into the water. Then I woke and it was day. Tell me, poets and prophets, what does this dream mean?*

127 (G 42). 'Dies zu deuten bin erbötig! . . .'
24th January 1889

(*Hatem:*) *Let me interpret. Have I not often told you how the Doges of Venice were wedded to the sea? Your dream makes me love you even more, because in it you are wedding me, a stranger, to your river and to your homeland; and here I shall live and love you always.*

Again two songs are related musically as well as verbally. Both are simple and unconstrained with a strong easy flow of appealing melody in voice and piano, presenting no difficulty and much delight to the listener. The first is a woman's song recounting a dream of drifting on the river. Nothing could suit it better than its delicate barcarolle movement. Hatem's reply takes its themes and transforms them with virile strength and tenderness, culminating in a joyous cry at 'hier soll bis zum letzten Kusse' (here to the last kiss) and a tenderly musing piano postlude.

NOTES. The thematic inter-connexion is evident at first hearing. Amusingly, it is at its strongest at the moment when in the second song (bars 13–16) the circumstances of the first (bars 1–4) are directly referred to. After the former passage the piano bar allotted to the falling ring is pleasantly apt.

128 (G 43). 'Hätt' ich irgend wohl Bedenken . . .'
26th January 1889

(*Hatem:*) *I would not think twice about making you a present of our great cities like Samarkand, with their gaudy pomp. But what if you asked our Emperor to give you them? He's finer and wiser than I am; but he doesn't know what loving is. Emperor, you'll never feel like giving that sort of present. To think of gifts like that you need to have a girl like mine and be a beggar like me.*

This has thematic affinities with the preceding song. Hatem is again in joyous mood. Again voice and piano vie in delighted melodies to a more or less orthodox accompaniment figure of triplet chords in the right hand. The bass line becomes ponderous and the music ironically perplexed when the oddly ungenerous views of the Shah are mentioned. But the melodies burst out all the more brightly later on, notably at the last ringing words 'und ein Bettler sein wie ich'. Then the piano postlude's bass octaves troll out magnificently in the long falling phrases that bring this enjoyable song to a close.

NOTE. It looks as if the Shah on his throne is awarded the 'loneliness' motif 15 at bar 11 et seq. Serve him right, one feels.

129 (G 44). 'Komm, Liebchen, komm! . . .'
25th January 1889

(Hatem:) Come, my love, come and put on my turban. Only you can wind it beautifully. Not even the Shah himself high on his throne could have his head enfolded so gracefully.

A turban was the headdress of Alexander himself. Well it pleased all the lords that succeeded him; and muslin is still the finest headdress, let jewels glitter as they will.

So wind this silver turban about my brow, my love; and then, if you look at me, I am a king.

This is a straightforward love-song. Melodies and harmonies are simple, the accompaniment orthodox, and the whole blended with Schubertian felicity. The music becomes more typically Wolfian at the praise of the turban – 'Ein Dulbend war das Band das Alexandern', etc. Lighter and cooler in texture, it goes spiralling sedately round in winding melodic figures and key-changes, culminating on the softly sustained last syllable of the word 'Musselin'. The first strain reappears and is taken to a rousing climax on the last words. At this passionate avowal of love the turban is forgotten. The long piano postlude recalls the measure and melody of the words 'Komm, Liebchen, komm'. The melody is extended, first appealingly then imploringly, in syncopated left-hand octaves under a persistent six-quaver measure of right-hand chords. At the close it hushes to a whisper; 'Come, my love, come' quietly, tenderly, 'Come, my love.'

NOTE. See note to 119, and note 2 to 163.

130 (G 45). 'Wie sollt ich heiter bleiben . . .'
23rd January 1889

(*Hatem:*) *How can I be carefree when parted from her? My only wish is to write; I have no taste for wine. When she drew me to her, no use for talking then. But as my tongue then faltered, so does my pen now. Come then, dear Saki, fill my cup in silence. I need say only 'Remember'; he already knows my wish.*

131 (G 46). 'Wenn ich dein gedenke . . .'
25th January 1889

(*Hatem:*) *When I am thinking of you, my cup-bearer always says 'Why so silent Sir? For Saki would gladly listen for ever to your teaching.' When I lie under the cypress tree, lost in my thoughts, he thinks nothing is going on. Yet it is at this moment that I am at my most profound, as wise as Solomon.*

Another pair of songs. The mood and music of each are similar in conception; in each persists a muted thought of the loved one. Both need interpretation of a high order before their beauties become manifest. Again the words are mirrored with great art by Wolf, and it is perhaps for this reason that the second song is less immediately successful. The first speaks of the thoughts of love; the second is, so to speak, concerned with the thoughts of the thoughts of love, and it sounds just that much more remote.

The dreamy, wistful lilt of the first catches the mood to perfection. It is questioning in the first two lines, mellow at 'Nun aber will ich schreiben' (my wish is to write). It melts into tenderness at 'wenn sie mich an sich lockte' (when she drew me to her) and is the very essence of wistfulness for the one word 'Gedenke' (remember) where the major triad is used for the first time, under a sustained high note. If in this song the mood is elusive it is nevertheless caught and held. In the second song the harmonies shift obscurely and the emotion, though detectable, never really succeeds in shining through the surrounding subtlety.

NOTES. 1. The rocking rhythm of the first song throughout suggests the dreaminess of motif 18.

2. The second song has thematic material (e.g. in piano bass and treble bars 1–2 and similarly throughout) much akin to that of some of the love-songs of the Spanish Songbook (see note to 122).

132 (G 47). 'Locken, haltet mich gefangen . . .'
29th January 1889

(*Hatem:*) *Let her tresses bind me fast within the circle of her face. I have nothing to match their dear golden coils.*

Except that this heart is still young and full of fire. From under the snow and mist of its peaks a volcano bursts molten out. You shame the bleak mountain side, like the blush of dawn; and once again I feel the breath of spring and the fire of summer.

Cupbearer! more wine! I pledge this bowl to her! When she finds a heap of ashes she will say – he burnt himself up for me.

133 (G 48). 'Nimmer will ich dich verlieren! . . .'
30th January 1889

(*Suleika:*) *Now I shall never lose you! Love gives strength to love. May you adorn my youth with your strong passion.*

How flattered I feel when I hear my poet praised! For love is what gives us life; and intellect gives life to life itself.

Yet another pair. The light and ironical passion of the first poem is a little exaggerated in the music; but convincingly so. From the very first bar the piano part tears away and the voice strikes in exultantly. The excitement is intensified for 'Nur dies Herz', etc. (Except that this heart . . .). Here the impetus of the descending left-hand theme, the storming rhythms of the right, the drive and fire of the voice part, all vividly suggest hidden sources of power bursting out. The first theme returns in a more restrained form and gradually reaches a new brightness for the sustained words 'Frühling' (spring) and 'Sommer' (summer). The song finishes with declamatory phrases which die away in mock pathos at the mention of ashes and revive in crescendo for the last words 'Der verbrannte mir'. The postlude emerges unscathed from the flames to relive the initial moment of the song. 'Locken, haltet mich gefangen' it says, in a passionate outcry.

Suleika is given a chance to reply in the second song. In Wolf's tumultuous setting the intellectual implications and overtones of the poem are brushed aside. The first strains are full of an acceptance as fiery and impassioned as the previous declaration of love. There is a smouldering quietude at 'Ach! wie schmeichelt's' (How it flatters) from which the music leaps up in a great climactic flare that makes a fitting finale to the passionate love-songs of the *Westöstlicher Divan*.

NOTES (to 132). 1. The left-hand opening theme has quavers on the off-beat; helplessness is suggested in the opening lines of the text (motif 2).

2. The rhythmic impetuosity equals that of *Feuerreiter* (56). It seems that at the reference to ashes the piano passages on the last page of that song (at 'husch! da fällt's in Asche ab') are deliberately quoted.

3. For the piano part at bars 8–10 see 122, note.

134 (G 49). Prometheus

2nd January 1889

Darken your skies with cloud, Zeus, and practise your thunderbolts on the mountains, like a boy lopping thistles.

You cannot harm my world, or my home, or my hearth whose fire you envy.

I know of nothing more wretched under the sun than you Gods. You eke out your majesty on burnt offerings and prayers, and you would starve but for the foolish hopes of children and beggars.

When I was an ignorant child I too used to look up at the skies as if there above dwelt One to hear my cries and pity me.

But who helped me against the insolence of the Titans? Who saved me from death, from slavery? It was my own courage and strength that saved me; small thanks to you asleep in the heavens.

I honour you? Why? When have you ever eased any man's pains, or dried any man's tears? Have I not been forged into a man by Time and Fate, my masters – and yours? Did you think I would hate life and run away, because not all my dreams came true?

Here I sit, making men after my own image, to suffer, to weep, to rejoice and to be glad. And to ignore you, as I do!

The demi-god, Prometheus, was represented as man's ally against the tyranny of the Gods. In some myths he is even the creator of mankind who to animate his creation stole fire from Heaven. His punishment was to be chained to a mountain in the Caucasus, with an eagle feeding on his liver; from this plight he was rescued by Hercules. He is an obvious symbol of humanist ideals, and of rebellion against harsh authority.

Goethe's great dramatic monologue inspired both Wolf and Schubert to magnificent music. Here, as in the next song, Schubert's setting is outstanding for human strength and nobility, while Wolf chooses to attempt to write above a mortal pitch. Everything about his *Prometheus* is larger than life. He orchestrated several of his songs, but only of this one can it be said that it is better so arranged. The piano part, magnificent though it is, seems inadequate as sheer sound to exploit the full range and resource of this prodigious music, which is almost that of Milton's Satan –

> ... 'unconquerable will,
> And study of revenge, immortal hate
> And courage never to submit or yield ...'

The long heaven-storming prelude has a Titanic defiance, like a huge clenched fist rising and shaking and striking at the gods. The music hushes to gather strength and is repeated in full with the voice part adding its snarling contempt 'Bedecke deinen Himmel, Zeus', etc.

This merges into unshakeable confidence – 'you cannot destroy my world'. Great massed octaves surge up invincibly and turn into an outburst of pride and rage again at 'beneidest' (envy).

Now the piano part begins to crawl with contempt at 'Ich kenne nichts Ärmeres' (I know of nothing more wretched). For some fifty bars a mock-whimpering motif sounds in the piano right hand. Under it the left hand marches in strong octaves as Prometheus sings, in slowly rising phrases or huge melodic sweeps, of the manifest inadequacies of the gods. Another rebellious climax is reached after 'erbarmen' (pity).

The music of the prelude returns at 'Wer half mir' (who helped me) as past wrongs are remembered and Zeus himself is again attacked in angry declamation. Here the whole giant frame of Prometheus shakes; and after 'Schlafenden da droben' (sleeper in Heaven) there is a stunning outburst of rage in the piano interlude, and of defiance as the resuming voice fairly shouts 'Ich dich ehren? Wofür?' (I honour you? Why?).

The initial quietude of the following indictment makes it infinitely effective. The piano has repeated triplet octaves in the right hand, as the voice sings its pitying melodies, and the ponderous octaves in the left hand are interspersed with contrasting outbursts in the angry rhythm of the prelude. The right-hand octaves thicken to chords, the left-hand octaves come surging up the keyboard as Prometheus asserts his parity with the gods at 'meine Herrn und deine?' (my masters – and yours). At this last word a triple forte is again reached for the fourth and last time. Gradually the rage dies from the music, the mood changes from defiance to affirmation. With 'Hier sitz ich' (here I sit) Prometheus is absorbed in his creative task. In the piano the strokes of hammer on anvil ring out. Now Zeus is irrevocably denied. The anger and pride of the prelude reappear; and the last words, 'wie ich', are echoed by strong hammering chords, as the forger of mankind with one gesture turns his back on Heaven and resumes his human creation.

NOTES. 1. It is sometimes supposed that the song is about 'Prometheus bound' and the piano prelude is 'about' a thunderstorm. There seems no good reason for the first assumption; and in view of Wolf's passionate identification, in his serious songs, with the character and drama of the poem, the prelude is also worth a closer look. It contains all the thematic material of the song; and the later uses of this make the meaning reasonably clear, in so far as it can be expressed in words. It could perhaps be analysed on these lines.

A solitary giant figure towers up (bars 1–4) and conscious of its strength becomes proud, angry, self-assertive (bars 4–8) and then moves through defiance (bars 9–16) to open rebellion and menace (bars 17–19). This is repeated in bars 20–38. For bars 39–49 the music changes. Two new themes appear; minim chords in a characteristic harmonic progression, followed by rising octaves. It will be noted how these chords in bar 39 are related to bar 9, and the octaves to bars 18–19. But since in each case the asperities of the original statement are changed and softened, the effect is now not of defiant threat but of unshakeable self-confidence. In this way the whole of this long song is built from the nineteen bars of character study in the prelude illuminated by and in turn illuminating the sense of the words in every bar. There is no space here for more detailed analysis; but the following points are perhaps of particular interest:

(a) The variations of rhythm and texture in bars 4–8, etc., 129–132, 140 and 144, etc. (piano left hand), and the way in which this rhythmic self-assertion culminates first in the massive anvil strokes of 160–162 and then in the final outburst of the closing bars.

(b) The melodic and harmonic guises in which the chords of bars 39–40 and 45–46, etc., reappear in bars 115–116, etc., 123–124, etc., 139–140, and the way in which the basic progression common to all of them is finally lingered out in the almost forgiving passages in bars 159–160, and recurs in similar mood in 167–9.

It is noteworthy how these two strands, perhaps corresponding respectively to the ideas of the Titan's anger and of something approaching filial respect or even affection, unite and part again, especially at the pivotal point of both words and music, namely the change of mood in bars 159–161 with the words 'Hier sitz' ich', etc.

2. The defiant ring of bars 9 et seq. has a milder parallel at bars 23–26 in *Ritter Kurts Brautfahrt* (97) where Kurt meets a foeman.

3. The rising octaves of bar 40, etc., are the apotheosis of the 'manliness' theme previously heard in the Eichendorff songs (motif 6). Here they find their last and truest use.

4. It will be noted how the 'menace' of bars 18–19 is related to the restless energy of motif 5 in a version already used in *Beherzigung* (103).

5. The falling bass of the first four bars, and later, suggests the idea of isolation associated with motif 15.

135 (G 50). Ganymed
11th January 1889

*In the radiance of the spring dawn-shine, the warm beauty of nature takes
hold of my heart. Would that I could embrace it in these arms; these my arms.*

*I lie here yearning, moved to tears by the flowers and the grasses. Now the
sweet winds of dawning come to slake my thirst. The nightingale calls from
the valley. I am called; I come; but where? where?*

*Above; my home lies above. The clouds float downwards, answering my
cry of love. Come to me, enfold me, take me to the skies, all-loving Father!*

Goethe takes the legend of the Trojan prince, Ganymede, gathered up to
Olympus by Zeus to be the cupbearer of the Gods, and puts it to profound uses as a symbol of union with God and Nature, mysticism and
pantheism. The poem therefore presents a more difficult task to a composer than its opposite counterpart *Prometheus* (134). The defiance in
that poem is one single impulse. But the self-surrender here is an infinitely more far-reaching concept. Wolf's and Schubert's settings are
utterly different from each other and still leave whole areas of the poem
unexplored. Schubert's Ganymede is a human figure, whose translation
takes place after the end of the song, as it were off-stage. Wolf has perceived more of the deeper significance of the poem. His song is all
symbol, at the outset already in a hovering trance of ecstatic communion
with Nature. The piano's soft high single quavers fall and rise and float
in languorous curves and suspensions. These move up from D major
through F sharp major to B flat major while the voice sings its warm
bright melodies based on the tonic triad of each successive key. D major
is again reached for the cry of 'Dass ich dich fassen möcht' (Would that
I could embrace you) for the voice alone, interspersed with slow expressive piano phrases and sustained rich chords with added dissonance, like
tears of joy.

Piano echoes voice at 'in diesem Arm'; and for the succeeding vision
of beauty in nature an almost voluptuous swaying movement begins. A
new semiquaver sighing is added in the left hand as the winds of dawning blow. The music is all yearning at the repeated 'wohin?' (whither?).
Then the first strains are repeated. From 'hinauf' to the end of the song
the music unifies appeal to Zeus with appeal to Nature. Rolling cloud-
struck tremolandi replace the original contemplative left-hand crotchet
rhythm. The song ends with a yearning postlude repeating the melody
of the cry 'In diesem Arm'.

Wolf himself justified his attempt at setting the poem after Schubert on the grounds that the latter had failed to understand it. But it may be that in a sense Wolf understood it too well. One can still prefer the strong sweetness of Schubert's music to the blissful masochism of Wolf's, superbly wrought though it is.

NOTE. The transcending effect of mediant key-change is particularly impressive in this song (motif 24).

136 (G 51). Grenzen der Menschheit: The limits of mankind
9th January 1889

When the Eternal Father serenely sows the benison of his lightnings from rolling clouds over the earth, I kiss the lowest hem of his garment in childlike awe.

For no man may measure himself with the gods. If he rise and touch the stars, then he finds no foothold; he is the plaything of clouds and winds.

If he stand strong and firm on the steadfast and enduring earth, then his stature cannot compare even with the oak tree or the vine.

How are the gods to be told from men? Before the gods the waves of time roll on, an eternal sea; us the waves lift for a little, then engulf and drown.

A little ring encompasses our life; and many generations link in lasting succession on the endless chain of their existence.

This final song of the Goethe volume explores the ways of the universe, and the nature of gods and men. Within this mighty music the conflicting moods of the two previous songs are absorbed and reconciled.

The piano begins with slow majestic chords; the voice part responds in adoring words set to a tranquil long-flighted melodic line. At 'Denn mit Göttern', etc. (for no man may measure himself with the gods) the music builds, climbs and then falls in both pitch and volume, in a new deliberate measured rhythm; the philosophic assessment is made graphically vivid. At 'Heb er sich aufwärts' (If he rise up) the piano part and voice together stir and gesture and strain upwards to a new climax at 'Sterne' (stars). Widely spaced octaves and augmented chords in the piano part speak with eloquence and grandeur of uncertain walking on sheer dizzying space. There is unsurpassed strength and solidity in the contrasting section at 'Steht er' (If he stand). The heavy and sustained crotchet tread of the wide-ranging bass part rings out under the repeated notes of the voice. The following piano interlude is deliberately merged into an everyday matter of fact theme.

It is worth considering what demands the poem makes on the composer in this passage. If he is to fashion a worthy musical equivalent for these splendid verses he must find music to speak first of exalted uncertainty, then of unexalted certainty, to compress into a few bars the whole human condition as Goethe conceives it. The music must first of all have grandeur but also a certain instability; then it must have complete stability and strength but also a certain matter-of-fact quality. The result is not likely to be part of a conscious thought-process; but it is a searching test of the depth of the song-writer's intuitive feeling for his art. Schubert and Wolf both succeed triumphantly.

To return: at 'Was unterscheidet Götter von Menschen?' the music recalls briefly the previous equivalent for 'no man may measure himself with the gods'. After a solemn pause, the gods themselves are evoked, or rather the endlessly flowing sea of time that rolls before them. The accompaniment billows up in a succession of great waves. The vocal phrases are first awe-struck, then heart-rending at 'verschlingt die Welle' (the waves engulf), then endlessly resigned at 'und wir versinken' (and we drown). After 'Ein kleiner Ring', set in a little ring of semibreves, the tolling rhythm of the first part of the song reappears in a chain of high widespread chords, as the huge intervals of the voice part plunge and rear. In the postlude the music dissolves into an eerie and sombre vision of an eternity beyond our imagining.

NOTES. I. The constructional use of rhythm in the piano part is far more extended than usual in Wolf. It seems for example that an even minim rhythm is associated with the gods, or eternity, and an even crotchet rhythm with mortal man, with rhythmic complication when the two ideas are interfused. This idea/rhythm correspondence can be charted thus.

Bars 1–27 the emotions aroused by the gods	$\frac{2}{2}$ ♩ ♩ | ♩ ♩
„ 28–35 men unlike gods	♩♩♩ | ♩ ♩ ♩
„ 36–43 men emulating gods	♩♩♩♩ | ♩ ♩ ♩ ♩
„ 44–73 the human condition	♩♩♩♩ | ♩ ♩ ♫ ♩ ♩
„ 74–77 men unlike gods	♩♩♩ | ♩ ♩ ♩
„ 78–95 men and gods in time	♫♫♫ ♫♫♫ | ♫♫♫ ♫♫♫
„ 96–99 a ring (!)	o
„ 100–126 the eternity of the gods.	♩ ♩

2. The 3 + 3 + 2 arrangement at bars 36–43 and 78–95 is found in *Ganymed* (135) above, dated two days later, and practically nowhere else in Wolf's work. The harmonic correspondence between bars 46–49 and 96–99 is perhaps also meaningful.

3. The pathetic augmented fifths of motif 23 are given the mysterious aspect of motif 19 at bars 44–50.

V. The Spanish Songbook

[Peters Edition 3149-52]

Emanuel Geibel (1815–84) and Paul Heyse (1830–1914) were among the North German poets who went to Munich in the early 1850's at the invitation of Maximilian II of Bavaria, who had a penchant for the society of literary men.

They both had a love of Romance languages and literature and a flair for verse translation. The result of their collaboration on translations from sixteenth- and seventeenth-century Spanish poetry, the *Spanisches Liederbuch*, was published in 1852. One would expect to find a few of their poems in a representative anthology of German verse, but their artistic talent was for perfection of form rather than for depth of content.

Wolf follows his poets in separating the *Geistliche Lieder* (sacred songs, Nos. 137–146) from the *Weltliche Lieder* (secular songs, Nos. 147–180). His selection is fully representative.

137 (S.g. 1). 'Nun bin ich dein . . .'

(Juan Ruiz, trans. Heyse) 15th January 1890

(A prayer to the Virgin Mary)

Now I am yours, you flower of all flowers. My only and continual song is of your praise; my one wish is to serve you for ever. To you all my hopes aspire, my inmost being is open to you; save me from the sin that so sorely besets me! Star of the sea, haven of bliss, through whom the afflicted have found salvation; before I die, look down from Heaven, Queen of the stars. The abundance of your mercy can never fail. You help him who is heavy laden. To cling to you, to lie at your feet, heals all grief and pain. My just punishment is very grievous; I am so afraid of having soon to sleep the sleep of death. I pray you, turn to me and guide me through this dark sea to Heaven my haven.

Heyse's translation consists of five verses in a somewhat self-consciously adroit rhyme scheme. Within this framework each line and each phrase speaks of a sinner's praise and prayer. In the strength and weight of Wolf's musical response all the frills of the versification are ironed out into a single simple penitential garment. There is then nothing to distract attention from the central theme of supplication which rings through this beautiful song like a litany. The means by which this effect is achieved are more apparent in study than in performance. But the unifying force of the basic $\frac{4}{2}$ rhythm ♩ ♩ ♩ 𝅝, and the sensitive inflections of harmony and melody, cannot escape attention at a first hearing. In spite of the slow tempo and unyielding rhythm there is no monotony. The opening bars make clear the mood, which is from then on created afresh in every bar. Even the postlude reaffirms this feeling anew. Into it is incorporated the vocal phrase with which the song begins, with the effect of resolving all that has gone before into unshakeable certitude – 'now I am yours'.

NOTES. 1. The piano melody that pervades this song here and elsewhere speaks of yearning (motif 12).

2. The treatment of 'Frau auserlesen' in bars 9–10 has characteristic affinities with motif 19.

3. The tonality in spite of its chromatic appearance is basically F major. The departure from this key in the third verse, 'Nie kann versiegen', etc., indicates the emotional climax of the song, especially at the lovely F sharp (G flat) major treatment of 'heilt allen Harm und Schaden' (heals all grief and pain).

138 (S.g. 2). 'Die du Gott gebarst . . .'

(Nicolas Nuñez, trans. Heyse) 5th November 1889

Mother of God, pure and undefiled, who have freed us from our chains; turn my tears to joy, for only your grace and mercy can save us. Turn me to you, Lady, so that this torment, this despair may have an end; that death may find me unafraid, and the light of Paradise not blind me.

You are immaculate and so are chosen to dwell in eternal glory; though suffering surround me I am not lost if you will but consent to save me.

Again the rhyme scheme of Heyse's translation seems contrived. The general comments on the previous poem and song are applicable. The unifying piano rhythm – here $\begin{smallmatrix}6\\4\end{smallmatrix}$ ♩ ♩ ♩ ♩ ♩ – is again inflected so as to avoid the impression of monotony while creating the impression of a single overmastering emotion. The two songs are complementary. This has fewer melodic felicities, and more control and austerity, than its counterpart.

NOTES. 1. Parallelism between the two songs extends to the harmonic structure. This song is in A minor almost throughout, the accidentals being only chromatic alteration of this basic key. The tonality diverges for a moment at the emotionally climactic passage 'dass der Tod mich furchtlos fände', etc. (that death may find me unafraid).

2. The musical material mentioned at note 2 of the previous song (motif 19) is also found here, e.g. at 'mach' mich fröhlich', etc., bars 9–12.

139 (S.g. 3). 'Nun wandre, Maria . . .'

(Ocaña, trans. Heyse) 4th November 1889

Joseph sings:
    You must journey on, Mary; it will soon be morning, and there is not much further to go now. Come along, my darling, my precious, we shall soon reach Bethlehem.

    Then you can get your proper rest and sleep; it will soon be morning and there is not much further to go now.

    Yes, Lady, I can see that your strength is failing, and that you are in pain. I wish I could help you more.

    But take comfort; we shall surely find some lodging there. It will soon be morning, and there is not much further to go now.

    If only your time were come, Mary, I'd give a good reward for the good tidings. I'd even give away our little donkey. It will soon be morning; come along then, there is not much further to go now.

166

The poem is in a long Christian tradition of devout imaginative embroidery on the Gospels. The source here is Luke ii. 1–5:

'. . . there went out a decree from Caesar Augustus, that all the world should be taxed. . . . And all went to be taxed, every one into his own city. And Joseph also went up from Galilee, out of the city of Nazareth, into Judaea, unto the city of David, which is called Bethlehem. . . . To be taxed with Mary his espoused wife, being great with child.'

We know that Christ will be born in Bethlehem; and that the only lodging they will find there will be a stable with a manger. But all Joseph knows in the poem is that they have had to undertake a long journey, and that his dear wife is in need of loving comfort. It is this human situation that Wolf's song re-creates, with ineffable tenderness, as if the music were a soothing response to a cry of distress.

The voice part lies mainly within the span of a fourth, B to E, within which the notes B, C sharp, D, E are heard repeatedly. Yet the typically Wolfian effect is one of shapely singable melody that lingers unforgettably in the mind. The dynamics in voice and piano are equally restrained. The song never rises above mezzo-forte, and that for only two half-bars; all the rest is marked piano and pianissimo.

The journeying figures of the prelude continue throughout the song. Companionable thirds in the right hand sound their steady equal quavers over a trudging bass, with a processional effect as the quavers rise from the lower to the middle register, suggesting an uphill journey. As they level out, the quiet comfort of the voice part begins. When the word 'Bethlehem' is reached, the movement is halted, hushed and reflective, as if brought to a standstill by a sudden vision of anticipation. Then, with an upward movement and a few semiquavers to give a hint of extra effort, the steady plodding resumes at 'Dann ruhest du' (Then you can rest). How intimately we are made to feel Joseph's helpless anxiety and solicitude at 'Wohl seh' ich, Herrin, die Kraft dir schwinden' (I can see that your strength is failing, Lady). There is extra effort and pain in the piano part; each step is a pang. But the troubled harmonies of this passage and the following interlude resolve into a brief bright A major at 'Getrost!' (Take comfort). The steady journeying resumes, the music is all solace. At the end, the piano part moves downhill and away. The voice is heard as if in the distance, singing 'Come, we are not far away now'. As the little procession moves out of earshot the piano postlude, in its lower register, finds and holds for the first time in the song the tonic major key, with a moving warmth and assurance of rest and sleep soon.

NOTES. 1. The music at 'Wohl seh' ich, Herrin', etc. and elsewhere is of the kind that occurred to Wolf in contexts suggesting 'mystery' (motif 19).

2. The parallel thirds here and elsewhere are sometimes used in contexts suggesting companionship (motif 16).

140 (S.g. 4). 'Die ihr schwebet um diese Palmen . . .'

(Lope da Vega, trans. Geibel) 5th November 1889

The Virgin Mary sings:

Angels hovering over the palm trees in the night wind – will you not hush the swaying of the tree tops? For my Child is asleep.

Palm trees of Bethlehem in the raging wind – why must you thresh so angrily tonight? Be still, lean calm and gentle over us. My Child is asleep.

How tired He was; weary with all the sorrow of the world. But now His pains are eased in peaceful sleep; hush, you trees, for my Child is asleep.

The winds blow grim and chill; and I have no covering for my Child. Oh all you winged angels thronging the wind, quieten the tree tops. For my Child is asleep.

The verses approach nearer to poetry than is usual in the Spanish Songbook, and they have an emotive effect in their own right. And for Wolf, it is not enough to present poetry; the mood and the scene must be recreated afresh. So the music for this song must speak eloquently of winds and wings and tenderness, prayer and lullaby.

The piano prelude sets the scene with a semiquaver winnowing of broken chords followed by a soughing melody in the left hand, in which the voice joins. The whole essence of the song is in these first few bars, the figurations and melodies of which persist throughout, in a ceaseless flow. Dynamic contrasts help to vary and depict the scene. At the words 'Ihr Palmen von Bethlehem' bass octaves storm up and the voice sings imploringly. The melody shines out over the dark winds and controls them for a while. A long easeful lull comes over the music until the winds blow down again grim and chill – ('Grimmige Kälte sauset hernieder'). But they are still, as it were, held in check by the high sweetness of the voice part, and are conjured into peace at the moment of final invocation. Here the composer's imagination is seized by the picture of winged angels riding the wind. Without any halt in the flow or change in the texture of the music the middle syllable of the word 'geflügelt' (winged) streams out over five beats. Then the miracle is made audible. The piano's semiquavers are hushed as the voice sings its last heartfelt appeal 'stillet die Wipfel! es schlummert mein Kind'. In the postlude the winds abate and are still.

NOTES. 1. Mediant modulations had special meaning for Wolf (motif 24). But it is a matter of conjecture whether they have a thematic significance in this song.

2. Brahms' setting of the same poem for contralto and piano with viola obbligato (Op. 91 no. 2) is also extremely beautiful in its less graphic way.

141 (S.g. 5). 'Führ' mich, Kind . . .'

(Anon., trans. Heyse) 15th December 1889

Lead me, holy Child, to Bethlehem. Thou art my God; I long to behold Thee. None has ever come to Thee save with Thy help.

Shake me awake, call me, and I will come. Give me Thy hand to guide me that I may be on my way.

Let me find Bethlehem, there to behold my God. None has ever come to Thee save with Thy help.

I am sore smitten with the sickness of sin. Without Thy aid I shall falter and fall.

Guide me to Bethlehem; Thou art my God; I long to behold Thee. None has ever come to Thee save with Thy help.

The idea of a journey to Bethlehem again evokes the undulating quaver thirds and occasional semitonal clashes of *Nun wandre Maria* (139). This song is perhaps overshadowed by the earlier masterpiece. But it has a radiance of its own. The poem dictates the ABABA form and Wolf easily achieves a formal perfection. In addition, the design adds significance to the verses. 'Führ' mich, Kind, nach Bethlehem', the main vocal melody entreats. The piano part is pining for the desired journey, already setting out. But there is a hint of anxiety at 'Wem geläng' es, wem, ohne dich zu dir zu gehn!' (none has ever come to Thee save with Thy help). In each of the contrasting B sections the musical material for this passage is extended and developed. At 'Rüttle mich' (shake me) the strong bass octaves are tinged with the previous anxiety. Later, at 'der Sünde schwerem Kranken' (the heavy sickness of sin) they have distressed augmented intervals, suggesting the unquiet thought 'Perhaps He will not come'. But after each passage an intimate reassurance returns. The momentous piano octaves are steadied, the tone hushes from *ff* to *p*, the journeying thirds reappear with their new melody, and the music believes again.

NOTES. 1. The companionable thirds are motif 16.

2. The bass octaves at, e.g., bars 10–11 are akin to the unease of motif 5.

142 (S.g. 6). 'Ach, des Knaben Augen . . .'

(Lopez de Ubeda, trans. Heyse) 21st December 1889

The Child's eyes are so clear and beautiful, and they have a nameless radiance that wins all my heart.

If He should chance to look with those eyes into mine, and see His own image there, surely then He would smile at me lovingly?

So I surrender myself to the sole service of His eyes, for they have a nameless radiance that wins all my heart.

The song itself has a heart-winning radiance. The plain thirds in both hands of the piano part achieve an extraordinary limpidity and grace of melodic rise and fall. The vocal line has an equally steady flow, mainly in repeated notes or by step. It is so beguiling as to distract attention from the broader melodies of the accompaniment. The whole song is a perpetual stream of tender melody in five, sometimes six, parts; a great outpouring of simple adoration. In the first verse the swaying, lulling piano part and the tender vocal line rise gently together. At 'mein ganzes Herz gewinnt' (wins all my heart), the voice part falls quietly while the piano goes chiming softly upwards. This is fine enough; but there follows a passage that, for melting tenderness and beauty, matches anything in Wolf's work. The change to A flat major from F major at 'säh' er dann sein Bild darin' (if He should see His own image there) is particularly magical. Wolf has infused into this simple music human tenderness as well as worship. The first strain, which is repeated at 'und so geb' ich ganz mich hin' (and so I surrender) is enriched by this dual idea. The postlude is a brief prayer and lullaby together.

NOTES. I. There is confusion at the half-bar. It seems probable that this song, like others in this volume, may have been conceived in terms of the accompaniment rhythm. The mating of piano and voice is melodically perfect; but the word-stress may sound faulty unless the song is in effect sung as if in $\frac{3}{4}$ with only slight stresses on the first beat of each bar.

2. The contour of the first long vocal phrase 'Ach . . . erschienen' has been heard in the Goethe songs, e.g. *Blumengruss* (109) where the same notes in the same key are also used in contexts of surrender and abnegation. Its use here may be an unconscious reminiscence; but it rings true and new-minted.

3. The consecutive thirds of 139 and 141 recur (motif 16), but here they add sweetness to the music rather than any particular idea.

4. For the verbal theme of this song see 44, note 2.

143 (S.g. 7). 'Mühvoll komm' ich und beladen . . .'

(Don Manuel del Rio, trans. Geibel) 10th January 1890

Full of toil I come unto Thee, and heavy-laden; receive me, Thou haven of mercy. See, I come in tears, humbly grimed with the dust of the earth.

Thou alone canst make me as white as the fleece of the lamb. Thou wilt take away the sin of him who repents.

Take then Lord my burden from me; full of toil I come unto Thee, and heavy-laden.

Let me kneel beseeching before Thee, that I may anoint Thy feet with sweet-smelling spikenard and tears, like the woman whose sins Thou forgavest, until guilt disperses like smoke. Thou who didst once say to a malefactor 'Today shalt thou be with me in Paradise'; receive me, Thou haven of mercy.

This song has won wide acclaim, and certainly it contains music of the very highest quality. Yet one may perhaps venture to question whether it stands as high in the canon as is sometimes contended. Wolf's genius lay in music which is not only masterly in itself, but gains lustre and meaning from an intimate connexion with the essence of the words. But here music and verse seem to be drawn from different sources, and the second part of the contract is left unfulfilled. In this song, the remorseful piety of the poem disappears in a welter of agony and self-inflicted torture. It all takes place, so to speak, within one personality, as one single obsession in one mind; there is little or no hint of any outside source of redemption. A great singer can create an escape from this imprisoning music into light. But it is not a song for those unfamiliar with Wolf's work.

Piano chords foreshadow the characteristic obsessive rhythm

The voice makes its anguished way, mainly in abject falling phrases, among the intensely rich chromatic dissonance of the accompaniment. A first emotional climax is reached at 'nimm denn, Herr' (take then, Lord). Here the tensions are resolved in a strong affirmation of the main theme in more diatonic terms. But this is re-absorbed into the chromatic texture at the repetition of the opening words 'Mühvoll komm' ich und beladen'. The music of the first page reappears, leading up again to the diatonic climax at 'O nimm mich an' (receive me). Here the voice is high and ecstatic for a moment before falling in submission at the closing words. The postlude repeats more quietly the obsessive rhythm that has resounded throughout the song.

NOTES. 1. This keynote of agonized obsession is illustrated in a way that is technically superb; a song-writer could return again and again to this song for enlightenment and instruction. In 69 bars of slow $\frac{3}{4}$ time, the two-bar piano rhythm is heard some thirty times. Discounting the piano prelude and postlude, the second thirty bars are essentially the first thirty repeated almost note for note – a semitone higher for sixteen bars and a tone lower for fourteen. Of the first thirty bars, the second four repeat the idea of the first four; the next two bars are twice repeated. Each idea is the same idea and that consists of repeated dissonant chords, repeated emphatic single notes.

2. The cyclic patterns of the piano's melodic line in this song (e.g. top notes of bars 19–24 and 49–54) are heard in later songs at moments of intense inwardness or constraint, e.g. in 218, 222, 240.

3. In the repetition of the second thirty bars certain variants occur according to the demands of the vocal line. But there seems no good reason why bar 17 should not be exactly parallel with bar 47; in which case one would have expected D sharps in the last left-hand chord of the former.

144 (S.g. 8). 'Ach, wie lang die Seele schlummert . . .'
(Anon, trans. Geibel) 19th December 1889

My soul has slept too long; the hour of waking is at hand.

My soul has slept as if dead, in Satan's power since it drank from the cup of sin. Yet now a longed-for light dawns, blinding the eyes; the hour of waking is at hand. Though the soul seem deaf to the sweet angel choirs, let it listen; it shall hear from on high the weeping of the Child Jesus. After a long night of sleep, a day of mercy dawns; the hour of waking is at hand.

Voice and piano join in providing a prelude in seven bars that resume the thematic material – a basic rhythm $\frac{4}{4}$ ♩ ♩ ♫ ♩ to a falling motif for the sleeping of the soul, and a rather jaded harmonic progression for its awakening. Then the falling sevenths and rising semitones sound softly in the piano part as the voice intones the soul's shortcomings. At 'Doch nun ihrer Sehnsucht Licht' (Yet now a longed-for light) the basic rhythm is strengthened by bass semibreves. The rhythmic phrases turn upwards, the voice sings out grateful melodies. In the second verse the soul's harmonies are a little more hectic and the diatonic contrast, when it recurs, even more soothing. All this is well enough, but this song is quite untypical of Wolf in its bland lack of correspondence between the transcendence of the subject and the gentility of the music.

NOTES. 1. There are evident rhythmic affinities between this song and the next, 145, dated some three weeks earlier. This suggests that Wolf, consciously or not, is recomposing an earlier inspiration. This curious phenomenon occurs elsewhere in his work, e.g. 222 is (perhaps consciously) based on 224, and part of 225 is (no doubt subconsciously) based on 214.

2. For other uses of rising semitones in analogous verbal contexts, see 32, note 1.

145 (S.g. 9). 'Herr, was trägt der Boden hier . . .'
(Anon., trans. Heyse) 24th November 1889

Lord, what will grow in this ground, watered with Thy bitter tears?
'Thorns, dear heart, for me; for thee, flowers.'
Then can a garden thrive where such dread streams flow?
'Yea; and know this – in it are many wreaths for the weaving.'
Lord, Lord; for whose head are those wreaths woven?
'Those of thorns are for me; those of flowers I hand to thee.'

This and its following counterpart (146) are great songs. They aim at, and very nearly achieve, the highest in music. This song in particular is an acknowledged masterpiece of deep emotion. Both are imagined discourses between the sinner and his Redeemer. Wolf reaches great heights in his treatment of the bittersweet dramatic paradox of the poems. The redeemed sinner questions in anguish, the Saviour answers from Gethsemane or Golgotha in tones of beatific calm and comfort. The solemn phrases of the piano prelude seem to suggest with each stab of pain an involuntary gesture of sympathy and love. Each time, the sharp dissonance is softly resolved as the voice asks its questions. At each reply the piano's rhythm strengthens, the harmonies are consonant and in a lower register; and the vocal melody warms and brightens, suffused with comfort. So the song proceeds until the last reply summons up all that has gone before into one lovely final phrase, first sombre with dark octaves in the piano at 'Die von Dornen sind für mich', then ineffably sweet with a simple chordal accompaniment at 'die von Blumen reich' ich dir'.

NOTES. 1. One has heard this song (and the next) performed as a duet for soprano and baritone – a practice which seems wholly indefensible.

2. The resolving dissonances of the piano prelude are reminiscent of Schubert's Rückert song *Dass sie hier gewesen* (Op. 59 no. 2), where the conjunction of sorrow and love, this time on the human level, is also the theme.

146 (S.g. 10). 'Wunden trägst du, mein Geliebter . . .'

(Jose de Valdivivielso, trans. Geibel) 16th December 1889

Thou art wounded, my belovèd Lord, and in pain; could I but bear that pain in Thy stead.

Lord, who has dared to hurt Thee so?

'These wounds are the price of redeeming thy soul; of these wounds I must die, for my great love of thee.'

Could I but bear those wounds for Thee, Lord, for they will be Thy death.

'Say, rather, that they will be thy life, my child, if this my suffering moves thee; my blood shall bring life to thee.'

Oh how my heart and mind ache with Thy anguish!

'Gladly would I endure far worse, to save thee; for He alone knows the strength of love Who has died for love.'

Thou art wounded, my beloved Lord, and in pain; could I but bear that pain in Thy stead.

This is a fitting finale to the cycle of sacred songs. It has much in common with the preceding song. But it stands nearer to the Passion; the agonized questions are now accompanied by the middle register of the piano, the comforting replies by the higher register, becoming at times remote.

Into this fine song Wolf pours a libation of all his previous devotional music. Without being at all derivative the music resumes and reunites the responses to love and compassion that resound throughout the cycle. The thematic connexions with 145 are obvious enough, and Wolf's music also suggests that the singer of this song, who was the pilgrim to Bethlehem of 141, who in 142 beheld the eyes of the Holy Child, was not unseen nor unrewarded. It is further implied, no doubt subconsciously, that these are the same person, and that person Wolf himself. In the best of these sacred songs, the work of different poets, translated by different poets, is unified and given profound meaning by Wolf's own musical and personal sensitivity.

NOTE. Two of the more evident thematic parallels are noted for interest:
  (*a*) Bar 10 – cf. 141, bar 8.
  (*b*) Bars 15–16, etc., piano melody – cf. voice part in 142, bars 1–2, etc.

147 (S.w. 1). 'Klinge, klinge, mein Pandero . . .'

(Alvaro de Ameida, trans. Geibel) 20th November 1889

Ring out, my tambourine; but my heart is elsewhere.
  If this gay instrument could feel my pain its every note would be a lament.
  I play my music for the wild dances, to silence my grief.
  But to the rhythm of the dance my heart seems like to break and my song
to be a cry of pain; for my heart is elsewhere.

The simultaneous musical portrayal of a tambourine ringing out gaily and a heart suffering in silence proves to be rather too much of a task even for Wolf. The piano thrums and jingles admirably in its solo passages, but in the rest of the song some of the singer's sorrow has got into the tambourine. The measured pulse of the piano part with incessant staccato semiquavers tinkling over a Spanish dance rhythm provides a strong framework within which the subtle and flexible vocal line has freedom to make its musical points. For instance the opening phrase 'Klinge, klinge, mein Pandero' is set to the obvious ¾ rhythm ♫♩♫♩♫♩|♩♩; but the balancing phrase at 'doch an andres denkt mein Herz' (but my heart is thinking of other things) is wistfully extended over four whole bars. The verses thrice introduce three consecutive rhyming lines the sense of which overruns the end of the line in some cases. In arranging for each rhyme to fall on the first beat of the bar, and allotting to each line two bars of ¾ time, Wolf makes space within the rhythmic scheme for the sense and sound of particular words to be brought out, e.g. the sustained 'Qual' (pain) in one verse, 'wild' in the next. Similarly the leaps and curves of the melody bring out verbal contrasts. The whole song gives the impression of creative intelligence fashioning and reshaping musical material which, though not itself of the finest quality, is memorably treated for pictorial, dramatic and emotive effects.

NOTE. Pianists may be reminded by the piano interludes in this song (e.g. bar 10 et seq.) of a well-known passage in the first movement of Beethoven's *Waldstein Sonata* (bars 62–63). This work has been described by J. W. N. Sullivan as 'of almost "purely" musical interest . . . even the qualities it expresses, apart from specifically musical talent, are of no particular significance'. Some might think this a rather harsh judgment; but it is of interest to note that Wolf should have had similar music in his head in a passage about trivial music unaffected by a simultaneous sorrow.

148 (S.w. 2). 'In dem Schatten meiner Locken . . .'

(Anon., trans. Heyse) 17 November 1889

In the shade of my long tresses my sweetheart has gone to sleep. Shall I wake him? Ah, no. Early each morning I comb out my flowing hair; in vain, for the wind blows it about.

Shadowing tresses, sighing breezes, have sent my sweetheart to sleep. Shall I wake him? Ah, no. I shall be told how I have tormented him by refusing him for so long, and how his whole life depends on the touch of my sunbrown cheek.

He calls me his tormentor, and yet he has gone to sleep by my side. Shall I wake him? Ah, no.

A justly famous and popular song, in the category of slight yet perfect work which is so typical of one aspect of Wolf's genius. The poem is not particularly attractive, but the composer was moved by it, in a fortunate hour, to make a song full of melodic enchantment and harmonic subtlety. The soft dancing rhythm of the piano's first bar persists through almost the whole of the song, delicately varied in harmony and tempo to suit the changing mood of the singer. The question-and-answer refrain 'Weck' ich ihn nun auf? Ach nein!' is delightfully interpreted by Wolf as finding the singer in two minds. Mischief and affection impel her to wake him, the music suggests. But tenderness, as of a mother watching a sleeping child, supervenes. The mischievous little rhythm slows down after the first two bars. 'Schlief mir mein Geliebter ein', is sung to a marked rallentando, slowly and lovingly. Mischief returns in a bright key; 'Weck' ich ihn nun auf?' The piano echoes the question 'Shall I? . . . Shall I?' 'Ach nein' sings the voice in sweetly falling melody. But the piano is not yet convinced. The chord under which the word 'nein' is sustained turns out to be the wrong chord, and is gently changed so that the piano can ask its question again, reaching, with the same small sigh, the same conclusion.

It is typical of Wolf at his best that elusive subtleties of this kind are not obtruded into the music. What is heard is a fresh flow of melody in brightening harmonic sequence. Intuitive forces are at work moulding the music into the shape of an idea, infusing it with the emotion of the idea, making the emotion audible. The dancing piano figurations reappear until a more even rhythm in spread chords is heard at 'schläferten den Liebsten ein' (sent my love to sleep), matching the preceding words. The tender musing question and answer are heard again, flaring into the brightness of F sharp major tonality for the words 'braune Wange' (brown cheek) before resuming in the original key. After the question and answer once more the song ends with a summary from the piano. Two bars of the gay characteristic rhythm suggest the temperament of the singer, one bar a question and the last two notes her answer 'Ach nein', this time subdued and without key-change; the final answer.

NOTES. 1. This song was incorporated by Wolf into his opera *Der Corregidor*. It is sung by Frasquita in Act I.

2. The mediant modulations which occur in the question-and-answer passages occur elsewhere in contexts suggesting the changing effects of light (motif 24). Here it is probably non-thematic; but the sense of Wolf's music would not be violated if one thought of these passages in terms of a brightening and a fading smile.

3. Brahms' youthful setting of these words (Op. 6 no. 1) is also charming. It is by no means eclipsed by Wolf's.

4. F sharp major tonality (here at 'braune Wange') is a feature of Wolf's music in moods of extreme elation.

5. For the dividing melodic lines that characterise the main theme see motif 14.

149 (S.w. 3). 'Seltsam ist Juanas Weise . . .'
(Anon., trans. Geibel) 14th November 1889

Juana's ways are strange. When I am sad, when I sigh 'today', she murmurs 'tomorrow'.

She is moody when I am gay; but she sings cheerily if I weep. If I say she is beautiful, she says she hates the sight of me. Such cruelty breaks my heart; when I sigh 'today', she murmurs 'tomorrow'.

If I look at her, she looks down, only to look up at me again as soon as I look down. When I call her a saint, she calls me a devil; and when I sigh 'today', she murmurs 'tomorrow'.

If I modestly mention some small achievement, she says I'm hopeless. If I dare hope for Heaven, she prophesies Hell. Yes, her heart is so icy that if she saw me dying of unrequited love, and heard my last sigh 'today', she would still murmur 'tomorrow'.

This song, odd and unattractive at first hearing, gradually insinuates its way into a place of lasting affection. The haunting refrain ' 'morgen' spricht sie leise' makes an immediate melodic appeal, and the whole song is endearing, especially if interpreted as wryly rueful and not without humour. The piano part has a wistful guitar-theme of spread chords, breaking off abruptly and lapsing into sad silence on the first beat of every other bar. It is at this moment that the plaintive two-bar phrases of the voice part begin. In this way the vocal line and the accompaniment overlap and alternate; but, like Juana and her lover, they never really come to terms. In much of the song the sole accompaniment of the voice is the aftermath of a quaver chord spun out by the sustaining pedal – as tenuous a relationship as the one described in the poem. The effect is one of recitative throughout. Voice and piano go their separate ways with a flawless delicate dovetailing which is irresistible if it is done properly. But the musical logic of the chromatic movement of the voice part can be kept convincing and interesting only by a singer with perfect intonation. It is a very searching test of musicianship, rarely heard in performance, and in good performance practically never. But it richly rewards closer study.

NOTE. The drooping sorrow of motif 22 so characteristic of the Goethe songs is here put to mock-tragic uses. 'Lebe wohl' sounds through this song as much as in the Mörike song of that name (48).

150 (S.w. 4). 'Treibe nur mit Lieben Spott . . .'
(Anon., trans. Heyse) 15th November 1889

All right, my dear; just go on mocking my love for you. One day, the god of love will mock you too. Go on mocking if it pleases you; women bring sorrow to all men, as well as joy. Mock on; some day it will be your turn. Though you are haughty now, you too will sue for love one day. Now you mock at my need, but one day the god of love will mock you. Let all mortals ponder this; Cupid may be sleeping now, but he will suddenly wake and wound you. Go on mocking then; it will be your turn one day.

This is no doubt intended as a pendant to the previous song; the key is the same, and the few spread guitar chords by way of prelude are common to both. The mood here is more incisive, but not without tenderness. A deliberate foot-stamping and finger-snapping dance measure dominates the song. The first vocal phrase has a strongly rhythmic shape $\frac{3}{4}$ ♫♫♫ ♫ ♫, no doubt suggested by the opening words. Voice and piano freely interchange rhythmic and melodic interest throughout. At the words 'Magst an Spotten nach Gefallen' (go on mocking if it pleases you), and again later, the piano snaps dissonantly in quicker and more emphatic rhythmic phrases that slow down and merge into the vocal line again as the refrain is repeated.

NOTE. In a song where mockery is mentioned one would expect motif 4; in this song, which is about nothing else, the thematic acciaccature are at times exaggerated into semitonal clashes (see 162, note).

151 (S.w. 5). 'Auf dem grünen Balkon . . .'

(Anon., trans. Heyse) 12th December 1889

Through her green lattice window my sweetheart is looking at me; her eyes are shining, but she gestures 'No'.

A lover's joys are never unalloyed: sometimes I hear flattery, sometimes petulance, when I come to her window.

How like a woman to mix a little sadness into my pleasure; her eyes are shining, but she gestures 'No'.

How can her coldness and my fire be reconciled? But she is my heaven, now bright, now dark: and to the winds I sigh that my sweet little love has never yet put her arms around me.

Yet she keeps me so delicately in suspense: her eyes are shining, but she gestures 'No'.

A justly famous song. It contains no great musical profundity: no great depths of passion or feeling are explored. Yet it is perhaps the most compelling song that even Wolf ever wrote. Once fall under its spell, and for days one cannot sing, play, listen to or think of anything but *Auf dem grünen Balkon*.

Many elements combine to produce this effect. First, the poem is attractive in its own right, and the charm and chime of phrase and rhyme-scheme clamour for musical expression. Then this pleasure is enhanced by the perfect matching of Wolf's vocal melodies and piano part with the sound and sense of the words, evoking an irresistible tenderness and exaltation. Add to this again, on the purely musical plane, the rhythmic understanding between the voice part and the piano part, each contributing to a continuing swing and sway. Yet again, add the ceaseless flow of lilting melody: not only the vocal line, not only the beguiling arabesques of the piano right hand, but the spread guitar-chords of the left, have a melodic role to play. And all these elements act and interact, play and interplay, and yet are marvellously brought together by the sheer quality of the musical ideas into one single organic whole, a continuous delight to the ear and the mind. Even in this Mozartian amalgam of craftmanship and melodic appeal there is still room for some special felicities. For instance, the tender shifting of the piano harmonies over and under the sustained note at 'Fensterlädchen' and later at 'meine' can linger particularly long in the memory. And Wolf, in sympathy with the singer's complaint, has ventured on a little prophecy. The song-form is ABABA, where A contains the sad 'she says no'. On its second appearance the piano melody is slightly shifted away from the first beat of the bar: on its last appearance this feature persists and a modulatory treatment is added, so that the effect is perceptibly less decisive each time. The point is also made by a significant change of verbal accentuation. The first appearance of 'Sagt sie mir Nein' is clearly 'she says "*No*".' The second is much less sure of itself. The third is 'She *says* "No" . . .' It is a very winning song.

NOTES. 1. The piano accompaniment stands up in its own right as a self-contained instrumental solo. There are certain indications that it was so conceived and that the song is an artificial construction.

2. There is a hint of the rising and falling sixths of motif 11, in the opening vocal melody and elsewhere.

152 (S.w. 6). 'Wenn du zu den Blumen gehst . . .'

(Anon., trans. Heyse) 1st November 1889

When you walk in the garden among the flowers to gather the loveliest of them for your garland, it is yourself you must gather. For you are the fairest flower of all.

The whole of a longish poem is devoted to this one theme. The opening words paraphrased above recur twice as a refrain. Wolf's extraordinarily rich and beautiful setting combines the fluency of Schumann's songwriting with the contrapuntal sureness of Bach himself. None of the Spanish songs is authentically Spanish, or is intended to be, but this one is quintessentially German. Musically, everything about it is a delight. Voice and piano begin together with a simple walking tune and an accompaniment like a two-part invention. Then at the words 'Ach wenn du in dem Gärtlein stehst' (Oh when you stand in the garden) the music is set flowering. In the piano the bass and alto parts of the initial walking music are recombined, a brief reminiscence of the loved one's entry into the garden. Over this the added treble part peals out in high notes and then chimes downwards. Now it is the voice's turn. At 'müsstest du dich selber pflücken' (it is yourself you must gather) the sedate walking is abandoned. These words are set to a curving melody that goes straying amazed among the bar-lines, as if the thought expressed were among the most novel and striking ever uttered. Now the piano accompaniment burgeons into a fourth voice, and so the song proceeds with strands of melody weaving and interweaving a garland of their own. The first words reappear, 'wenn du zu den Blumen gehst', and with them the melodies of which one can never tire. At the final repetition of 'müsstest du dich selber pflücken' the music indicates that the singer has now grown a little more used to this idea. It seems to him now not quite so breath-taking, but more familiar and more beautiful, and the voice part overflows in a new melody that breathes adoration. Two bars of piano postlude say dulcetly 'wenn du zu den Blumen gehst' as the song ends with a quiet meditation on the opening melody.

NOTES. 1. This is the lyric equivalent of the 'dramatic' music of *Auf dem grünen Balkon*. The two songs are closely akin in key, structure and texture.

2. *Frühling übers Jahr* (113) has the same mood and the same central idea. (Wolf's settings are both in his springtime key, A major.) His art creates a song of the same high order of excellence from these trivial verses as from Goethe's fine lyric.

3. See note 1 to 153.

153 (S.w. 7). 'Wer sein holdes Lieb verloren . . .'

(Anon., trans. Geibel) 28th October 1889

Whoever has lost his loved one through not understanding love – better if he had never been born.

I lost her there in the garden, where she was gathering flowers. She blushed and smiled at me, and spoke of love.

But I, the biggest of all fools, made no answer. I wish I had never been born.

I lost her there in the garden as she spoke of love and its heartache, for I dared not tell her how I am hers, and hers alone. She sank down among the flowers.

But I, the biggest of all fools, not even then did I dare put my arms round her. I wish I had never been born.

Whoever has lost his loved one through not understanding love – better if he had never been born.

This is another song of great charm, in which the singer's misfortunes are described plaintively but not without humour. The doleful phrases of the prelude are almost all within a compass of two semitones, a melody fully as inhibited as the hapless hero. Wistful vocal lines combine with the piano's sad little phrases and soulful leaps in a tuneful outpouring of self-reproach. And somehow the music also suggests an enduring love. The piano interludes after 'Und von Liebe sprach sie mir' (she spoke to me of love) and 'In die Blumen sank sie hin' (she sank down among the flowers) are replete with tenderness.

N   181

NOTES. I. Thematic affinities, and the order of this song in the volume, suggest that it was intended as a sad sequel to 152. (Both songs were scored by Wolf for inclusion in his unfinished opera *Manuel Venegas*.) But it might be unwise to juxtapose the two in a programme. A proper performance of the former would have suggested the contented and articulate lover, and the lament of this song can hardly be made convincing thereafter.

2. The time signature of $\frac{2}{4}$ is perhaps not quite accurate. In practice the tonic stress is felt on the first beat of every other bar, as if the song were really in $\frac{2}{2}$ time with extra bar-lines inserted.

154 (S.w. 8). 'Ich fuhr über Meer . . .'
(Anon., trans. Heyse) 31st October 1889

I roamed over land and sea without ever finding happiness. Others found it; not I.

I sought it, and found sorrow. I hoped and dared, but no joys prospered for me.

I bore my lot without complaint, thinking those times would pass. They do not; but happy times have passed by so swiftly that I have never overtaken them.

The verses are a tedious series of complaints, unrelieved by any illuminating thought or insight; a hard luck story that offers very little of substance to the musician. Taking his cue from the first words 'Ich fuhr über Meer, ich zog über Land', Wolf attempts to infuse a passionate intensity into the song by means of a restless driving theme worked out in the piano part. But he has to hold this rhythm back by extensive and repeated rallentandi in order to match the limp pathos of the words. This saps the vitality of the song, which must be reckoned amongst Wolf's comparative failures.

NOTE. Some form of the 'unrest' of motif 5 is to be expected here. Indeed the song is practically fashioned from it.

155 (S.w. 9). 'Blindes Schauen . . .'
(Rodrigo Cota, trans. Heyse) 26th November 1889

Seeing, yet blind; shining, yet all dark; joyful, yet weeping; sweet, yet bitter; such is love. I thought it a blessing, but it is a curse that robs me of my rest.

The motif that Wolf devised for the piano part of this song is of great strength and unifying force. Perhaps it deserved a better fate than that of uneasy yoke-fellow to these verses. There is no attempt at a musical equivalent for the literary device of oxymoron, the idea of bitter-sweetness, though no one was better equipped for this than Wolf. Instead, the cue is taken from the last sentence. The shining, the joy and the sweetness are forgotten. From the very first bar the music begins to rage and tear; the piano postlude is an outburst of thwarted anger. The song has superlative dramatic effect, but not quite the same order of musical quality.

NOTES. 1. The piano part was perhaps preconceived. The introduction of its rhythm $\frac{4}{4}$ ♩ ♩. ♪ ♩ into the vocal line at the words 'Liebe, falsch' and again at 'da dein Fluch' is not motivated by the scansion of the words. The inversion of the right-hand theme earlier in the piano part at 'süsse Galle' is not motivated by the sense of the words. Each is felt to be an instrumentalist's rather than a song-writer's conception in the ordinary sense.

2. One may speculate on whether Wolf may not after all have found subconsciously an equivalent for the paradox of the poem. The left-hand rhythm is certainly strong, but its strength is concentrated on the weak beats of the bar, in a way reminiscent of the musical ideas associated by Wolf with weakness in other songs (motif 2).

156 (S.w. 10). 'Eide, so die Liebe schwur . . .'

(Anon., trans. Heyse) 31st March 1890

Lovers' vows make poor witnesses on oath. When love sits in judgment the verdict is never by justice but by favour.

Lovers' vows make poor witnesses. In the court you'll find wretches bound by vows that are no more steadfast than winds or the flowers of the field.

Lovers' vows make poor witnesses. As clerks of the court you'll find vain thoughts, trembling so much that they can't keep the records straight.

Lovers' vows make poor witnesses. The judicial procedure is 'sentence first – verdict afterwards'; but nothing is ever decided.

Lovers' vows make poor witnesses.

The verses are in a rhythmic pattern similar to those of 157, dated some five months earlier; but Wolf has no improvements and few changes to suggest. The nature of the verses prevents the composer from deploying his most characteristic gifts. There is no musical equivalent for allegory, and no one particular emotion can be identified, let alone rendered in musical terms. The result is just a song, unilluminated by the usual Wolfian perceptions, with an uneasy and rather portentous playfulness that runs parallel to the sense of the words without really intercommunicating with them. The music is of course quite adequate for its purpose. The strong running bass lines in dotted rhythms are enjoyable; and occasionally, where Wolf finds a verbal phrase that pleases him (e.g. at 'die Blumen auf der Flur' – the flowers of the field) the musical result is most appealing.

NOTE. At bars 9–11 appears the sort of rollicking music that Wolf often contrived to write in F sharp major tonality. In this song in B minor he need make no special effort to reach it; the rollicking is itself rather lackadaisical.

157 (S.w. 11). 'Herz, verzage nicht geschwind . . .'
(Anon., trans. Heyse) 19th November 1889

Do not despair too soon, my heart, just because women are women.

Always be on your guard against them though. They think of themselves as shining stars, yet they burn like sparks of fire. But do not despair too soon, just because women are women.

Be particularly wary of anything like wheedling. This is designed by women to hoodwink you; because they are women.

They are always in league together; they are doughty fighters with their tongues as weapons. They love to chatter and waste time; because they are women.

And how contrary they are! If you praise anything, they will instantly criticize it even though they really agree with you; because women are women.

The words certainly suggest misogyny: and one has heard concert performances of the song with more snarls than smiles. But the music is teasing; it is never more than wry, and never that for long. Behind this apparent condemnation of women in general lies an exasperated but tender affection for at least one woman in particular, as well as a certain light-heartedness. The opening mock-solemn recitative recurs throughout, interspersed with passages of great charm combining pretended disapproval from the voice with a twinkling effect in the piano part. The refrain 'weil die Weiber Weiber sind' is subtly varied at each repetition, first sad, then tender, then declamatory, and in its final version drawn out and almost sentimental. The postlude chuckles indulgently and is clearly about to drop its guard when it is suddenly brought back to its right frame of mind by a final interrupting chord.

NOTES. 1. This song was later allotted to the philandering Corregidor, in Act II of Wolf's opera.

2. The sense of the concealed melodic line in the dotted rhythm that occurs throughout – in particular in the postlude – is closely akin to that of Wolf's love-music (motif 13); the recurrent rising triplet figure speaks of gaiety (motif 7).

158 (S.w. 12). 'Sagt, seid Ihr es, feiner Herr . . .'
(Anon., trans. Heyse) 19th November 1889

Tell me, sir; aren't you the young gentleman that was dancing and singing so nicely with us not long ago?

Wasn't it you that sang so loud and talked so grand?

Yes, it was you, I'm sure of it, that did all that dancing and singing.

And weren't you telling us how you never really understood the castanets and the songs, and how you had never really known love, and how you shunned women?

Yes, it was you; and I bet you have held many a girl tight, dancing and singing.

And didn't you keep on performing innumerable dances and songs, until you fell down exhausted?

Yes, it was you; I'd know you anywhere. All that dancing and singing!

This is a soubrette song; a very delightful piece of coquetry. The left-hand piano part has a routine accompaniment figure in even quavers. Over it the staccato right-hand part, and the voice, go dancing and singing. These two continuous melodic lines unite, part, meet again, bow and curtsy, in an outpouring of bright melody. Technical device is lavished on making the point 'Ja, Ihr seid's' (Yes, it was you). This central idea has a harmonic equivalent (it is always in the home key of G major every time it occurs), a melodic equivalent (the insinuating motif of the piano introduction – 'I'm pretty sure it was you') and a rhythmic equivalent (the four accusingly accented crotchets in, e.g., bar 8 – 'Of course it was you'). The young gentleman thus identified must surely have been more delighted than embarrassed at having his prodigious feats (in the gypsy encampment?) recalled in this ebullient and charming music.

NOTE. Mediant modulations are a feature of the song. In other contexts these have thematic significance (motif 24), but probably not here – unless he danced and sang all night?

159 (S.w. 13). 'Mögen alle bösen Zungen . . .'

(Anon., trans. Geibel) 3rd April 1890

All those wicked tongues can go on saying what they please; I love him who loves me, I love and am loved. Those tongues whisper wicked slanders; but I know they are only out for innocent blood. So I'll never care, say what they like; I love him who loves me, I love and am loved. Those who enjoy slander are the disappointed ones, that no one wants. I am proud to be wanted; I love him who loves me, I love and am loved. If I were made of stone, then I could be deaf to a lover's pleading. But my heart is soft, as God made it; I love him who loves me, I love and am loved.

Wolf has taken these rather solemn verses and deftly transformed them into a bewitchingly light-hearted and delicate song. The poem with its recurrent refrain enables him, as so often in the Spanish Songbook, to achieve a design more common in instrumental music than in song. Here the pattern is a simple alternation of two successive strains each related to the other and each delightfully varied on repetition. After a short introduction announcing the basic rhythmic phrase ♪♩♩, and its two possible places within a bar of $\frac{3}{8}$ time, the lilting song begins. The piano's staccato right hand suggests chattering tongues, and the left-hand rhythm already heard suggests cheerful unconcern, while the voice part in words and melody combines both ideas. Then the delicate staccato single notes of the piano give place to light staccato chords at the refrain 'Wer mich liebt, den lieb' ich wieder' (who loves me, I'll love in return) as if applauding the sentiments expressed. In the second strain the staccato chattering is allotted to the piano left hand under slight repeated chords from which the voice picks out its melodic line. These two alternate with charming effect. There are the usual felicities, e.g. at the tenderly modulating spread chords and rising phrases at 'Liebesgruss und Liebesflehn' (a lover's greeting and pleading), before the final repetition of the main theme.

NOTE. This song is usually sung earnestly, as if true love were its theme. But other interpretations may be permissible. Wolf has a reminiscence of the prelude to this song in the prelude to *Tretet ein, hoher Krieger* (181) (also in D major), a song which hints at coquetry; and the piano phrase heard in the two bars preceding 'Zur Verleumdung' has off-beat bass octaves as in *Ich hab' in Penna* (180), q.v. – at bar 9 et seq. – a song which is an unabashed avowal of coquetry. And even if these musical analogies are not very compelling, it is still true that the words of this Spanish song are somewhat equivocal, and that its music has not only gaiety but something very like mischief.

160 (S.w. 14). 'Köpfchen, Köpfchen, nicht gewimmert . . .'
(Cervantes, trans. Heyse) 31st October 1889

(Preciosa's prescription for headache:)
Don't whimper; hold your head up. (Patience is a good prop for the purpose.) Remember to hope, however bad it is; and don't take anything too seriously, especially stories that might make your hair stand on end. To avert that, say a little prayer to the good Lord and the great Saint Christopher.

Preciosa is the heroine of a story by Cervantes. The song is a pleasant trifle into which the composer has put a disproportionate amount of deftness and wit. The clashing single quavers in the accompaniment suggests a series of tiny but persistent pangs, easing at the mention of patience ('Geduld'), and recurring but in a modified and less poignant form at 'Hoffnung' (hope). The small discords resume at the warning against hair-raising stories, but the music becomes firmly diatonic at the final moment of intercession. In the postlude the tiny top notes are tapped out delightedly free from any suspicion of semitonal clash; the prayer is answered, the headache cleared.

NOTES. 1. The high staccato minor seconds of motif 3 fit the idea of a childish predicament and prayer and also evoke tiny stabs of pain. It is not surprising that this song is liberally sprinkled with this chord and interval; it occurs in one form or another about fifty times in obviously thematic use in the song's forty bars of $\frac{2}{8}$ time. This ubiquitous idea is put to still further use. At the mention of hair standing on end the minor second is graphically transformed, in the voice part, into the wide rising interval of the minor ninth.

2. The childlish nature of the song is given additional emphasis by the off-beat rhythm of motif 2.

161 (S.w. 15). 'Sagt ihm, dass er zu mir komme . . .'
(Anon., trans. Heyse) 4th April 1890

Tell him to come to me, for the more they scold me the more my love grows.
For nothing on earth can stop love. Their anger and envy cannot harm it, for the more they scold me, the more my love grows.
They have locked me in my room many a weary day, and punished me cruelly. But my love gives me strength to bear my afflictions, and the more they scold me, the more my love grows.
My tormentors often say I must quit you, but this only makes us cleave to each other more. Even if I had to die for this, it would be bliss to die for love; the more they scold me, the more my love grows.

This is a colourful and passionate song with a hint of manufacture in its musical construction. Apart from the phrases that recur as a refrain, the verses have a basic rhythm of a line of four syllables followed by a line of eight, the lines rhyming alternately. Wolf's musical pattern irons out this rhythm into two or three bars of quavers in $\frac{3}{4}$ time. To avoid monotony semiquavers are added in the first bar, the result being $\frac{3}{4}$ ♫ ♫♫♫ ♫. This rhythm throbs throughout the song as obsessively as the love it expresses. The music is perhaps a little laboured; but lovingly so. Intricate variations of harmony in Chopinesque chromatics combine with the undeniably vital rhythmic force of the main motif to make a compelling song.

NOTES. I. Wolf's passionate love-motif 13 is strongly in evidence, e.g. in the piano interlude of bars 20–21.

2. Songs in the key of B minor ending on the dominant are a marked feature of the Spanish songs in a bittersweet mood.

162 (S.w. 16). 'Bitt' ihn, o Mutter . . .'

(Anon., trans. Heyse) 26th November 1889

Mother, tell Cupid not to aim at me any more; he will kill me.

Mother, oh Mother; love mocks yet soothes me, draws and repels me.

Last Sunday I saw two eyes, a miracle of Heaven, yet a bane of the world.

Like a basilisk's eyes they have brought death to my heart.

So please tell Cupid not to aim at me any more; he will kill me.

In both words and music there is over-insistence on somewhat jaded themes. But the music goes with a fiery impetus, there is strong erotic feeling in plenty, and the song is superbly effective for a dramatic soprano.

NOTE. It looks as if Wolf was reminded, perhaps by the idea of Cupid in both poems, of a song dated eleven days earlier, *Treibe nur mit Lieben Spott* (150). The key, the opening melodies, and in particular the chains of first inversions with added semitonal clashes (at 'was man sagt, o Mutter' here, and at 'Magst an Spotten nach Gefallen' in the earlier song, are the very same chords) make it clear that the same material is being used again. This may have been intentional, to suggest that the singer of this song is the girl addressed in 150, and that the prophecy that she in turn will be mocked by Cupid has been duly fulfilled. On the other hand it was Wolf's normal practice in the songbooks to juxtapose songs where the thematic relationship is deliberate; and the words of these two songs have no emotion in common.

163 (S.w. 17). 'Liebe mir im Busen zündet . . .'

(Anon., trans. Heyse) 2nd April 1890

Love has set my heart aflame; bring water, dear Mother, before it burns away.

Do not blame Cupid; he cooled my soul so gently, but then it burst into bright flame; bring water before it burns away.

But where is the flood that could quench this fire? Not all the seas would suffice. And yet I weep with delight for it; bring water before my heart burns away.

The poem is frankly silly, and the setting is not fine enough to redeem it. But musically the *tour de force* effect is irresistible. From the spanking chords and bright melody of the opening phrases a tear-away rhythm goes like fire through the piano part, cooling down and flaring up as the words dictate.

NOTES. 1. The unrest of motif 5 occurs at bars 11–12, etc.

2. At bar 23, etc. where the music describes cooling, its texture is, no doubt by coincidence, akin to the accompaniment of the passage praising muslin as a headdress in *Komm, Liebchen, Komm* (129).

164 (S.w. 18). 'Schmerzliche Wonnen . . .'

(Anon., trans. Geibel) 29th March 1890

Blissful sorrow, and sorrowful bliss; tears in the eyes, fire in the heart; pride on the lips and a sigh in the breast; love is a mixture of honey and gall.

When the soul leaves the body, St Michael tries to guide it up to heaven. But the devil tries to pull it down to perdition. Neither will give in, and they tussle for it.

So the soul is pulled up and down between heaven and hell, and being in love is just like that.

And, oh mother, I at seventeen have already felt it, and have renounced it with tears of remorse. Yet already I am in love, already in love again!

Wolf's comparative lack of success in dealing with allegory has already been noted. In this song he is at least given an understandable central theme to deal with. But this asset is counterbalanced by the episodic nature of the verses, which deal sometimes with the emotions induced by love, sometimes with love itself, including a long discursive story by way of illustration. The composer is left in a state of some confusion, and the result is a rather curious mélange of music, drama and narration, none of which is particularly deeply felt. The song is spirited and effective enough, but tends to pall.

NOTE. The affinities between this song and others sound like jaded echoes of previous inspirations. A few examples are recorded for interest:

(a) piano left hand, bars 3–9, etc., cf. *Lied eines Verliebten* (55) and note to 122.

(b) At 'oft, wenn ein Seelchen vom Leibe geschieden' the 'isolation' and 'separation' of motif 15 comes so pat as to sound almost absurd.

(c) At 'aufwärts und abwärts', etc., are echoes from *Der Rattenfänger* (96) with a nod in the direction of the mystery motif 19.

(d) The end of the voice part recalls the same moment in *Hätt' ich irgend wohl Bedenken* (128).

165 (S.w. 19). 'Trau' nicht der Liebe . . .'

(Anon., trans. Heyse) 28th March 1890

Put no trust in love, my love; take care! It will make you weep, though you laughed today.

As the moon wanes, so does happiness; and as for love, take care! It will make you weep, though you laughed today.

As the crickets chirp in summer and then are silent, so love will make you weep, though you laughed today.

Mark well what I say; Cupid is cruel. Time passes by and love will make you weep, though you laughed today.

It is not always bright, not always dark, but the sparks of joy fade so fast. Cupid is false-hearted – take care! He will make you weep, though you laughed today.

This is another of the masterpieces of technique and felicity so characteristic of the Spanish songs. Clearly it would be impossible for the song-writer to rely on a re-creation of the sense of the words, since they have so little and are repeated so often. Instead Wolf finds a charming melody for them, and a countermelody and a handful of gay lilting phrases for the piano. There are all the deft touches of his mature craftsmanship. Thus, when the refrain recurs at the word 'gelacht' (laughed) a little phrase in staccato quavers goes twinkling down the middle register of the piano and disappears like a fading smile. The extended piano interlude that follows at this point throughout the song makes the same point over again quite delightfully; its happy laughter is cut off gently but firmly by a sforzando chord.

NOTE. The song has the typical wistfulness of Wolf's A minor music for a woman's voice.

166 (S.w. 20). 'Ach, im Maien war's . . .'
(Anon. trans. Heyse) 30th March 1890

It was in May time, when the warm breezes blow and each seeks his love.
I alone poor wretch lie languishing in a dungeon cell, and I cannot tell
when day dawns or when night falls.
But I used to know by the singing of a bird outside my prison – until a
guard killed it. May God send him the worst of rewards!

This enchanting song is the great puzzle of the Spanish Songbook. Its
lilting melody and thrumming guitar-like accompaniment are not related to the situation and mood of the verses in the way one would normally expect in a Wolf song. This is perhaps a song within a song; a
ballad describing a singer singing an old tale of sorrow from long ago.
The grief is transmuted into an occasional touch of mild melancholy.

NOTES. 1. The guitar accompaniment is clearly akin to that of the later *Ein
Ständchen Euch zu bringen* (208). The piano postludes of these two songs, and
also of *Der Rattenfänger* (96), have much in common. Their effect is so striking
and so unusual in keyboard music that one wonders whether Wolf was reproduc-
ing a particular kind of virtuoso guitar-playing familiar to him from his own
experience.
2. The death of the bird is still of course the emotional climax of the song as
the changed harmonies at this point demonstrate.
3. The vocal melody is the basic inspiration of this song, and a very fine
one; but it does not seem to have been designed for this text. It may even have
been an instrumental conception; note how the melodic line at 'war's in Maien',
heard again in *Nein, junger Herr* (198) pays tribute to the last movement of
Schubert's violin and piano sonata Op. 137 no. 1.
4. Wolf has mistranscribed the poem; 'im Maien' on the fourth page should
read 'im Baume'.

167 (S.w. 21). 'Alle gingen, Herz, zur Ruh . . .'
(Anon., trans. Geibel) 2nd November 1889

All things are at rest, my heart. All sleep, save you alone. For hopeless
sorrow robs you of rest, and your thoughts fly in speechless grief to your love;
to your love.

This fine song is achieved with the utmost economy of means and refinement of technique. The music combines the mood and style of some
of the Mörike songs, both devotional and amorous, with the poignant
harmonic treatment so characteristic of the Spanish volume. A basic
rhythm ♩ ♫♩♫ etc. suggesting the beat of the sorrowing heart is

announced in the prelude and continues throughout the song. Like a heartbeat it is unobtrusive, almost unnoticed, until a moment of passionate stress. Even then it never distracts from the richly expressive cantilena that is the singing voice in this exquisite duet for mind and heart. At first it is heard through quiet chords as an accompaniment figure while the voice sings its rich opening melody. It is transferred to the right hand in octaves at 'Denn der hoffnungslose Kummer' (For hopeless sorrow). Gradually it rises in pitch and is transformed into fuller chords with a quickening rhythm at 'und dein Sinnen' (and your thoughts). It reaches a climax as the voice sings its last repeated phrases, first passionately then tenderly. The piano postlude incorporates allusions to the opening vocal melody before hushing into silence.

NOTES. I. At 'Denn der hoffnungslose Kummer' bar 7, etc., appears the Wolfian coinage for wakefulness at night (motif 17).

2. Similar heartbeats are heard at the end of *Geh'*, *Geliebter* (180).

3. The harmonies at the second 'seiner Liebe zu' may perhaps have been in Wolf's mind when two years later he came to set the closing words of *Dass doch gemalt* (195), in the same key of F major, in which music of this kind so frequently presented itself to him.

168 (S.w. 22). 'Dereinst, dereinst, Gedanke mein . . .'

(Cristobal de Castillejo, trans. Geibel) 11th April 1890

Some day, some day, my mind, you will be at peace. Though now you know no relief from the pangs of love, you will sleep well in the cool earth. There without love or sorrow you will be at peace. What you never found in life will then be granted. Then, free from pain and sorrow, you will be at peace.

The verses in German are maudlin. Wolf's noble music enriches and redeems them. The abject sorrow, the yearning for release, are implied rather than stated; the mood created by the composer is that of immense weariness of the spirit. The continuing slow accompaniment rhythm $\frac{3}{2}$ ♩ ♩ assists this impression; but what makes it unforgettable is the falling of the vocal and accompaniment themes. Falling tones, falling semitones, sound throughout, as if the melodic lines themselves were being flattened and crushed by an intangible but intolerable burden. When the voice sings of the coming lightening of this load, the melodic line counteracts the pressure sufficiently to allow it to rise somewhat, though slowly and with palpable effort, step by step up the scale for three notes. This happens at the first 'ruhig sein' (be at peace) echoed by the piano, at 'schläfst du gut' (you will sleep well), and at 'wird dir's gegeben' (it will be granted). Elsewhere the vocal line either falls or has its attempts to rise thwarted by this great weight of weariness. Even the two further repetitions of the key-phrase are compounded of

two falling semitones  . This no doubt

was the composer's central concept, the germ-theme from which this whole beautiful song develops.

NOTES. I. The song has striking thematic kinship to the music with which Wolf invested Goethe's Harper (86–88). Indeed the poem here on its lower level expresses exactly the underlying mood of the Harper songs and not surprisingly finds a similar musical equivalent (motif 22).

2. At the first 'ruhig sein' and later is the childlike submission of motif 2.

169 (S.w. 23). 'Tief im Herzen trag' ich Pein . . .'
(Camoens, trans. Geibel) 12th April 1890

Deep in my heart I bear my grief, unseen to outward view. I hide my dear grief well away from the world; it belongs to the inmost soul alone. As sparks of fire lie hidden in flint, so I bear my grief deep within.

We are told little about the nature of the poet's grief and nothing about what causes it. One can see difficulty in finding a musical equivalent for so unknown and unknowable an inward sorrow; the marvel is that Wolf succeeds so well.

The song is a treasure. It is mysteriously and hauntingly sad, like a Chopin mazurka (indeed it might very well pass for one of the finest). This strain sounds in the opening piano part as the voice sings its veiled phrases. It stops and turns to recitative accompaniment as the spark-in-flint simile is sung to warmer harmonies – 'Wie der Funke frei und licht sich verbirgt in Kieselstein'. Here a gleam of the E major triad is heard before darkening into C minor again as the voice sings, most movingly, the last words 'trag' ich innen tief die Pein'. Then the solemn mazurka theme reappears, strange and elusive in its sadness, to end the song.

NOTE. Wolf's songs bear many indications of the influence of Chopin. Another mazurka-like invention (again a particularly fine one) is heard in *Mein Liebster singt* (206).

170 (S.w. 24). 'Komm, o Tod . . .'

(Comendador Escriva, trans. Geibel) 14th April 1890

*Come death, shrouded in night; but come quietly so that my joy in
embracing you does not recall me to life. Come as lightning comes crackling
from a clear sky unheralded by storm, dealing a double blow. So suddenly
may you be vouchsafed to me, stilling my longing so quickly that my joy
in embracing you does not recall me to life.*

'Half in love with easeful Death' is the mood of this marvellous song.
The sombre colouring of the piano prelude yields, as the voice enters, to
a rich melodic flow from both voice and piano. Lulling rhythmic piano
phrases persist throughout, reaching a dynamic climax at 'Schlag'
(blow), then hushing again in a sweet yet unsentimental yearning. The
repetition in the last verse allows Wolf to repeat the music of the first
page, with a varied vocal line. This is rounded with a postlude epi-
tomizing the whole song, which is a perfect unity and a masterpiece of
its kind.

NOTE. The persistent accompaniment figure is a brother of Wolf's sleep music
(motif 18).

171 (S.w. 25). 'Ob auch finstre Blicke . . .'

(Anon., trans. Heyse) 16th April 1890

You looked at me angrily, but no one can deny that you have looked at me.
  *Your eyes have wounded my heart, but there is no sorrow which is not
requited by the joy of seeing you.*
  *I have suffered mortally from your anger; but no one can deny that you
have looked at me.*

This little song of hopeless devotion may make no very striking impression at first hearing, but it becomes a favourite in time. The voice echoes
a wistful prelude in a sequence of sad melody made sadder by the
neutral accompaniment chords. A major chord gleams briefly at the end
of the refrain, 'du hast geblickt nach mir' (you have looked at me)
before fading again into the wistful theme of the prelude. The deeper
meaning of this theme is made manifest by its use in the vocal line at
the words 'gibt's ein Leiden', etc. (there is no sorrow). Then the first
strain resumes, delicately varied and more fervent, shining out into the
dominant chord again until the wistful theme of the prelude appears
once more to end the song.

NOTES. I. The identity of piano prelude, interlude and postlude is a favourite device of Wolf's for songs devoted to one single idea. The theme here recalls one of the melodies of the *Italian Serenade* for string quartet, a work clearly written with some emotional context in mind, to the inner meaning of which the words of this song may perhaps provide a clue.

2. The song appears to be a typical Spanish Songbook construction. The confusion of the verbal stress at the half-bar shows clearly enough that the rhythmic instrumental concept is the basic one.

3. In Wolf's songs in B minor ending on the dominant there is a similar mood of lingering bittersweet (55, 175).

4. See 180, note 1.

172 (S.w. 26). 'Bedeckt mich mit Blumen . . .'
(Anon., trans. Geibel) 10th November 1889

Strew me with flowers; I am dying of love. Lest the breezes rob me of their sweet scent, cover me. For the breath of love and the scent of flowers is all one. Make ready my grave here of jasmine and white lilies; I am dying. And if you ask me why, I answer – in sweet torment I am dying of love; of love.

From this pot-pourri of sickly yearning, Wolf makes a most beautiful song, lush yet never sentimental. The piano has a languorous melody sustained in Chopinesque style over light repeated chords. The voice, like a second violin, adds a counterpoint; and the two proceed together intertwining continually, with the voice part constantly varied and renewed to match the inflections of the words. Thus, at successive mentions of the word 'Liebe' (love), the melodic curve reaches a high F (the highest note in the song, held in reserve for these moments); then for the last 'Liebe' the voice descends to a lower register in ineffable yearning, dying away under the opening piano melody which in turn dies away.

NOTES. I. The yearning of the piano treble in the first two bars, etc., is motif 12.

2. The Italian song *Sterb' ich, so hüllt in Blumen* (219) is a more austere musical treatment of a similar poetic idea.

173 (S.w. 27). 'Und schläfst du, mein Mädchen . . .'
(Gil Vicente, trans. Geibel) 17th November 1889

Awake my love, arise, and open the door; for the time has come, we are leaving. No matter if you are unshod, for our way lies through the deep swift-moving waters of the Guadalquivir. The time has come. We are leaving.

The fierce urgency of the words is abated by Wolf's setting, which is of no surpassing musical value. But it is an attractive vignette. Despite the quick tempo the persistent ⁶⁄₈ rhythm ♫♩ ♩. gives the impression of a barcarolle. The melodies are delightful and the piano part full of characteristic harmonic touches, e.g. the mysterious darkening of the tonality at 'Und bist ohne Sohlen' (if you are unshod) and the corresponding lightening at 'geht unsere Bahn' (our way lies).

NOTE. It is an odd coincidence that a song ending 'wir wandern von hier' should finish with exactly the same plain piano chords, very uncommon in Wolf, and in the same key, as the Mörike song *Auf einer Wanderung* (27).

174 (S.w. 28). 'Sie blasen zum Abmarsch . . .'

(Anon., trans. Heyse) 13th December 1889

The bugles are sounding for the regiment to march off, dear mother. My lover must leave and I am left alone.

The stars have scarce faded from the skies, and already there's the sound of rifle-fire in the distance. He fastens his pack and marches off, my heart with him. My lover must leave and I am left alone.

I feel like a day with no sun; my pain will be long healing; I care for nothing any more save a long communion with my grief.

My lover must leave and I am left alone.

Like *Klinge, klinge, mein Pandero* (147) this delightful song is a duet for two aspects of a situation, and again interpretation is a vital factor. The veiled pathos of the words and vocal melodies is set off admirably by the bright bugle-calls and clear drum-taps of the accompaniment. The temptation to the pianist to play the brilliant military march themes with evident enjoyment and gusto is wellnigh irresistible. But if the contrast is made too pointed, the effect is lost; the piano part needs to hint at the underlying sadness.

The quietly summoning staccato thirds of the prelude lead into soft bugle-calls as the voice part enters – 'Sie blasen zum Abmarsch'. The simple drooping melodies linger wistfully among the preparations for departure. At 'lässt mich allein' (leave me alone) the voice is left alone for a moment. Then drum-taps are heard and the piano prelude swells out, in military band fashion, before fading and marching away at the re-entry of the voice 'Am Himmel die Sterne sind kaum noch geflohn' (the stars have scarce faded). Then the refrain is repeated to sighs and a sad echo from the piano. Now a grieving reverie intervenes. The vocal melodies are muted; the piano's march, now some distance away, is interspersed with muffled drum-taps and troubled harmonies, slowing down until the refrain is again heard drooping into the last word 'allein'. The piano postlude takes over the military march theme, a tempo, very softly – quite gaily at first, then softer with little harmonic clashes, then receding into the distance, fading into inaudibility. The singer is left alone.

NOTES. I. The pathos of this song can be compared with the tender gaiety of *Ihr jungen Leute* (202) on exactly the same theme, with similar effects, but creating a very different impression. In each song occur the companionable thirds of motif 16.

2. At the end is the processional exit effect very dear to Wolf, e.g. in *Epiphanias* (104).

175 (S.w. 29). 'Weint nicht, ihr Äuglein . . .'
(Lope de Vega, trans. Heyse) 29th March 1890

Weep not, dear eyes; how can one who can kill with love weep with jealousy?

   How can one who can bring death, wish for death? Whoever can resist his tears would be won over by his smiles.

   So weep not, dear eyes; how can one who can kill with love weep with jealousy?

The mood of the verses is unclear. Wolf alternates between earnest and jest, with beguiling melodies at the beginning and end, and troubled chromatics in the middle section. Numerous changes of tempo are directed. It seems that Wolf has found some elusive musical mood that he does not wholly succeed in communicating in this short song. One wishes it were longer. The main themes have an ingratiating way with them, like those of the *Italian Serenade*.

NOTES. I. The *Italian Serenade* for string quartet is also brought to mind by 171 above. The two songs seem to have affinities. Both are in the same minor key ending on the dominant, but otherwise the purely musical similarities are not striking. Yet these two songs and the *Italian Serenade* seem to have some indefinable element in common; as if each was differently derived from the same emotional source.

2. The gaiety of the piano interlude after 'Liebe' calls for F sharp major tonality. Here there is not very far to go to reach it.

3. Wolf's songs in B minor ending on the dominant have a quality of bitter-sweet.

4. See 180, note I.

O   197

176 (S.w. 30). 'Wer tat deinem Füsslein weh . . .'

(Anon., trans. Geibel) 5th December 1889

'Who has hurt your little foot, la Marionetta, your snow-white heel, la Marion?'

I will tell you what hurt me, not one little word will I withhold. I went to a rose tree at night to pluck a rose. I trod on a thorn as I went, la Marionetta, and it pierced my heart, la Marion.

I will tell you all my grief, my friend, and will not cheat you. I went into a wood alone to pluck a lily. A sharp thorn pricked me, la Marionetta, it was a sweet word of love, la Marion.

I will tell you, in all sincerity, of my sickness and of my wound. Today I went into the garden where the loveliest carnation grew. A splinter hurt me there, la Marionetta, the wound still bleeds, la Marion.

'I, dear lady, am a doctor skilled in the treating of wounds. I shall cure yours so tenderly that you will scarcely feel it. You will soon be healed, la Marionetta, soon free of all pain, la Marion.'

Wolf is clearly attracted by the refrain 'la Marionetta . . . la Marion' which comes tripping and dancing in with a vivacity so irresistible as to disarm criticism. There is much wit and resource in the thrumming and tinkling guitar-effects of the song's captivating melodies, and its elated rhythmic pulse. Nevertheless the song is perhaps overlong for what it has to say; and as it is also not particularly easy for either performer it is all too rarely heard.

NOTES. I. For the melodic curve of the left-hand piano theme (bars 2–9, etc.) in other love-songs, see note to 122.

2. The thorn-in-the-foot symbolism of unhappy love recurs in the Italian Songbook – *Ich esse nun mein Brot* (210).

177 (S.w. 31). 'Deine Mutter, süsses Kind . . .'

(Don Luis el Chico, trans. Heyse) 2nd April 1890

When your mother bore you, my sweet child, she could hear the wind in the trees. For you were born as fickle as the breeze, choosing a lover one day and discarding him the next. Yet it would be foolish to chide you for your infidelity. Fate was against you, my sweet child. Your mother when she bore you could hear the wind in the trees.

A waywardly syncopated dance rhythm –

– strums throughout the guitar-like accompaniment, with harmonies veering between dark and bright. The inflections of the voice part suggest affectionate reproof rather than scolding. The song as a whole is highly wrought and charming in its decorative effects but adds little to Wolf's stature.

NOTES. 1. The writing is derivative, taking its colouring and some of its melodic ideas from *Auf dem grünen Balkon* (151) dated some five months earlier. In mood and occasionally in material it is not unlike another finer song on a similar theme, *Lied eines Verliebten* (55).

2. A hint of Wolf's passionate love-music (motif 13) is heard in the piano part at bars 1–2, etc.: and a clear statement of it when the words become forgiving at bars 21–22.

3. The accompaniment hugs the off-beat – because of 'Kind' in the first line perhaps (motif 2)?

178 (S.w. 32). 'Da nur Leid und Leidenschaft . . .'
(Anon., trans. Heyse) 20th April 1890

Since all I have known with you is sorrow and passion, I shall offer my heart for sale. Now, does anyone want it?

If I am to value it – three farthings would not be enough. It was never the wind's plaything, it remained constant.

But driven by necessity I'm offering it for sale, cash down to the highest bidder. What am I bid?

Each day it silently grieves me, so away with it and its whims; I am offering it for sale. If it were gay, I should keep it, but as it is – what am I bid?

Once I sell it I can live without care – any offers? Once more before the hammer comes down; I am offering my heart for sale. So make up your minds.

Now – going, going, gone! Well done; may it bring you happiness; take it – my sweetheart – brand the slave mark into it with a hot iron. I shall give you my heart even though you don't want to buy it.

We have already noted that Wolf finds difficulty in dealing with verses that contain extended figures of speech. Here the whole poem is a singularly trivial allegory, so that the composer has no opportunity for changes of mood and indeed little success in establishing what the prevailing mood actually is. There is some racy and effective piano writing, for example the 'going – going – gone' effects at 'Nun zum ersten und zum zweiten', etc. The accompaniment was no doubt the primary concept, but on the whole it is conventional, leaving all the burden of expression to the voice. A song on this basis is hardly viable unless it has broad melodic appeal, which is lacking here. The accentuation is faulty, the musical material slender. The whole song is overlong and must be reckoned among Wolf's failures.

NOTES. 1. Again the song is derivative; but the echoes are hardly worth noting.

2. Bars 20–24 have the typical racy mood that suggested F sharp major tonality to Wolf.

179 (S.w. 33). 'Wehe der . . .'

(Gil Vicente, trans. Heyse) 27th April 1890

Woe to the woman who lured away my lover.

The German poem has more words than these, but no more meaning. A highly skilled dramatic soprano, with a ringing high A and a sufficiently menacing aspect, could make this song very effective. Short of this it is difficult to believe in a word of the poem or a note of the music.

NOTE. Once again Wolf uses A minor for a woman's song portraying a mood of distress.

180 (S.w. 34). 'Geh', Geliebter . . .'

(Anon., trans. Geibel) 1st April 1890

You must go now, my love; it is dawn.

Already there are people in the streets and in the market place; already pale morning is spreading its white wings. And I am fearful of the neighbours and the scandal, for they do not know how truly we love one another. So you must go now; it is dawn.

The sun will soon be drying the pearls of dew from the grass, and I must weep and lose the pearl that was my treasure. Day will seem like night to me, for our parting darkens my life. But you must go now, my love; it is dawn.

Leave my arms, for if you let the time slip by we shall pay with long sorrow for our brief joy. Now we are in Purgatory, but one day we shall behold the radiance of Heaven. So you must go now, my love; it is dawn.

The operatic breadth and sweep of this long marvellous song make a fitting conclusion to Wolf's most highly wrought songbook. A village Romeo and Juliet situation is brought to passionate life in a setting of flawless construction and great depth of feeling. It is a measure of its power and quality that the music even justifies the dramatic convention of the poem. 'Go now', the song commands, and goes on commanding for some hundred bars of moderate ⅜ time. No listener would wish the order obeyed earlier.

There is a short piano prelude which contains in a mere three bars the whole essence of the song. The first bar establishes an urgent cajoling rhythm. The second holds it back with tenderly drooping quaver semitones. In the third bar, without any change in the feeling or the texture of the music, the two ideas are combined – pressing rhythms in the left hand, gently falling quavers in the right; a command and a caress. The scene is set for the entry of the voice to a melody as apt as it is beautiful. It too combines the elements of warmth and urgency from which the whole song is compounded. It shifts off the beat and briefly out of the key only to plunge and reappear warm and vibrant at 'dämmert' (dawning). Then in a brief interlude the gestures of affection melt into tenderness on a high bright arpeggio. All this in eight words and eleven bars; but they comprehend a whole world of feeling and drama.

What follows is evolved by a process of continuous creation which is impossible to describe, but unforgettable when heard. There is sumptuous melody at the quiet section beginning 'Wenn die Sonn' am Himmel', etc. (when the sun in the sky); urgent grief at 'Fliehe denn aus meinen Armen!' (Leave my embrace); and an overflowing of love and sorrow in the repeated refrain 'Drum, Geliebter, geh' jetzt!' (so leave me now, my love). In the postlude tenderness and anxiety hush to a murmur of heartbeats and an empty embrace. All this may sound exaggerated; but those who are familiar with this song are more likely to think it a culpable understatement.

NOTES. 1. The drooping semitones of the piano prelude right hand had a particular meaning for Wolf in the Spanish songs. They appear in nearly the same notes and similar tonality in 171 and 175 (e.g. piano prelude and bar 22 in each), both dated about the same time. These passages are related to Wolf's loving and grieving music of motifs 13 and 22.

2. The heartbeats in the piano postlude are as in 167, *passim*.

3. There are surprising musical affinities between this song and Mignon's *Kennst du das Land* (94). An involuntary reminiscence can probably be ruled out because of the difference in date of the two compositions. There is no obvious parallel between the two situations, but Wolf seems to have been convinced of their essential similarity. The shape of the refrain here suggests motif 11, which is unequivocally used in the Goethe song. And there is more to it than this. Even setting aside such evident affinities as the keys and key-changes of the two songs, their common ¾ – ⅜ rhythmic structure, the falling quaver semitones (after 'wohl' in 94, here throughout), there is an unmistakable feeling of identity of impulse behind the music.

A particular example of this will be found in a comparison between the passages at 'Kennst du es wohl' in 94 and at 'fliehe denn', etc., in this song. Wolf's writing at the high creative level common to both songs was never superficial; and there is clearly room for speculation about the reasons for their musical kinship. There is no evidence that Wolf had imagined Mignon as being passionately in love with Wilhelm Meister and thinking of this love as guilty or illicit (though it is fair to say that there is much in Goethe's novel to support this view). Perhaps it is simply that 'Geh, Geliebter' reminds Wolf of 'möcht ich mit dir, o mein Geliebter, ziehen' in Goethe's poem.

VI. The Keller songs

[Peters Edition 3153, Nos. 7–12]

We have already met Gottfried Keller (1819–90) for his pleasant valediction to Mörike (p. 35). He is known mainly as a novelist and short-story writer; but he was also a not inconsiderable poet with something of Goethe's eclecticism, and of Mörike's verbal magic.

These six poems are taken from the collection known as *Alte Weisen* or, as one might say, old songs resung; each is by or about a woman. The settings were intended as a tribute for the poet's seventieth birthday. But Wolf was late in starting, the music did not flow as freely as usual, and Keller died before the songs were completed.

181. 'Tretet ein, hoher Krieger . . .'

25th May 1890

Enter, tall warrior; you have surrendered your heart to me. Now you must put off your crimson cloak and gold spurs. Yoke your charger to my father's plough, and give me the rich saddle cloth as a carpet. The gold and gems of your sword-hilt will adorn me; the blade can be a poker; and the white plume on your red cap will make a useful fan in summertime. The Marshal must learn how to bake bread and slice meat. Recommend your soul to Christ our Lord, for your body is sold and cannot be redeemed.

An odd poem, and an odd setting. The fate of the captive knight in bondage is set out in verses so colourful and attractive that one is unprepared for the real menace of the last lines. Wolf offers no solution to this problem, which is perhaps intractable if taken seriously. Instead his music is charming and almost coquettish; it can be greatly enjoyed for its own sake once possible problems of interpretation are discounted.

NOTES. 1. Wolf may be using the poem as a lay-figure round which to drape preconceived material. This procedure is unobjectionable, and indeed extremely difficult to detect, if the fit is good. But this one is bursting apart at the seams. When words like 'in', 'und', 'auf' and even the second syllable of 'Vater' are allotted to the first beat of a strongly metrical bar in a Wolf song, something is very wrong. It is clear that the voice part is in the main wrongly barred, the stress being felt irresistibly at the half-bar, while the piano part is felt as written. The effect is a kind of unintentional rhythmic canon at the half-bar. This confusion is a notable feature of some of Wolf's writing. It seems likely that the songs in which it occurs almost throughout are in some measure contrived, in the way suggested. This is of course not necessarily a blemish. The point is that Wolf has conceived the piano part in rhythmic terms before finding a correspondingly complete idea of the vocal line. When this procedure succeeds it does so with astounding brilliance. Otherwise, as here, the result is puzzling.

2. The piano prelude echoes the prelude to *Mögen alle bösen Zungen* (159), q.v.

182. 'Singt mein Schatz wie ein Fink . . .'

2nd June 1890

If my love sings like a finch, then I'll sing like a nightingale; if he is a lynx, then I'll be a snake. Bring him back to me from far away, or my heart will break. Give me back that proud man; he must surrender meekly to me. Then he shall see how love can become a fiery sword.

Wolf seems unusually baffled and ill at ease. In the first few bars, the piano part is given up to a somewhat trivial rendering of finches and nightingales. The song is mainly notable for a chromatic accompaniment with drooping semitones. This persists throughout and seriously outstays its welcome, despite lavish accelerandi and crescendi and a climax at 'ein feurig Schwert' (a fiery sword) which is finely effective in its way.

NOTES. 1. As in 181 above there is a slight confusion at the half-bar, e.g. at 'ist mein Liebster ein Luchs'. This might suggest a preconceived accompaniment, but for the dullness of the one provided.

2. The nightingale is also allotted semiquaver triplets in the same key in *Philine* (93).

3. In the piano postlude is the passionate love-music of motif 13.

4. Wolf was very scathing about Brahms' setting of these verses (Op. 69 no. 8 under the title of *Salome*). But there seems little to choose between them.

183. 'Du milchjunger Knabe . . .'

16th June 1890

Young man, why do you look at me so? What a question it is that your eyes have asked.

Not even the councillors in the city, not even all the wise men in the world, could answer the question in your eyes.

But there's an empty snail-shell lying in the grass; just put it to your ear and you'll hear something whispering.

We, too, have a question – what is it about this simple poem that has suggested such curiously convoluted music, such subtle emotional overtones? A wistful questioning begins in the piano part

and persists until it is transmuted at 'Schneckhäusel' (snail-shell) to the gentle meaningless murmur which is all that is offered by way of reply. With its wistful delicacy, its tentative groping for the key, the music seems to be an exquisite portrayal of calf-love. On this view it is the young man, in effect, who is singing. The song is all question, murmur, and mystery, representing the effects of the words on their naïve hearer. The words seem almost a reverie in reported speech – 'This is what she said to me'. There is little trace of the woman's affectionate and mature teasing. Admittedly the song is clearly for a woman's voice and on this interpretation becomes impossible to perform.

The practical approach therefore is to ignore difficulties for the sake of some tenderly beautiful music.

NOTES. 1. The suggested evocation of young love in the music is somewhat supported by its mild resemblances to *Nimmersatte Liebe* (21) and *Wie lange schon* (197). The same impulse is perceptible in each.

2. Brahms' splendid setting of an earlier version of this poem under the title *Therese* (Op. 86 no. 1) is a straightforward rendering of the idea with no attempt at subtlety; an interesting contrast to Wolf's.

184. 'Wandl' ich in dem Morgentau . . .'

8th June 1890

When I walk in the dewy morning through the flower-filled meadow I am so shamed by all I see.

The dove on the church roof, the fish in the millstream, all feel and say 'Love'.

Bright apple-blossom mothering little fruit to come; the butterfly-pair dying joyously so early in the year – Lord, what have I done, that I must die unloved?

Keller sets the composer another intractable problem by bringing in the notion of death at the end of this poem. Wolf again deals with this, very sensibly, by ignoring it. It would have been outrageous to disturb with tragedy the lilting longing of this song in Wolf's favourite spring key of A major. The ⁶₈ rhythm ♩ ♪♩♫ – perhaps suggested by the first words of the German text – dominates the music. The dipping and lifting phrases of the piano prelude introduce a series of appealing vocal melodies. In the last verse 'Gott, was hab' ich denn getan', yearning is portrayed with characteristic delicacy.

NOTES. 1. Here the Italian songs are directly foreshadowed. For example the piano part at 'Braut' has the same essence as the similar phrase in *Wir haben beide* (205) at the words 'die Engel Gottes'.

2. Both aspects of Wolf's love-music are contained in this song; 'Agape' (motif 14) throughout and 'eros' (motif 13) in the last four piano bars.

185. 'Das Köhler weib ist trunken . . .'

7th June 1890

The collier's wife is drunk again. She is singing in the wood; you can hear her voice echoing hoarse and shrill among the trees. Once she was a beauty, courted by rich and poor. She queened it, head in air; choosing a husband

*was too much trouble. Then red wine overmastered her; how transient all
things are!*

*The collier's wife is drunk again. She is singing in the wood; you can hear
her voice echoing hoarse and shrill through the twilight.*

The poem is full of pity, the music full of bitterness and mockery.
'What a shame,' says Keller. 'Serve her right,' says Wolf. The song
begins in a splendid piece of original and incisive rhetoric, with a brilliant evocation of wild singing and laughter. Even in the reminiscence of
'sie war die schönste Blume' (once she was the fairest flower) we are not
allowed a moment of real tenderness. The new theme clearly associated
with queening it and strutting about

is disapprovingly introduced long before the poem mentions it; and
this same 'theme itself conveys more than a hint of a coming loss of
decorum. Indeed after 'fiel ihr zu schwer' (was too much trouble) it sags
blowsily and collapses; and the original incisive theme takes over and
dominates the song. Even the regretful words 'wie müssen alle Dinge
vergänglich sein' (how transient all things are) are swept away in the
blazing bitter crescendo that summons the music back to the opening
strains for the repetition of 'Das Köhlerweib ist trunken' and leads on
to the climax of the song and the piano postlude; which with absolute
mastery conveys unforgettably the vivid impression of mirthless and
terrible laughter.

NOTE. The song resounds with something very like the mocking laughter of
motif 4.

186. 'Wie glänzt der helle Mond . . .'

5th June 1890

An old woman speaks:
   *How cold and far away the bright moon shines; but farther still is the
beauty I had once. Far away the sea beats on the shore; but farther still is
the youth I had once. Soon now I shall be going away to Heaven. There I'll
see Mary on her throne, with her Blessèd Son asleep in her lap, and God the
Father feeding the Holy Ghost from His hand with the grain of Paradise.
And there I'll sit in my silver veil just looking at my newly white hands.
Only St Peter will take no rest: he'll be squatting by the Gate cobbling old
shoes.*

Wolf had no sympathy for the drunken collier's wife in the previous song. But his heart went out to the old peasant woman in this one. The result is the masterpiece of the Keller songs and one that takes an assured place among the best of Wolf's work.

By his own standards it is open to criticism; for example, the ABA song-form has no obvious relevance to the poem. This is partly Keller's fault. The old woman is of a literary turn of mind in the first two couplets, and this is hardly consistent with the naïve simplicity of her later description of Heaven, touchingly expressed though it is. But the underlying thought is coherent enough; and the sheer quality of the musical material as a whole defies criticism. Soft open repeated chords in the piano's upper register suggest the heights and spaces of the night sky. The vocal melodies end with a rising inflection for the first part of each of the two comparisons and then droop again for the second, making the point most movingly – 'the moon – my beauty; the sea – my youth'. A whole world of tranquillity and resignation lives here. The idea of Heaven is then depicted in sweet strong chords over an affirming bass, as if this idea were going to be allowed to come true because of an old woman's great faith. At 'in meinem Silberschleier sitz' ich dann' the original themes and figuration return, and Wolf proceeds without incongruity to round off the music with a graphic illustration. The final section, beginning at 'hockt vor der Tür' (squats by the Gate) and continued in a short piano postlude, contrives by the simplest of means and in a short compass to suggest the tableau of St Peter working in the otherwise motionless radiance of a picture-book Heaven.

NOTES. 1. For high piano chords in the same context as the beginning of this song see the end of *An die Geliebte* (44).

2. The curious affinities between this song and *Dank des Paria* (115) have already been commented on in the note to the latter; even more interesting are the less marked but detectable affinities between this song and that extremely unflattering vision of the religious life *Geselle, woll'n wir uns* in the Italian Songbook (200 q.v.).

VII. The Italian Songbook

Paul Heyse has already been mentioned (p. 163) as a gifted translator from Romance languages. His *Italienisches Liederbuch* published in 1860 consists mainly of translations of anonymous Italian lyrics. They are usually short, often repetitive and sometimes trivial; but the collection as a whole succeeds in creating a vivid picture of a true and real world. There is occasionally a certain artifice in Heyse's renderings that might suggest an idealized summer landscape 'wo die Zitronen blühn'. But in the main his fidelity to the original Italian lyrics preserves their intimate sense of close communal life, the living reality of the street, the church, the market place, and above all, the men and women, gay or sad, in love or in despair, accepted or ostracized. The poems that Wolf selected retain this quality. Even their first lines, by which the songs are usually known, illustrate this personal and intimate background – 'They tell me . . .', 'I'm told', 'I asked them and they said . . .' Practically the whole songbook is about what 'I' or 'you' feel, what 'they' say or do. From this Wolf creates an apotheosis of popular song, raised to the highest pitch of art.

187 (I 1). 'Auch kleine Dinge . . .'

9th December 1891

Even little things can bring joy and be loved. Think of the beauty of pearls, the savour of olives, and the sweet smell of roses.

A justly famous song, simple in style and yet deeply moving in effect. It was chosen by Wolf to stand at the forefront of a collection containing many of his rarest masterpieces; and the world has applauded his choice ever since. Yet the meaning of the song presents difficulties. It is certainly not a mere advertisement for pearls, olives and roses; and the feeling goes too deep for a love of miniature things as such. On the whole the music suggests that this was, for Wolf, a love-song; a humble avowal of lonely and perhaps hopeless love.

The piano prelude is a marvellously subtle foreshadowing of the thematic material to be used as accompaniment throughout (broken chords in semiquavers in the right hand, a falling melodic line in the left). The vocal line is among the finest of Wolf's many similar inspirations; it is all delicacy and restraint, yet makes an instantaneous and unforgettable appeal as sheer melody.

NOTE. Some additional pointers to the view expressed above:

(*a*) A melodic line in the left hand, falling away from a steady level of figuration in the right, is often used by Wolf in contexts suggesting separation or loneliness (motif 15).

(*b*) This melodic line is in itself very closely parallel to that of a later song of humble love (215).

(*c*) The left-hand piano part centres on the weak beat of the bar in a way often associated in Wolf's music with the idea of childish dependence (motif 2).

(*d*) The moving gentleness and simplicity in the quiet climax of the last few lines and in the piano postlude is typical of the Italian love-songs; see in particular 204, note 2.

188 (I 2). 'Mir ward gesagt . . .'

25th September 1890

They say you are going on a long journey. Oh tell me when you are going, my darling, and where, so that my tears and thoughts can go with you. Think of me sometimes and give me hope. My tears and thoughts will always be with you. Think of me, do not forget me, dear heart.

The sadness of the music adds poignancy by suggesting that this may be a final farewell. The piano right hand with steady slow quaver chords in common time provides the focal point of the song. The voice part emerges from and is sustained by these chords, while in the piano left-hand a melody in single notes, with a poignant discord on the first beat of the bar, goes grieving downwards on its separate way. So the song continues. The steady rhythm, the troubled harmonies, and the dividing melody suggest a journey, a sorrow, and a separation; and all three are blended by great art into exactly the emotion described in the verses. All this is moving enough; but there is still an emotional climax to follow. For the final words 'vergiss es nicht, mein Herz!' the steady movement of the accompaniment is halted. From a few notes for the voice and a few simple chords in the piano, the composer, with the magic so characteristic of this songbook, conjures a farewell phrase so loving and resigned as to win any heart at once and forever. And the song ends quietly and hopefully.

NOTES. 1. The piano part of the whole song is motif 15.

2. The final phrase gains immeasurably in effect by its diatonic harmonic treatment, in contrast with the preceding chromaticism; this favourite procedure of Wolf's is a clear indication, if one were needed, that the last line is the emotional climax of the song.

3. The discord on the first beat of the bar is reminiscent of the opening of *Wie viele Zeit verlor ich* (223), and suggests a somewhat similar mood.

4. The text does not define the sex of the singer: but the song is usually thought of as a woman's.

189 (I 3). 'Ihr seid die Allerschönste . . .'

2nd October 1890

You are the loveliest in all the land, lovelier than the flowers of May. Not Orvieto's cathedral or Viterbo's fountains rise in such majesty.

So great is your enchantment that even Siena's cathedral must bow before you. So rich are you in grace that not even Siena's cathedral can compare with you.

This is decidedly not one of the great songs. The tonality and rhythm are square, and the responses to the text conventional (e.g. the rather tiresome fussing in the piano part at the mention of fountains). The composer is given nothing to bite on; no phrase of the verse has real distinction, and the music achieves none, though it has great charm.

NOTE. The marked speed of ♩ = 100 seems too fast. On the second page Wolf himself gives several indications of restraint. 'Poco rit' is marked, but these passages clearly need to be taken at a very moderate tempo, which makes the original tempo too great a contrast.

190 (I 4). 'Gesegnet sei, durch den die Welt entstund . . .'

3rd October 1890

Praise to Him who created the world. How finely He wrought it! He made the sea and its fathomless depths; He made the ships that sail upon it; He made Paradise with its everlasting light; and He made beauty, and your face.

The basic material of this masterpiece is simplicity itself. The piano part has an ordinary rhythm ♪ ♩, a motif of falling octaves or fifths, quietly moving chords, repeated seconds rising by step. The voice part sings repeated notes or scale-passages or the simplest of sequences. It is an elementary treatise on the rudiments of musical theory, set out in seventeen bars of common time. And yet, by some unimaginable magic, it is a music impossible to hear, or even to read, without emotion. It passes comprehension how these undistinguished verses could have been transmuted by these slender means into one of the world's greatest songs; yet so it is.

There is power in the falling piano octaves of the first bar, and great strength in the rising bass. At 'wie trefflich schuf er sie' (how finely He wrought it) there is an exultant fanfare. The voice rings out here, in the supposed climax. Only later do we learn that there is a greater glory still. The meditation continues – 'Er schuf das Meer . . .' (He made the sea). Here the right-hand piano part is neutral orthodox accompaniment giving greater clarity to the creating gesture of the falling fifths in the left hand. This figuration continues in rising semitones, and then the real climax is reached. 'Er schuf die Schönheit' (He created beauty); and now the composer makes us believe that at this instant the thought of the loved one's face takes possession of the singer's mind, and takes his breath away. The voice first swells out triumphantly and then hushes in adoration. 'Beauty; your face'; it is a whisper. In the postlude the piano goes on meditating on that moment.

NOTES. 1. The sudden decrescendo at 'Schönheit' should not be made to sound too contrasting by a previous exaggeration of tone. The word 'Licht' should be taken not louder than mezzo-forte.

2. The lordly gesture of the falling fifth has been heard in *Der Sänger* (95).

3. The piano postlude is comparable with that of *An die Geliebte* (44) where the same mood is expressed; see notes 1 and 2 to that song.

191 (I 5). 'Selig ihr Blinden . . .'

4th October 1890

Blessèd are the blind, who cannot see the charms of women; the deaf, who cannot hear the lament of lovers; and the dumb, who cannot speak their heart's need. And blessèd the dead, who can no longer suffer the pangs of love.

The composer takes this text very seriously. To counterbalance the hyperbole of the verses he gives them a strong foundation of music expressing unshakeable conviction of the truth of the sentiments expressed. Over a persisting pedal point the accompaniment marches in diatonic or chromatic scale-passages in an unrelenting four-in-a-bar crochet rhythm. The effect is of strength and simplicity throughout, with a suggestion of organ tone to match the Biblical echoes of the poem. This treatment gives the words of the song a new sincerity and makes them almost believable. The first strain is announced as an uncomplicated statement in voice and piano, rising in pitch and increasing in chromatic intensity as the song proceeds. At last at 'selig ihr Toten' (blessèd the dead) the music invests all that has gone before with an added solemnity. High sustained notes now toll out in the treble as well as the bass, while the voice sings its long lament. The piano postlude grieves briefly for lost love and then recovers control as the strong descending scale passages take charge and end the song.

NOTE. The dispassionate treatment which is here given to an exaggerated text is the saving grace of this song, and redeems it wholly (as in 193). There are some unfortunate examples of what happens when Wolf gives verse of this kind a more passionate expression than it has strength to bear, creating an imbalance fatal to the musical integrity of the song, e.g. *Wehe der* (179) and *Verschling' der Abgrund* (231).

192 (I 6). 'Wer rief dich denn? . . .'

13th November 1890

Who called you here? who bade you come? Why come at all if it is a burden to you? Go to your other sweetheart, follow your thoughts. Yes, go to her; I gladly absolve you from coming to me. Go to the sweetheart you prefer – who called you here? Who bade you come?

This is a good example of the way in which Wolf treats the often trivial material of the Italian poems, interpreting the text and interfusing it with subtleties of illustration and vocal stress.

The song opens with a gesture of defiance in the piano prelude. The voice is then directed to sing its opening questions scornfully, punctuated by sharp little chordal interventions. These are followed by some trivially gay phrases from the piano, which cease as the voice falters at 'wenn es dir zur Last' (if it is a burden to you). The 'wenn' is stressed – *if* it is a burden to you. The voice recovers, but falters again; in an expressive phrase at 'wo du die Gedanken hast' (where your thoughts are), at 'will ich gern dir schenken' (I gladly absolve you), and most movingly of all, at the last words. Here with the plainest of harmonies and vocal lines the music is suddenly in tears. The piano postlude recovers and finishes the song in defiant vein.

NOTES. I. Wolf was never afraid of writing music that seemed banal if the poetic and interpretative context called for it, as in this song. What at first sight seem trivial equivalents for defiance and nonchalance are seen to be masterstrokes of depiction standing for simulated defiance, pretended gaiety. This is a procedure that stands at the limit of song-writing. It would hardly be possible to take it any further than in this song while remaining in the domain of musical expression. But Wolf's touch was never surer than in the first part of the Italian Songbook, and here this device is used with great effect.

2. For another song where the meaning of the music is the contrary of that expressed in the words, see *Wie soll ich fröhlich sein* (217).

3. The German text does not define the sex of the singer; but the song is clearly a woman's.

193 (I 7). 'Der Mond hat eine schwere Klag' . . .'
13th November 1890

The moon is sore aggrieved, and has laid a complaint before the Lord. She feels she cannot continue in the sky, because you have robbed her of her lustre. She says that when she last counted the serried stars, two were missing; you have stolen two of the loveliest – your eyes, whose light has blinded me.

The mood of this masterpiece is quiet, the tempo slow; in the accompaniment are repeated phrases, in the voice part repeated notes. Yet the total effect is not of monotony, but of a trance-like rapture, leading up to a moment of almost unbearable poignancy.

This song does not perhaps make its full impact at first hearing. At first one is perplexed by the treatment of the words. The poem is no more than a quaint conceit; but Wolf treats it with hushed reverence and awe. His musical response to poems about the beauty of a woman's eyes was always heartfelt. Here the music suggests that he found this particular poem not only believable but almost literally true. In the piano part, the simple chordal pattern of falling two-bar phrases in an unchanging slow rhythm are austere gestures of grief and resignation in a pavane for lost stars. The depth of the singer's underlying emotion is hinted at in the momentary warmth of major harmony at 'du habest ihn um seinen Glanz gebracht' (you have robbed her of her lustre), the first hint of the poem's real meaning. The pavane resumes as before; but when this meaning is again approached, at 'zwei von den schönsten' (two of the loveliest), the music moves with inevitable rightness into the sweetness of the major key. When the point of the poem is reached, at 'die beiden Augen dort', etc., these words are hushed, the pervading rhythm is unchanged; yet, by the simplest of harmonic means – a few chromatically altered notes, a slight shift of tonality – the music seems momentarily to falter and fight for control until the quiet final chord of the short postlude is reached.

NOTES. 1. The change of key-signature to three sharps from six flats looks much more dramatic than it is. The three sharps are simply a convenient way of writing G flat minor. A similar progression, in the same notation, is found in *Mignon* (Kennst du das Land) (94).

2. The chordal rhythm ♩. ♫. ♪, etc., has already been heard in the first *Peregrina* song (45, note), the words of which are also about the beauty of a woman's eyes (44 note 2).

3. The melodic line of the piano accompaniment is closely akin to the 'sorrow' of motif 22.

194 (I 8). 'Nun lass uns Frieden schliessen . . .'
14th November 1890

Let us make peace now, my dearest, my own. We have quarrelled too long. If you will not yield, I shall; how could we two make war to the death? Kings and princes make peace, and shall not lovers? Princes and soldiers make peace, and shall two lovers fail? What these great lords can achieve, shall not two loving hearts?

The text, with the repetitions common in this songbook, has a simple lulling effect. Wolf overwhelms it in music of matchless sincerity and serenity. Soft moving broken chords are interspersed with little tender falling melodies that echo or reflect the voice part; and this is sensitive alike to the inflection of the words and to the lilt of the accompaniment. There are also moments of heightened emotion. The questioning at 'auf den Tod bekriegen?' (make war to the death?), at 'wohl missraten?' (how could we fail?) and in the last word of the song, is tenderness itself.

The piano postlude is tranquil and reassuring. 'Of course we shall', it says softly, 'of course.'

NOTES. 1. The first 16 bars of the piano are repeated almost note for note. The exceptions, for two quavers at the word 'Soldaten', are practically a treatise on song-writing.

2. For a possible sequel to this song see 205.

195 (I 9). 'Dass doch gemalt . . .'
29th November 1891

If only a picture were painted of your beauty, and a heathen prince found it, he would bestow great gifts on you; he would lay his crown in your hands. All his kingdom would have to follow the true faith. It would be proclaimed throughout the land; – all must become Christians and love you. Straightway all the heathen would be converted and become Christians, and love you.

This innocuous and faintly ridiculous poem sets the composer's mind ablaze with music.

The song presents the verses as a series of thoughts passing through the mind and turning into music as they pass. It is as if every moment of every bar were an immediate quickening in response to a great love. There is no prelude – the voice is impatient to begin. Broken chords and a breathless vocal line in crescendo announce the first idea as if it had just at that moment occurred to the singer. Then the voice hushes at 'fände' (found) thinking of the beauty of that picture. There is increased intensity of expression conveyed in the chromatically changing piano chords that follow. At the renewed quietude after 'in deine Hände' (in your hands) the song comes to a half-close. But now (and again the music suggests that a new idea has just occurred) the repeated quavers are taken up in insistent repetition over a strong bass line, clearly foreshadowing some important pronouncement. Voice and piano combine to illustrate the universal nature of the imagined conversion. And now (again a new idea) the clarion call rings out in the piano rising to the vocal climax of the ringing proclamation 'Christ soll ein Jeder werden' (all must become Christians). The music then hushes, as if amid all this panoply the occasion for it had been almost forgotten and then remembered – 'und dich lieben' (and love you). This is the emotional climax of the song. It is followed by what seems like a full close. Another composer might have treated the last sentence as a dynamic culmination. Wolf's different way is infinitely more expressive and convincing. What follows is a quiet statement giving the sense of 'Yes, that is just what would happen; they would all become Christians and love you.' Indeed, one would go with him to see, hoping it might be so.

NOTES. 1. This song marks the beginning of a new creative period. Like *Der Tambour* (17), which began the Mörike outburst, it teems with invention which within this more limited compass of an Italian song almost bursts its musical framework.

2. For the verbal theme see 44, note 2; for the harmonies in the last line see 167, note 3.

196 (I 10). 'Du denkst mit einem Fädchen . . .'
2nd December 1891

You think you've only to look at me and I'll fall in love with you. That's what I wanted you to think; I've caught others even more sure of themselves than you, so you shouldn't trust me too far. No, you're not the first I've caught. But you're quite right, in a way. I am in love – though not, as it happens, with you. I am in love – but not with you!

This is not one of the truly great songs, although it can be redeemed to some extent by interpretation. Even the tiny piano prelude has a contrived air, like the kind of overture that consists of a potpourri of themes from the opera. The opening words 'Du denkst mit einem Fädchen mich zu fangen' (you think to catch me with a thread) give the composer an idea for some dangling threads of melody. They change, at 'ich fing schon andre' (I've already caught others), and again when these words are repeated, into the assertive themes heard in the piano prelude – the theme of the catcher, not the caught. But their deployment in the first section seems to lack some of Wolf's usual constructional logic and musical *raison d'être*. There is no attempt at sensuous melodic or harmonic appeal, so that if the dramatic and interpretative effect fails there is very little left. In the second section of the song however Wolf is himself again. The first 'I am in love, but not with you' is decisive – 'Ich bin verliebt', then gay – 'doch eben nicht in dich'. For the second 'verliebt' the voice goes swooning up an octave in pretended bliss and breaks into outright laughter for the rest of the phrase. 'So there' says the piano, and the song is over.

NOTE. For better or for worse, this music has a compelling originality. Its few themes in few bars crackle with invention, and it is not surprising that this song follows 195 as the second of a new, though short-lived, creative period.

197 (I 11). 'Wie lange schon . . .'

4th December 1891

How long I have yearned – if only a musician were fond of me! Now may the good Lord grant my wish and send me one with cheeks like milk and roses. And look! here he comes, with a delicate air, with bowed head, playing the violin.

This is a splendid piece of evocative writing. The verses have a certain absurd charm of their own; but the music gives them a whole new dimension of sympathy and humour.

The piano begins with repeated slow drooping wistful phrases, , the melodic and rhythmic shape of which in various forms dominates the song. There is a lesson in song-writing in these three notes, which form the perfect musical equivalent for the theme of the verses – a simple basic idea taking a somewhat unusual form! A slight syncopation, and a chromatically altered note effect this change, which gives to the whole song its characteristic savour of affectionate burlesque. These little phrases in the piano sigh feelingly, moving in sympathy with the vocal line, throughout the first part. But with the answering of the maiden's prayer, a delightful change comes over the music. The left hand of the piano indicates in measured staccato semi-quavers the delicate new arrival on the scene. In the right hand the little phrases appear in a new time and rhythm 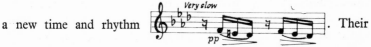. Their speed, suddenly doubled, indicates a quickening of interest; they have become decidedly more alert. Over this accompaniment the voice sings its grateful phrases, not forgetting the original germ-theme at 'sanfter Miene' – (delicate air), until at the last words, 'die Violine' the piano takes over. Now the song ends with an entrancing postlude, one of Wolf's finest comic inspirations, which in its context gives a vivid impression of the young violinist, playing his little piece 'with great diffidence and hesitancy' – conscious of the ever-present possibility of a sudden appalling wrong note. His solo ends con bravura with a trill – only it has to be a slow and rather laborious trill, as the composer indicates. One imagines however that the subject of this shy serenade is in an uncritical frame of mind.

NOTES. I. Consciously or not, Wolf is here engaged in self-parody. The main theme is a burlesque of his own frequent equivalent for moods of sorrow and deprivation (motif 22).

2. The singer is thought of as a very young girl – no doubt a contemporary of the heroine of *Ich esse nun mein Brot* (210).

3. There is a faint echo of *Das verlassene Mägdlein* (19) at the word 'gut' (piano, bars 12 and 13).

4. The young violinist's solo seems very like a charming melody that occurs briefly in the Schubert song *An eine Quelle*.

198 (I 12). 'Nein, junger Herr . . .'
7th December 1891

Oh no, young sir, this won't do at all; people should behave properly. I'm good enough for a workaday sweetheart, you think; but you look out for something better at holiday-time. Oh no, young sir; if you carry on like that, your daily sweetheart will be giving in her notice.

As usual, Wolf has looked behind the words to the mood. Here he has discovered, behind the ostensible gaiety, a hint of distress. But it is only a hint; nothing can be allowed to trouble for long the delightful lilt of this music, and gaiety prevails. The prelude announces the vivacious rhythms that characterize the song. The main theme, occurring in voice and piano at the first words 'Nein, junger Herr', to the sound and sense of which it is designed to correspond, is subtly varied to accord with the mood of the voice part. Both melody and accompaniment are set swaggering about parodistically at 'Feiertagen' (holidays). The first strain returns at the repetition of the first words. Now comes the hint of distress as the tempo is held back; but the music recovers itself at the end of the voice part and goes dancing off in a laughing postlude.

NOTES. I. The frolicking at 'Feiertagen' is in the typical Wolfian F sharp major tonality.

2. For some reminiscences of the main vocal melody see 166, note 3.

199 (I 13). 'Hoffärtig seid Ihr . . .'
8th December 1891

You are haughty and proud with your suitors. If you are spoken to, you scarcely deign to reply; it is as if a kind word would cost you too much effort. Yet you are no princess; no kingdom will be your dowry. Then if you don't want gold, take dross; if you don't want love, take contempt.

As so often in this songbook Wolf's music throws new light on the verses.

These suggest merely petulant anger throughout. The jabbing rhythms and speed of the piano part and the vehemence of the vocal line convey this admirably as the song begins. But suddenly, at the words 'als kostet' Euch zu viel ein holder Gruss' (as if a kind word, etc.), the texture of the music is changed, and the voice falters in wistful tenderness. When the angry phrases resume, words and music have been enriched by this almost unwitting admission of continuing love. But this procedure has its dangers, and the composer himself has perhaps been caught in two minds. The extreme vehemence of the setting of the final words 'willst du nicht Liebe, nimm Verachtung hin' is a brilliantly effective finale that nevertheless seems to go too far in the other direction. Making an artistic unity of this rage and this tenderness within twenty brief bars is an exacting task for the singer.

NOTES. 1. The key phrase mentioned above 'Als kostet' Euch', etc., is Wolf's passionate love-motif, 13.

2. The song is in a sense the male counterpart of *Wer rief dich denn* (192).

200 (I 14). 'Geselle, woll'n wir uns in Kutten hüllen . . .'
5th December 1891

Now, my friend, what do you say to getting ourselves up in friars' cowls and robes – and leaving the world to the worldly? Then we could go knocking from door to door, whining 'alms for a poor monk, for pity's sake'.

'Oh father,' they'd say, 'come again when the bread is baked. Come later, father, my young daughter is ill.'

'Then I must go and see her; she must not die unshriven. Oh I must certainly go and see her, she must confess all her sins. See to it that all the doors and windows are shut, and that no one disturbs us, while I'm hearing the poor child's confession.'

This song is unique in Wolf's work. The character of the bogus friar with his pretended concern for the spiritual welfare of young girls might easily find a place in the pages of Chaucer or Boccaccio. The composer in music as attractive as it is ingenious, presents a richly comic yet inoffensive commentary on boundless fraudulence and guileless piety.

This is mainly achieved by the successive presentation of various aspects of the piano theme announced in a short prelude

Here it exudes a false geniality. After the monstrous hypocrisy of 'die Welt dem lassen, den sie mag ergötzen' (leave the world to him who delights in it) it slides about in unctuous chromatics in both hands, like the rubbing of fat greasy palms. Its first two notes are then heard knocking in the piano left hand at 'Dann pochen wir an Tür', first tentatively, then with more confidence. And the theme reappears, wheedling, at 'gebt einem armen Mönch' (give to a poor monk). The voice of the gullible parent replies – 'O lieber Pater', etc. But the basic quaver rhythm and texture are unaltered. It is clear that this section is not simply an impression of the actual words and tone to be expected, but a heartless parody of them by the bogus friar. When his own voice is heard again at the first 'Und ist sie krank' (if she is ill) the original theme returns in the piano left hand, very pleased with itself. At the second 'Und ist sie krank' it begins a rollicking so outrageous as practically to constitute a breach of the peace. Then, as if suddenly aware of the danger of giving the game away, it relapses into a more general tone of sanctimonious humbug. The imagined errand of mercy successfully completed, the theme trots off in the piano postlude in search of an actual victim.

This song is a field day for the singer, who has ample opportunity for displaying interpretative artistry. The music is so appealing that it is quite possible to derive a good deal of enjoyment from one hearing of this song without knowing what the words are about, let alone what the music is about. Later the song reveals itself as perhaps the finest of its genre ever written.

NOTES. I. There are interesting thematic resemblances between this song and that perfect piece of true piety *Wie glänzt der helle Mond* (186 q.v.) dated eighteen months earlier. The parental voice in this song (e.g. at 'ein Töchterlein von mir') sings in the tones of the devout believer in that song. The central figure here has a distinct musical resemblance (e.g. at 'gebt einem armen Mönch' and elsewhere) to the figure of St Peter in the Keller song. The earlier themes of piety are here caricatured. See also 115, note.

2. For the sliding chromatics of the piano interlude after 'ergötzen', see motif 20.

201 (I 15). 'Mein Liebster ist so klein . . .'
3rd December 1891

My sweetheart is so small that his hair sweeps the floor. When he went into the garden to pick jasmine, a snail frightened him. As he scampered back indoors to recover, a fly knocked him spinning; then a bumble-bee gave him concussion.

A curse on all flies and bees – and on all girls whose sweethearts come from Maremma. A curse on all gnats and midges – and on all girls who have to stoop for a kiss.

The men of Maremma are proverbially tiny. But this song is not a protest; it is a love-song, full of affectionate teasing and pretended dismay. It is not one of Wolf's best, if only because the words would hardly sustain a masterpiece. Yet it is very endearing. The idea of the minuscule hero, for all his misfortunes, is treated with a certain dignity in the music (e.g. the postlude) – Wolf, after all, was a very small man himself.

The prelude is taken from a passage heard later in the song at the mention of having a sweetheart from Maremma. The music illustrates the idea of smallness, with tiny intervals and finicking rhythm; but it is very far from being simply pictorial. What it is 'about' is not so much the little man as the singer's thoughts of him. The composer's direction 'sehr zart' (very tenderly) makes the intention clear. The voice begins with a melody as small in its intervals as it could well be. This makes its way over the diminutive piano themes which stretch upwards in vivid pantomime. The comic episodes are graphically treated in voice and piano; and the climax of affectionate exasperation at 'Verwünscht sei'n alle Fliegen' (bad luck to all flies), melts into a revealing tenderness at the last words 'so tief muss bücken' (must stoop so low).

NOTE. In this song the minor seconds of motif 3 could hardly fail to be in evidence. Perhaps the most striking example is the piano part at 'da warf ihn eine Fliege übern Haufen'.

202 (I 16). 'Ihr jungen Leute . . .'
11th December 1891

Now, you young soldiers going off to war, you must take good care of my sweetheart. See that he bears himself bravely under fire; this will be his first battle.

Don't let him sleep in the open; his chest is weak. Never let him sleep out of doors. He'd die; he just isn't used to it.

The verses are pleasantly teasing and affectionate, addressed perhaps to the same lad by the same girl as in the previous song. Wolf matches them with a little tune arranged as a sort of para-military march. This is introduced and interspersed with rather diffident drum-taps, and later on becomes for a moment or two decidedly dejected before marching off into the distance. The voice part picks out and sings the various delightful melodies latent in this evocative background. For the rest the wit and freshness of this music are their own commentary, renewed at each hearing.

NOTES. 1. *Sie blasen zum Abmarsch* (174) is worth comparing as a more serious treatment of the same theme, again complete with military march. The consecutive thirds that go marching off throughout the piano part of both songs are an aspect of motif 16.

2. The augmented fifths at 'schlafen' and 'bestrafen' are motif 23.

3. The marked tempo, crotchet = 104, makes it wellnigh impossible for the average pianist to give the necessary precision to the drum-tap rhythm ♪♪♪ ♪. It may be worth while to sacrifice a little of the speed in order to get this right. The rhythm itself may be thought, by analogy with its counterpart in *Der neue Amadis* (108), to suggest the idea of 'playing at soldiers'.

4. Compare the piano interlude after 'Leben' with the piano part at 'echte Blum' und Perl' ' in 75 (note 2).

203 (I 17). 'Und willst du deinen Liebsten . . .'
4th December 1891

If you would see your lover die of love, then unbind your hair, my darling, and let it float down free over your shoulders, like threads of pure gold.

How beautiful your hair is; like golden gossamer stirred by the wind, like countless gossamer threads of shining silk and gold. How lovely it is; how lovely you are.

This is one of Wolf's finest songs; it breathes ecstasy and adoration. It begins with soft spread piano chords that evoke rapt contemplation; the voice expresses it in almost motionless melody. At the description 'wie goldne Fädchen, die der Wind bewegt' (like golden gossamer stirred by the wind) the soft brightening arpeggios waft and float, in a supreme matching of image and music. 'Very soft and delicate', the composer's direction here, is scarcely necessary; the music itself is all softness and delicacy, entranced and entrancing, down to the simple and beautiful setting of the final words and the postlude's brief moment of adoring love.

NOTES. 1. In the piano part the rhythm of the first page, used in diminution in the second (♩ ♩ ♩ becoming ♪ ♩ ♪ etc. at a reduced tempo), is motif 1.

2. In the piano part, notably the postlude, the theme associated by Wolf with adoring love finds perhaps its finest use (motif 11). See also 47, note 1.

204 (I 18). 'Heb' auf dein blondes Haupt . . .'

12th December 1891

Lift up your fair head, and do not sleep, and do not be lulled by slumber. I have four important things to say to you; you must not miss any one of them.

The first is that my heart is breaking for you; the second, that I am yours alone; the third, that you are my one salvation; and the last, that with all my soul I love you and you alone.

The verses suggest that someone is being kept awake in order to hear four separate weighty pronouncements that need concentration to be understood. But this beautiful love-song is almost a lullaby.

The piano begins with a persistent lulling rhythm in four-part chords, so arranged that there is always a slightly shifting melodic line in progress. Through this the voice sings, in gently restrained yet lilting phrases, to the same basic rhythm. Whenever the voice part comes to rest, whether at the end of a phrase or on a prolonged word, the piano changes to singing octaves, giving the effect of continuous shared melody, as befits the emotions and the scene portrayed. This long chain of melody is linked by the unbroken rhythm, down to the closing words 'das letzte – dich allein liebt meine Seele'. Here the climax of the song is reached, as so often in the Italian songs, in a hushed murmur. The piano rhythm relaxes, for one delicate moment, as if to listen to the voice's last word. The postlude, in the most gentle and loving of strains, softly offers the melody that was the hidden heart of all the preceding music.

NOTES. I. The rhythm and barring need careful handling in performance. Wolf avoids the banal rhythm of the poem by a subtle shifting of the metrical stress. This not only gives new life to the verses, but also throws new light on the possibilities latent in $\frac{12}{8}$ time. But the metre of the poem nevertheless imposes itself on the music. This is felt most clearly at 'Herze bricht' where the musical accent makes the singer say that his *heart* is breaking, instead of, more sensibly, that his heart is *breaking*. Here and there elsewhere in the song a tonic accent is felt on the second beat of the bar. Indeed the composer himself takes the view that his melody still makes sense construed in this way, as is clearly shown by a comparison of, say, bar 3 with the fourth bar from the end. Perhaps one should play and sing almost without accents except where the cadence of the words justifies it. Certainly one should avoid at all costs any great emphasis on the first beat of each bar as written.

2. There is a detectable affinity between the music of the final vocal phrases here and in *Auch kleine Dinge* (187) – another reason for supposing that song to be a love-song.

3. In the opening bar of the piano is the narrative-reflective harmony of motif 21.

4. The marked off-beat accent on 'vier' in bar 5 is surely better omitted. There is no real point in the fact that there are *four* items.

205 (I 19). 'Wir haben beide . . .'

16th December 1891

We had long kept silent; then in a moment speech returned to us.

Angels flew down and brought peace again after war; God's angels flew down and brought peace with them; love's angels came by night and brought peace to my heart.

Another masterpiece, in which the contrast between sullen silence and tender speech is made movingly vivid and true. The first few bars evoke the numb sadness of estrangement. The piano rhythm is slow, tolling, in drooping octaves; the harmony is obscure; the vocal melody is monody, with the word 'lange' prolonged over the bar-line, to suggest 'so unbearably long a time'. Each element yearns for speech, each gradually thaws to give a hint of coming new life. Then the music quickens; new rhythms appear in voice and piano, the harmony resolves into simple chords, and melody comes flooding into the song. At the first mention of angels the music becomes seraphic, a strain of the purest heartsease. The piano part begins to sing for joy, to an infinitely simple phrase of four notes, a marvel of originality

etc. By the second mention of peace the key-changes have reached the tonic of E flat major for the first time in the song, with an ineffable sense of coming home. Here the singing piano melodies rise higher in the keyboard; the voice falls to its lowest point at 'Frieden eingezogen' (peace came in) and suddenly soars to a softly sustained high note on the first syllable of 'Liebesengel' (love's angels). Now the piano melody, chords outspread, hovers protectively over the hushing voice; the postlude repeats this melody as if loath to leave it, and then sleeps.

NOTES. 1. The sense of the music is the amazed tenderness expressed in *Nun lass uns Frieden schliessen* (194), 'how could we have quarrelled, you and I; how is it possible?' In the one word 'wieder' (bar 4) this mood is wonderfully concentrated. The rising minor third is almost a question; and it echoes the questioning of the same interval at the two central moments of the earlier song; to which this one could be a natural sequel.

228

2. The downward curve of the piano's opening bars is an analogue of the sorrow motif 22.

3. In the second part there is an occasional suggestion of the loving tenderness of motif 14 (e.g. piano treble and tenor, bar 12).

206 (I 20). 'Mein Liebster singt . . .'

12th December 1891

Outside in the moonlight my lover is singing, and I must lie listening here in bed. I turn away from my mother and weep tears of blood. And now I have wept all night, and cannot tell, for tears, whether it is day. Tears of longing I have wept; tears of blood that blind me.

A world of drama and passion is made explicit in the tiny compass of this masterly song. Wolf adds a new dimension to the words by incorporating the lover's serenade into the piano part. This is so bewitchingly tender and sad, and so independent in construction, that it might well pass in a solo performance as one of the finest of Chopin's mazurkas – which it strongly recalls in mood without being in any way derivative. The vocal line of the song is equally expressive and independent. Yet the two are combined into a perfect unity; the song of the lover and the thoughts of the listening girl are one shared sorrow.

NOTES. 1. If thematic kinship within Wolf's work is any guide, then the piano part at, e.g., bars 8–9 says quite plainly that the burden of the serenade is a passionate plea for elopement; this music has clear affinities with the piano part of *Und schläfst du mein Mädchen* (173), dated more than two years earlier.

2. Another 'mazurka' theme is heard in 169.

207 (I 21). 'Man sagt mir . . .'

23rd December 1891

They say your mother disapproves. Stay away then, my darling, do as she says. Oh no, my dearest, don't do as she says, defy her, come to me secretly. No, darling, take no notice of her, defy her; come more often than ever. No, don't listen to her, whatever she says. Defy her, my love, come every day!

From a piano motif  that resounds obsessively throughout, and a vocal line that freely follows all the inflections of the words, Wolf has created music that explores every possible aspect of the mood of the singer of these verses, from petulance to anger, from tenderness to gaiety. The surrender of the opening lines is only pretended; from the very first bar the piano part is defiance itself. But somehow it is a child's defiance; a stamp of the foot, a thwarted gesture. As the voice sings ingratiatingly 'so bleibe weg, mein Schatz' (stay away then, my darling), the piano part's gestures grow persistently stronger, accurately predicting an immediate change of mind – 'Ach Liebster, nein!' Then the voice becomes pleading again at 'besuch' mich' (come to me), and, with the help of some sliding chromatics from the piano, conspiratorial, at 'im Stillen' (secretly). Voice and piano now move through warmth to passion, the quoted theme being given a slight upward turn. At the exultant conclusion the word 'alle' (every) is sustained in crescendo for two bars over a fourfold quickening repetition of the defiant motif. The postlude has a high-spirited conclusion in the major, indicating that the situation is perhaps not so desperately serious after all.

NOTES. 1. The piano part at 'Stillen' reminds one of the piano part at bar 6 of *Geselle woll'n wir uns* (200), dated some three weeks earlier. A few other passages suggest a thematic use of sliding chromatics in association with the idea of deceit or cheating (motif 20).

2. The end of the postlude has something of the élan of the parallel passage in *Ich hab' in Penna* (232) – and perhaps something of the same significance.

3. For some different equivalents for 'defiance' see 134, note 2.

208 (I 22). 'Ein Ständchen Euch zu bringen . . .'
10th December 1891

I've come to sing a serenade, if that's all right with the head of the household. You have a lovely young daughter – it would surely be better not to keep her indoors so strictly? I expect she's already in bed, so kindly give her a message. Tell her that her true lover has passed this way, that he thinks only of her, day and night, and that he misses her for twenty-five hours out of every twenty-four.

Wolf catches to perfection the superb self-possession and swagger of the poem. The light tuneful vocal cadences are emphatically echoed in the gay strumming of the accompaniment. At 'dass ihr Getreuer' (that her true lover) the guitar playing begins to dance and race to the song's zestful conclusion. The serenader is young enough to be very amused by his humorous exaggeration at the end. The guitar figuration in the accompaniment exults and chuckles in the postlude, before dying away into the distance.

NOTES. 1. The mood of badinage is akin to that of Thyrsis in *Die Spröde* (111) and shares his accompaniment.

2. Note in the opening bars the narrative of motif 21.

3. At 'und liegt sie schon im Bett' the music has the look of the 'separation' of motif 15!

4. For the guitar music see 166, note 1.

209 (I 23). 'Was für ein Lied . . .'
30th April 1896

Where shall I find a fitting song to sing, one worthy of you? I should like best to delve it from the deep earth, a new song never yet sung; a song that no man or woman, not even the oldest, has ever heard or sung till this day.

From these simple verses Wolf has fashioned a great love-song, itself the answer to the question posed by the first line. The music is instinct with tenderness; the composer's mind is clearly dwelling as much on the woman to whom the song when found is to be dedicated, as on the song itself. Indeed the prelude says so. Although sure of its rhythm (which is to pervade the song) it is uncertain of its key, until, like a thought taking possession of the mind, it establishes beyond doubt, in one of Wolf's well-loved phrases, a home tonic. In this key the piano begins to muse, trying out melodies suitable for such a song. Against this background the vocal melodies voice their tender and devoted thoughts. The devotion is made apparent by, for example, the treatment of the words 'deiner würdig sei?' (worthy of you). Here the first syllable of 'deiner' is lovingly sustained and stressed, giving the sense of – 'worthy of *you*? how could it be, however beautiful?' Then the tonality deepens in the piano part at the words 'Am liebsten grüb' ich es tief aus der Erden' (best to delve it from the deep earth) and comes sighing up again to resume its musing at 'Ein Lied, das weder Mann noch Weib' (a song that no man or woman). Here it joins with the haunting vocal melodies that in searching for and describing a beautiful song become such a song. At the end the piano postlude is left with its musing theme. The music is still creating new melodies to weave into the text as if not wholly satisfied with what has been achieved. But listeners will be satisfied.

NOTES. 1. The piano prelude should be compared to that of *Schon streckt' ich aus* (213) dated a month earlier. The underlying musical 'idea' of each is the same.

2. Wolf was often inclined to think in terms of four-part piano harmony.

Here, as elsewhere in the last Italian songs, notably in *O wüsstest du* (230), the effect is that of string-quartet writing.

3. It is instructive to compare bars 5 and 13. These are identical except for one note, the third in the tenor part, which is varied from G flat to C to avoid a dissonance which would be meaningless in the later bar.

4. For the pervading rhythm see 224, note 2.

5. In the piano's main theme is a hint of the adoration of motif 11, with the sixths sounding together. The narrative-reflective motif 21 is also here in a refined form.

6. Whether by unconscious reminiscence or not, the vocal phrase at 'Am liebsten grüb' ich', etc., is closely akin to that at bars 5–6 of the first *Peregrina* song (45, note 1) of 1888. The idea behind the words is similar in each case.

7. This song provides a good example of Wolf's harmonic practice. The emotional climax comes with the variation of basic harmony at bars 9–12.

210 (I 24). 'Ich esse nun mein Brot . . .'

25th March 1896

I shall never be happy again. There's a thorn in my flesh. I look around in vain to find someone to love me.

If only there were an old man to show me a little love and respect. I mean a well-set-up honourable old man, of about my own age. I mean, to be perfectly frank, a little old man of about – fourteen.

What little point these verses have lies in the last word. But Wolf takes a much more sympathetic view of them, and lavishes every refinement of his art on their sleazy humour. In the first section the drooping semitones sob and sigh with an exaggerated mock-turtle pathos which is yet not unreal. The second section in the major at 'Wenn's doch auch nur' (If only there were) borrows one of the previous melodies and uses it for a little processional march theme of the utmost charm and good humour. At the same time the vocal melodies become broad and gay, at the idea of finding a suitable sweetheart. The singer is imagined as first sitting about despondently, then getting up and marching about pantomimically and finally marching off to an effectively calculated exit line. Wolf leads up to this final announcement with every possible dramatic resource of hesitation and sleight of hand and follows it with a spirited comment from the piano – all in five bars.

NOTES. 1. This song and its companion piece *Wie lange schon* (197) on the same theme and with the same structure are basically serious-minded, musically speaking. It is a travesty of the composer's intention to treat them as comic songs in the ordinary sense.

2. In the E flat major section the piano part takes on the shape of an earlier pantomime song, *Epiphanias* (104).

211 (I 25). 'Mein Liebster hat zu Tische . . .'
26th March 1896

My lover asked me to dinner. But he had no house, no fuel, no hearth and no oven; and the cooking pot was broken in two. No wine, no glasses; the table was mean, with a tablecloth to match; the bread stone-hard and the one knife quite blunt.

The craftsmanship of this song is impeccable. Every point is made, from the rather bewildered resentment of the piano prelude to the strong sense of ludicrous outrage expressed in voice and piano at the last words of this lamentable history. These points lend themselves to effective interpretation. But there is little hint of any fresh musical invention, and much reliance on previously conceived thematic material.

NOTES. I. The staccato accompaniment figure that makes its first appearance in bar 6 is borrowed from the postlude to *Jägerlied* (16). The whole song, in particular the last four bars, is in debt to *Spottlied* (89).

2. The sliding chromatics of the prelude here may suggest the idea of 'deception', motif 20.

212 (I 26). 'Ich liess mir sagen . . .'
28th March 1896

I asked after handsome Toni, and was told he was starving to death. Ever since he felt the pangs of love, it seems, he has cut down to seven loaves at a sitting. After this he fortifies himself with a large sausage and another seven loaves. Clearly unless Tonina eases his pain there'll be an outbreak of famine and starvation in the land.

Much of the commentary on the preceding song is relevant. The music is perhaps even more effective and strong, and markedly more original in conception, though still basically relying on previous themes. But unfortunately the text is intolerably silly. Although Wolf contrives to cram his music with all the meaning of the verses and a lot more besides, the result is nevertheless hardly viable.

NOTE. I. This song pays a certain tribute to *Der Schäfer* (107), also in C minor; the poems are similar.

2. See 218, note 3.

213 (I 27). 'Schon streckt' ich aus . . .'

29th March 1896

No sooner had I stretched out my weary limbs in bed than I beheld you in vision, my sweetest.

So I rise again straightway and put on my shoes, and go out walking through the town with my lute.

I sing and play and the streets resound. Many a girl listens; I am soon past. Many a girl has been moved by my song; while already the sound of my singing and playing has blown away in the wind.

There are songs written at about the same time as this one (211, 212, 218) in which Wolf seems to be using stock procedures without any perceptible new creative impulse. The inference might be that his powers were declining, if it were not for the fact that there also dates from this period a whole succession of resplendent masterpieces. This is the first of them in date-order. For sheer beauty of sound and perfection of organization it has few parallels. As with all great work, its surprises and delights are not all revealed at first hearing. It must be performed and read through as well as heard if its full savour is to be extracted.

The first surprise comes at the first chord of the piano's slow introduction. The key-signature of four flats is immediately contradicted by two chromatic alterations. As a result the ear hears an allusion to a chord in a remote sharp key. It is as if the tranquillity of A flat major were being troubled by some bright dream. Peacefulness is achieved in the second bar of the prelude and continues until the word 'Bildnis' (vision). Here the chord already hinted at shines out softly in arpeggio for a moment and then fades back into the basic tonality. One wonders where else in song so much is said, so feelingly, and in so short a compass, simply by one harmonic excursion. Now the tempo quickens a little, and more arpeggio chords are heard, at 'Gleich spring' ich auf' (I rise up straightway). These anticipate the lute serenade, and also refer back to the vision that inspired it. The arpeggios become more gently insistent as the voice lilts on its way to the word 'Laute' (lute). Then, after a bar of quietude, the serenading begins. The rest is pure enchantment. Anything that might have been thought of as odd or absurd about the poem is forgotten. The listener is wholly caught up and made one with the lone walker in the night, singing and playing his songs of love and longing. Even here, at this pitch of art, the composer is still inventing and re-creating the mood at every bar. Thus, at 'so manche lauscht – vorüber bin ich bald' (many a girl listens – I am soon past) the unexpected G flat on 'lauscht' magically suggests the idea of intent listening to a half-heard melody; the semiquavers at 'vorüber bin ich bald' float elusively past like that melody itself and its maker in the night; and the melting tenderness of voice and piano at 'gerührt' (moved) is a vivid evocation. In the lovely postlude little snatches of the serenade are heard as they waft away in the wind.

NOTES. I. The music, apparently so strikingly varied in each of the three sections of the song, is all derived from the same simple motif. Thus in the first

section, at bar 3, is heard  . During the second, from

bar 7, this becomes first ⟨notation⟩, then ⟨notation⟩ and in the final serenade

at bar 13 ⟨notation⟩.

2. The worshipping rhythm of motif 1 accompanies the serenade from bar 13 to the end.

3. Mediant modulation is a marked feature of this song. Elsewhere this has thematic significance (motif 24) in association with changes of light. It is tempting to suggest that Wolf thought of this song as taking place in successively brighter moments – the darkened room, the moonlit streets, the singing dispersed by the winds of dawn.

4. For interpretative purposes it may be worth remarking that there is absolutely no suggestion here of despairing love; all is peace and contentment.

5. For a parallel to the piano prelude see 209, note 1.

214 (I 28). 'Du sagst mir . . .'
30th March 1896

You tell me I am no princess; well, you're not exactly of the blood royal yourself. No, my dear, you get up at dawn to work in the fields, not ride in the State coach. You mock at my humble station; but poverty is no disgrace. You mock me for having no crest or coat of arms; but all you have to ride on yourself is Shanks's pony.

In other Italian songs on a similar theme (e.g. the next) there is sadness and tenderness underlying the verses, and the composer has been able to concentrate on these emotions and re-create them musically. In these respects, however, this poem is deficient. It is neither very tender nor particularly mocking, and there is no window to let the music in. The setting, despite the many felicities in the vocal and instrumental lines, is felt to be much too rigidly symmetrical and rather uninteresting.

NOTES. I. Wolf himself seems to have expressed unconsciously a certain dissatisfaction. Less than a month later he unwittingly began to recast some of the same material in *Gesegnet sei das Grün* (225).

2. A comparison between the two halves of this song is instructive. Each has eight bars (not counting the last of the postlude). Each bar is similar to but never exactly the same as its counterpart, in both voice and piano.

215 (I 29). 'Wohl kenn' ich Euren Stand . . .'
9th April 1896

I know your station in life is far above mine. You have no need to demean yourself so far as to love a poor humble creature like me, when the fairest of all bow before you. You easily conquered even the finest of men, so I know all too well that you are trifling with me. They tried to warn me that you are only making fun of me; but oh you are so fair to look upon – who could chide you?

This song of humble and hopeless love is one of Wolf's most original conceptions. The music is devotion itself, made stronger by the absence of any bitterness. The string-quartet texture of the piano part is typical of many of the later Italian songs; and it gives an air of remoteness to the essentially simple structure of the music. From the opening vocal melody the 'viola' part of the accompaniment goes sadly away down the keyboard in a gesture of renunciation. Halfway through, at 'Die schönsten Männer leicht besiegtet Ihr' (You easily conquered the finest of men) the mood changes. A great tenderness sounds in the assuaging quaver triplets of the piano and the curving vocal melodies. The music reaches a restrained climax at the last words 'Ihr seid so schön' and then, softly, 'Wer kann Euch grollen?' After this the lulling accompaniment breaks off abruptly and pauses as though needing a moment or two for control. Then the postlude sums up the song by combining the loneliness of the first melody with the offered embrace of broken triplet chords.

NOTES. I. This song is usually thought of as sung by a woman. But this is by no means clearly indicated in the text, and the emotional content of the music seems comparable to that of the Italian songs for a man's voice. There is one obvious echo of a man's song (213, dated eleven days earlier) at the vocal phrase in the second half of the fourth bar in each case – though this may of course be coincidental.

2. The left-hand piano melodies at the beginning of this song and of *Auch kleine Dinge* (187) are in their emotive effect very close to each other and to motif 15.

3. See 218, note 3.

216 (I 30). 'Lass sie nur gehn . . .'

31st March 1896

Let her go then, if she must act so high and mighty, as if she were some rare flower from fairyland. You can see where her bright glances go straying; she takes a new lover every day. She behaves just like Tuscany's river that every mountain stream rushes to follow; just like the river Arno, now with many followers, now with none.

On the whole the music fails in a strenuous effort to point and illuminate a barren text. The musical construction of this late song is as taut and epigrammatic as ever; but the musical material and its treatment seem alike banal, at any rate in the first section. At the words 'Sie treibt es grade wie Toscana's Fluss' (she is just like that river in Tuscany) Wolf puts his theme to more effective use. The strong sweeping rhythm and flashing demisemiquaver runs of this finely rhythmic passage, and the fervent declamation of the voice, make amends for any previous short-comings. The song becomes a dramatic triumph, culminating in a tumultuous postlude.

NOTES. 1. A footnote in the Peters Edition points out, by way of explanation of the last line, that the river Arno is deserted by its tributaries in the hot summer months.

2. At 'das Wunderkräutlein aus dem Blumenfeld' is the 'mystery' motif 19, rather slackly used.

3. In bars 2 and 3 the piano has the sliding chromatics of the 'deceit' motif 20.

217 (I 31). 'Wie soll ich fröhlich sein . . .'

12th April 1890

How can I be happy and even laugh, when you spurn me so openly?

You come to see me only about once every hundred years, and then reluctantly. Why come at all, if your family resents it? Give me my heart back and go your ways. Live at home with your own people in peace; for whatever Heaven wills shall come to pass.

Live in peace with your own people at home, for the will of Heaven shall be done.

This song is a masterpiece of construction; and had the verses been only a little more evocative, it might have been a masterpiece at the emotional level also. As it is, Wolf distils every drop of meaning and feeling from the text without quite achieving the sum of pure quality required to match the other marvels of the Italian Songbook.

'Wie soll ich fröhlich sein?' the song begins – 'How can I be happy?' The piano part is in measured minims to let these words stand out. The falling inflection of the vocal line indicates that this is a rhetorical question, a statement – 'I shall never know happiness without you'. The rhythm of these words 𝅘𝅥 𝄾 𝅘𝅥𝅯𝅘𝅥𝅯 𝅘𝅥𝅯𝅘𝅥𝅘𝅥 dominates the piano part like an involuntary confession. There are traces of petulance. The tempo quickens at the complaint 'Du kommst nur einmal', etc. (You come to see me so rarely), and a little impatient motif 𝅘𝅥𝅮𝅘𝅥𝅯𝅘𝅥𝅯 makes a brief appearance. But this disappears when the explanation for his absence is offered – it must be the family's fault, he is really forgiven. Again the setting belies the words at 'dann magst du weiter gehn' (then you can go your ways). This starts off very decisively, but falters tenderly in both voice and piano; the thought of parting is not to be borne. Similarly, in the following passage 'Daheim mit deinen Leuten' (live at home with your own people), says the voice, but the little expressive piano phrases say 'Wie soll ich fröhlich sein?' The song ends in strong recitative in a last attempt to convey the impression of conviction. Yet as the voice sings its last strong note of renunciation, the postlude proclaims with passion the rhythm and meaning of the opening words.

NOTES. 1. Several of the Italian songs suggest the background of a family feud. In *Man sagt mir* (207), the singer's direct invitation to defy the parental ban represents what the singer of 217 really means, but is too proud, or too unsure of herself, to say. It is practically impossible to make the meaning of this song clear in an isolated performance and it is, no doubt for this reason, not often heard on the concert platform.

2. Although the words of this song are applicable to either sex, the situation and the music surely indicate that it is intended for a woman's voice.

218 (I 32). 'Was soll der Zorn . . .'
20th April 1896

Why this rage, my love, that so consumes you? How have I sinned against you? Rather than this anger give me death. Pierce my heart with a knife; or with a sword, so that my blood gushes up to Heaven. Or take a dagger, and let all my anguish be washed away in my life-blood.

In some of the late Italian songs there seems to be a slight but perceptible waning of Wolf's creative powers. Usually the music is as majestic as ever, but sometimes the song-writing techniques appear to go awry, and procedures that were, in former contexts, inspirational and subtle seem to be in danger of becoming formular and bizarre. This song is, it must be confessed, a case in point. It is odd to choose these unattractively melodramatic verses for musical treatment, and odder to translate their suggestion of masochistic surrender into something more like a threat. True, there is some threatening in the poem; but there it is off-stage. Here it almost dominates the scene; and not even Wolf could convey in twenty bars the separate ideas of two emotions so wholly disparate as the anger and submission described.

NOTES. 1. The confusion at the half-bar (compare bars 3 and 4 with bar 11) and the uncertainty of accentuation (why 'tritt zu *mir*'?) suggest, as in some of the Spanish songs, that the piano part is preconceived.

2. Very remarkable is the way in which the piano part at bars 9–12 is a prolongation and extension of the piano at bar 3. For the cyclic pattern of the piano melody in bars 9–10 and 12–14, see 143, note 2. Here it is decidedly more of a mannerism than a deeply felt theme.

3. The piano part recalls, in the same key, a harmonic progression found in each of two slightly earlier songs – 212 and 215. Oddly enough, these similarities appear in bars 15–16 of each of the three songs.

219 (I 33). 'Sterb' ich, so hüllt in Blumen . . .'
13th April 1896

When I die, strew my limbs with flowers; dig no grave for me. Lay me under the sky where I loved to be. Lay me down in rain or wind; I die gladly if I die for you, dear love. Lay me down in sunshine and rain; I die in peace if I die for your sake.

Here is a late masterpiece, in which the music transfigures the verses. The left hand has a syncopated A flat octave pedal-point throughout, in gentle allusion to the off-beat rhythm which is allotted to the opening words 'Sterb' ich'. Over this background the piano right hand and the voice pursue their separate but engaging ways in lifting and dipping lilts of melody. The tranquil resignation in the piano's falling fifths, the easy flow of the voice's declaration of love are deeply felt; and they show how seriously Wolf is taking the text. The song follows this gently musing course until the first mention of the loved one. Then the piano's falling fifths are transmuted into a new caressing theme which, though essentially a restatement of the old, gives the song a new life. The original figurations briefly resume. Then, again as the loved one is mentioned,

239

the piano phrases float and fall as before in blissful tranquillity, and go lingering on in the piano postlude.

NOTES. 1. The music sings of great love, faithful to the death; not of death itself. It is an artistic error to sing this song funereally.

2. Note the release of motif 8 in the rising piano-passage at 'grabt'.

3. The theme of the verses is the same unsavoury potpourri as that of *Bedeckt mich mit Blumen* (172), here treated with even greater refinement.

4. The persistent piano rhythm is a novel and compelling variant of the self-surrender of motif 1.

220 (I 34). 'Und steht Ihr früh am Morgen auf . . .'

3rd April 1896

And when you rise at dawn, you chase the clouds from the skies, you charm the sun up from the hills; and eager angels vie to bring your shoes and clothes.

Then, when you go to Mass, you draw all the people with you; and when you near the sanctuary, your glance lights the lamps. You take holy water, make the sign of the Cross, then wet your white brow, and bow, and kneel; how like an angel.

How angel-lovely God made you; the crown of beauty is yours. How angel-sweet you move through life; surely the palm of all beauty was bestowed on you.

The fresh tenderness of this adorable song speaks for itself. The piano begins with an easy flow of single quavers. They rise up, another part is added in the left hand, and then the voice chimes in; reverently restrained at first, but becoming gradually brighter and freer as the piano chimes up through Wolf's beloved mediant modulations, from E major through A flat major to C major. The piano's higher octaves sing out alone briefly. Then they stoop down into E major again as the voice resumes with the words 'Dann, wenn Ihr ausgeht in die heil'ge Mette' (Then, when you go to Mass). The piano figurations and vocal melody are then taken through the same progressions again, but with a different effect. The piano part, though recognizably the opening theme, is now processional, with the open fifths set walking in the bass. The voice is sweet and solemn, hushing into sustained choir-chords at 'Weihwasser nehmt Ihr' (You take holy water) and easing back into the flow of even quavers for the last section. Here the voice shines out in some of Wolf's loveliest melodies, culminating in the closing words 'der Schönheit Palme ward an Euch gegeben'. These are set to a few simple notes and chords, at first strongly sung and then at the thought of this beauty hushing gently, echoed by the piano in which the chiming motif lilts upwards and ends.

NOTES. I. One would never suspect just from hearing this song and its continuous melodic flow in voice and piano the subtlety and profundity of its construction, which will repay close study. In particular one is struck by the evocative use of the flattened seventh of each successive tonality; and the way in which this effect is intrinsically related to the whole melodic and harmonic structure, and the meaning and emotion of the words.

2. The piano accompaniment figure is the genesis of the vocal melody of *Benedeit die sel'ge Mutter* (221) dated later the same month.

3. The mediant modulations with which this song is illuminated (motif 24) seem here to indicate as it were an intensification of spiritual light.

4. It might be possible to infer from a certain unease about bars 21–26 that Wolf was not wholly at home with the idea of devotional ritual. It is of course only in the context of this splendid song that this section is somehow not quite satisfactory; there is no question of its musical inadequacy.

5. For the motif that resounds throughout the piano part, see motif 14.

6. Bars 13–16 (a journey to Mass) are closely akin to the basic figuration and rhythms of *Nun wandre Maria* (139) (a journey to Bethlehem).

221 (I 35). 'Benedeit die sel'ge Mutter . . .'

21st April 1896

I bless the happy mother that bore you so sweet, so elect in beauty; my longing flies to you. You so sweet of gesture, the most beautiful on earth; you my jewel, my joy; a blessing on you.

When I yearn from afar and think of your beauty, how I tremble and groan past concealing. In my heart I feel strong fires rising that destroy my peace. I shall go mad with love.

I bless the happy mother that bore you so sweet, so elect in beauty; my longing flies to you. You so sweet of gesture, the most beautiful on earth; you my jewel, my joy; a blessing on you.

The first section of this famous song is simple and diatonic; the second, complex and chromatic; and the third is the first repeated note for note and word for word. This is an unheard-of procedure in Wolf's songs and not wholly a successful one. If the passion of the middle section is made convincing the recapitulation brings too great a contrast. This difficulty has to be resolved by interpretative art, and seems to be a slight blemish in an otherwise fine song, especially memorable for the vocal melody of the opening and closing sections.

NOTES. I. The repetition of the first verse is Wolf's, not Heyse's. The resulting

ABA contrast is exemplified by the main thematic component of each; devoted love (motif 14) in the major section and passionate love (motif 13) in the minor.

2. Bar 11 is almost a separate study. Logic demanded a direct repetition of bar 3. True, the first G in the treble has become an octave higher because of the voice leading. But there seems no real reason why the shape and pitch of bar 3 could not have been reverted to at this point – except perhaps that the note C on the third beat to which the word 'du' (you) is sung would have sounded clumsy with this accompaniment. For whatever reason, the upper register is preferred, with octaves momentarily replacing the chords; and the result is pure magic. The high E flat octave lights up the word 'du', which can now be sung with the necessary slight emphasis without disturbing the dynamics of the song.

3. See 220, note 2.

222 (I 36). 'Wenn du, mein Liebster . . .'
24th April 1896

When you go up to Heaven, my love, I shall meet you, offering my heart. You will embrace me lovingly, and we shall lie at God's feet. And when He knows of our unhappy love He will make one heart of our two loving hearts; He will join our two hearts into one in Paradise, all shone about by the radiance of Heaven.

A fine song, but quite eclipsed by its earlier counterpart, 224.

The piano accompaniment is laid out on the same lines but the right-hand octave melody here tends to recur too emphatically. The great climax in the postlude with its inevitable tremolandi may also be thought to lack the more purely musical appeal of the hushed conclusion of the earlier and more original work. The poem is less tender, more theatrical. It is a woman's song, and for these Wolf rarely found the same depth of intensity that he found for the men's songs in the Italian volume.

NOTE. The piano melody tends to cyclic patterns throughout (see 143, note 2) much more markedly than in the freer melodic flow of the similarly designed 224. See also notes 2 and 3 to that song.

223 (I 37). 'Wie viele Zeit verlor ich . . .'
2nd April 1896

How much precious time I have lost in loving you! If only I had loved God in all that time, I should have earned a place in Heaven by now, with a saint sitting by my side. But because I loved you and your fair fresh face I have forfeited the light of Paradise; and because I have loved you, my sweet flower, I shall never now gain Paradise.

These verses present an interesting problem. Are they intended as a serious complaint – 'you have sundered me from Heaven', or as an over-gallant compliment – 'you are more beautiful than Paradise itself', or as affectionate teasing – 'I could have had a saint at my side instead of a sinner'? To judge from Wolf's music his own interpretation was deeply serious; in this lovely song a lost Heaven is made manifest, and at the same time it is suggested that this loss is compensated by this love. He has taken what was no doubt intended only as a courtly fancy and turned it into a cry of despair and joy together. This is achieved by the simplest of means. Quiet repeated chords accompany the moving melody of the voice part. This is hushed over chords in a lower register at 'hätt' ich doch Gott geliebt' (if only I had loved God) rising to a crescendo, then hushing again. The lower chords resume at the first 'Und weil ich dich geliebt' (and because I loved you) and lead into the soft climactic moment for the words, 'Und weil ich dich geliebt, schön Veigelein'. Here the plain chords and melody melt in tenderness before the singer can master his voice and resume and end, leaving sad repeated phrases from the piano to round off this masterly song.

NOTES. 1. There is an evident correspondence between the melody and harmony at 'Schön Veigelein' and that at 'mit ew'gem Licht' in *Gesegnet sei* (190).

2. The piano postlude's drooping phrases are of the kind associated by Wolf with despair (motif 22).

3. See 188, note 3.

224 (I 38). 'Wenn du mich mit den Augen streifst . . .'
19th April 1896

When you look up at me and smile and then bow your head down – I beg you to tell me first so that I can control my heart; so that I can keep my heart in check and not have it burst with its great love; so that I can keep my heart still in my breast and not have it break out with its great joy.

This is another great love song. The means employed are simplicity itself. Over a persistent but gently yielding rhythm in the bass, the piano's treble octaves and the vocal line flow together in a continuous stream of melody. At first they are interdependent, with the piano echoing the shape of the vocal line. Then, at the first mention of the heart, they develop separately; yet each always sustains and enhances the other, making the words true and vivid. There is no describing this song; but with its immediacy of appeal it has only to be heard to be recognized as a consummate masterpiece.

NOTES. 1. As usual Wolf responds profoundly to the idea of physical beauty (see 44, note 2).

2. This music, so simple yet so deeply felt, seems in turn to have made a profound impression on the composer. Its rather ordinary rhythm 𝄴 ♩ ♫ ♬ throughout, and the very ordinary harmonic progression at the last words, are heard again in later songs, with similarly heightened effect. This rhythm pervades both the derivative companion piece 222 and the masterly and original *Was für ein Lied* (209). The harmony reappears not only in 222 but (in the same key) in *Wohl denk' ich oft* (240), at the last words in each case.

3. The persistent bass rhythm is the 'worshipping' motif 1.

225 (I 39). 'Gesegnet sei das Grün . . .'
13th April 1896

A blessing on green and its wearer. I shall have a green dress made for me. The meadows wear green in Spring. My true love wears green; green was ever the huntsman's wear, and it is my love's too. For green beautifies all things; all sweet fruit grows from green.

The song is appealing, but not first-rate Wolf. The opening strains seem somewhat jaded. But when the words first speak of springtime, at 'Ein grünes Kleid trägt auch die Frühlingsaue', a freshness comes into the music. A chiming motif starts up in the piano part. This is later modified to a suggestion of hunting horns, matching the sound and sense of the grateful melodic line. The chiming figures reappear and continue meditatively in the piano postlude.

NOTES. 1. The strong thematic connexions between the first four bars of this song and those of *Du sagst mir* (214) may mean that Wolf thought of both as being sung by the same character. But the resemblance seems more accidental, as if Wolf were recomposing the first four bars of the other song (dated only a fortnight earlier) in the belief that this was a new inspiration.

2. The horn passages of motif 8 are obvious enough for the mention of 'Der Jäger'.

3. The chiming motif recalls *Und steht ihr früh* (220) and *Benedeit die sel'ge Mutter* (221). This song seems to share their restrained mood of almost parental affection; the postlude suggests motif 14.

4. Also in A major are the Keller spring song *Wandl' ich in dem Morgentau* (184) (with which this song has certain affinities), the Goethe spring song *Frühling übers Jahr* (113) and the spring chorus from the unfinished opera *Manuel Venegas*.

226 (I 40). 'O wär' dein Haus durchsichtig . . .'
12th April 1896

I wish your house were transparent like glass, my darling, when I tip-toe by. Then I should always see you; how lovingly I should look at you! How many heartfelt glances I should give; more than there are drops of water in the river. How many times I should look at you; more than there are raindrops in all the rain.

Though this is not among the greatest of Wolf's songs, nor an instantly appealing one, it has a special place in the canon by virtue of its sheer formal perfection and unity. The accompaniment figuration announced in the piano prelude [music] is heard throughout this delicate and delightful song except at the word 'vorüberstehle' (tip-toe by), when the music tip-toes too [music]. The strange effect of this persistent accompaniment, in its context, is to create a vivid impression of glassy transparency and clarity. Through this background passes a fine-drawn line of sheer melody. There is no climactic moment in the voice part; both voice and piano are fused into the same substance.

NOTES. 1. The 'worshipping' rhythm of motif 1 sounds throughout.

2. At each 'Wie viele Blicke' the piano part is reminiscent of the postlude to *Und willst du deinen Liebsten* (203) and its adoring motif 11.

3. The accompaniment figure and its variants are found nowhere else in Wolf, so there is no guide to a possible connotation. But he elsewhere uses bare octaves and fifths in contexts suggesting transparency, 'disappearing into thin air' – e.g. the end of *Rattenfänger* (96) and *Die Geister am Mummelsee* (59), and throughout *Nixe Binsefuss* (57). The present phrase is so eloquently and so precisely used that it seems to have the additional property of a clear reflection of the inner feelings of the singer.

227 (I 41). 'Heut' Nacht erhob ich mich . . .'
25th April 1896

I rose at midnight to find that my heart had secretly fled away. 'Heart,' I asked, 'where are you going so fast?' It said it had gone to see you. Now see how it must be with me; my heart leaves my breast to look for you, my love.

With this 18-bar miniature Wolf achieves and crowns his series of short yet perfect songs. It does not perhaps yield up all its secrets at first hearing, but, once assimilated, it is an abiding joy. The perfection of Wolf's craftsmanship in this work is nearly as moving as its tenderness. Exquisite melodic lines in voice and piano are given extra poignancy by the string-quartet texture of the music. But the heart of the song is in the harmonies through which these melodic lines pass, becoming dark and bright by turns. The piano begins with a musing melody in octaves. This darkens into D minor chords, and turns out to be the idea of the opening words, for which the first two piano bars are repeated; – 'I rose at midnight'. From now on there is ceaseless invention in the writing. Simple falling chords in upward-tending progression are followed by a bright E major chord. This darkens again at the surging 'wohin stürmst du so mit Macht?' (where are you going so fast?) into D minor. And heart replies, warm and bright in D major, 'Nur Euch zu sehn' (just to see you). With this, new melodic invention crowds in within the limited space of a few bars and the song concludes with a reaffirming piano postlude, in the D major language of the heart. As so often in the Italian songs anything that might be thought of as odd about the verses is forgotten. With this music, the poem is great art.

NOTES. I. The joining and dividing melodic lines of motifs 13 and 14 sound throughout the song.

2. It was to be expected that somewhere this song would be related to *Wenn du mich mit den Augen streifst* (224). The harmony at 'Nur Euch zu sehn, sei es entwichen' here can be compared with that at 'ausbrechen will vor grosser Lust' in the earlier song.

228 (I 42). 'Nicht länger kann ich singen . . .'
23rd April 1896

The serenader:
I can sing no more, for the wind blows strong and taxes my breath. And I fear that the time passes profitlessly. If I were sure of her love, I should not now go home to bed. If I knew for sure, I should not go home lonely and lose this lovely time of night.

229 (I 43). 'Schweig einmal still . . .'

23rd April 1896

The listener:

> *Do be quiet; you'll drive me mad with that damned singing. Even if you kept it up till morning, you'd never achieve a decent song. So do be quiet and go to bed; really, I'd rather be serenaded by a donkey.*

The two songs must be considered together. True, the second could perhaps be understood in isolation sufficiently well to justify separate performance. But the first loses much of its meaning and its very real poignancy unless we know the cruel sequel.

Both songs stand high in sheer musical quality. In the musical expression of dramatic irony they surely stand supreme. Wolf's music deals not with the actual situation, but with two very different attitudes to it. Thus we never hear the melody of the serenade itself, though we can guess at it. What is heard, in the piano prelude of the second song, is an exasperated parody. It is not the song so much as the singer that is getting on the nerves of his audience. This spite is vented on what was no doubt an inoffensive and unpretentious serenade, which is held up to ridicule by a heartless burlesque

This theme is heard in the accompaniment of the first song thus

Here the phrases are teased apart, float in the air, and are blown away in the wind with a weary pathos like leaves of rejected manuscript. This pathos is notably increased by the words and their sensitive melodic line, and by our knowledge of the reception the serenade is going to get.

The diminished intervals that recur in each song – D sharp to A – suggest a donkey's bray. The point is made explicitly in the second song by the word 'Esel' in the last line, and by the grotesque braying of the piano part at that point and in the postlude. It is made implicitly in the first song, and adds to its pathos. Our serenader is made to appear a bit of an ass. But this song is not at all comic. The fragmentary phrases in the piano, the gasping accents in the voice at 'macht dem Atem was zu schaffen' (taxes the breath), the dramatic irony, above all perhaps, the string-quartet texture of the music, suggest an aloof other-worldly passion, wasted on its audience. Uncannily, these two songs in the same key, the same time, and with the same themes, are made to illustrate the ill-assortedness of the pair. The second song is enjoyably caustic and down to earth, with none of the magic or strangeness of the first.

NOTE. The braying motifs are a refinement of an effect previously used in No. 237 in the same key.

230 (I 44). 'O wüsstest du . . .'

26th April 1896

Oh if only you knew, false traitress, of my nightly suffering for your sake. While you lay in your locked house I was outside.

I knew rain and storm while I kept watch over you. My bed was under your eaves; the sky my covering; your threshold my pillow. I poor wretch, what have I not endured.

This song has some thematic connexions with the previous pair, suggesting that Wolf thought of the poem as the complaint of the unlucky serenader of 228 above once he knew how his efforts had been received. But we seem nevertheless to lack the key to it. The poem is a passionate lament for lost love and wasted time. But the mood of this song is no more than wry, with an almost austere detachment from the sense of the words. The music as such is admirable, but here more than anywhere else in Wolf the impression is one of absolute music conceived instrumentally, having no need of words and contributing little or nothing to the text used.

NOTE. This development is the logical outcome of a trend already noted, particularly in the Spanish songs; the independence of the piano part finally parts company with the verses.

231 (I 45). 'Verschling' der Abgrund . . .'

29th April 1896

May a chasm engulf my lover's house; may a sea pour over it. May a poisonous snake sting him who has proved faithless; may a snake swollen with venom bring death to him who thought to betray me.

The vehement piano part, though effective enough in its way, only emphasizes the song's lack of balance. Given a dramatic soprano with the fine quality of forte needed for the sustained high A on 'Tod' (death), and a pianist capable of disguising the abject banality of much of the material, one can imagine this song appearing to rank among Wolf's finer efforts. But otherwise it is best left for the study.

NOTE. This is in many ways the opposite counterpart of the previous song. Here the piano part is meaningless, except as an adjunct to the drama of the voice and the words.

232 (I 46). 'Ich hab' in Penna . . .'
25th April 1896

I have a lover in Penna, another in Maremma, another in Ancona, another in Viterbo, another in Casentino, another in my own town; and yet another in Maggione, and four in La Fratta, and ten in Castiglione!

The Italian Songbook ends with a brilliant little display masterpiece for soprano, combining prodigious effectiveness with high musical quality. The words count for nothing except the cumulative effect; the music adds a notion of irrepressible gaiety. The bouncing piano part begins neutrally with thirds in the left hand alone. The entry of the voice with its gay melodic line prompts the piano right hand to join in conspiratorially with discreet canonic echoes. There is a brief mock climax before and after 'Zum Vierten muss ich nach Viterbo wandern' (for number four I must go to Viterbo) with the twofold effect of heightening both the musical and dramatic interest. The effect hereabouts is that of a naughty child's gleeful recital of some small misdeed to an indulgent parent – 'Ask what happened next?' it says. And the music is gleeful and excited in just the same way: very pleased with itself at 'ein andrer wohnt in Casentino' (another lives in Casentino) and again reaching a temporary climax before going on 'and there's yet another. There's four!' (and a whole bar's pause like an excited child's pause for breath) . . . 'There's *ten!*' And here on this word the voice rings out bright and exultant over the repeated quavers with which the song began, now in full chords in both hands: and so with the words 'in Castiglione' the voice ends. Now the piano part, fully convinced of the excellence of the joke, bursts out into a riot of delight: the pianistic effect alone is unforgettable. Unfortunately it is often inaudible as well, since after a properly spirited performance the audience will also have burst out into delighted applause at the apparent full close of the voice part. The postlude should be heard not only for its astounding musical brilliance, but also for its dramatic point; all these lovers, it comments, and she doesn't care twopence for any of them.

NOTES. I. The felicitous combination of melodic charm and dramatic point is vividly evocative of the art of Mozart. The words of the song suggest one example of this in particular – the catalogue aria from *Don Giovanni*. There is a third point in common to both songs: the tripping downward scale passages (here at 'wieder einen hab' ich in Maggione').

2. The reader who is in any way convinced by the discovery of childlike excitement in the music of this song may be interested to note the little bouncing bass notes on the off-beat in bar 11 et seq. (motif 2).

VIII. The last published songs

Three songs to words by Reinick

[Peters Edition 3154, Nos 23-25]

233. Gesellenlied: The apprentice's song
24th January 1888

'Masters don't fall from Heaven', the proverb says. It's a good thing they don't; there are quite enough of them here already. If more came down, there'd be more beatings for apprentices.

'Masters don't fall from Heaven.' Nor do their wives, praise be. Oh please, dear Heaven, if you have one booming away up there, keep her in bliss, make sure she doesn't fall!

'Masters don't fall from Heaven.' Nor do their little daughters. I'm reconciled to that, but – what joy if a young and pretty and gay one fell for me, and took me for her sweetheart!

'Masters don't fall from Heaven.' It's really a comforting thought. When I become a master, and marry, let my life on earth become a heaven from which a master won't fall.

Each verse begins 'Kein Meister fällt vom Himmel'. This is set to a hearty tune with a bluff pompous musical truism as accompaniment. As the voice part continues, the piano proceeds to a deft parody of this opening phrase, demonstrating by a revised rhythm, a lightening of texture, and a little added trill, that the following reflections on this theme are not going to be unduly solemn. In the second verse the piano part joins with the voice in its appeal to Heaven to retain any masters' wives who happen to be there. In the third verse comes the real delight of this song. The idea of the master's young daughter clearly had a special appeal for Wolf. 'Young and pretty and gay', the poem describes her. The vocal melodies and the scintillating piano part vie together in high spirits and melt together in tenderness at this moment of the song to recreate most memorably these imagined charms and their effects on the singer. The final verse is bold and effective with a resounding conclusion. But it relies perhaps overmuch on themes and treatment which have already been allotted to the second verse and are not appropriate to both contexts.

NOTES. 1. For obvious reasons, Wolf is reminded of Wagner's Die Meistersinger. The resemblance is mainly in mood and style, although the strongly marked rhythm in the bass at bars 5 and 7 cannot fail to recall the opening bars of the overture to Wagner's masterpiece.

2. The whip-like treble runs that illustrate the beatings are recalled in *Selbstgeständnis* (64) in a similar verbal context.

3. Note the 'companionable' thirds (of motif 16) at 'wollt' mein Herzlieb sein'!

234. Morgenstimmung: Morning mood
8th September–23rd October 1896

Night will be over soon; already I feel the morning air. The Lord says 'Let there be light.' Then all darkness must vanish. Angels come down from the skies and fly over all the earth, singing for joy. Sunlight flames through the universe. Lord, let us strive, let us conquer.

In a revealing letter the composer wrote: 'Today is a specially happy day for me, for a song that has been pursuing me for years, and for which I was wholly unable to find the right setting, has at last been achieved. True, there were several stops and starts, and a great many difficulties in writing it (a quite exceptional thing for me), but it has turned out splendidly. The point was that Reinick called his poem "Morning song". But to me the poem was not like a song; that was the trouble. So I rebaptized it "Morning mood" and things were different straightaway.'

This very late song, one of the last Wolf was to write, is finely constructed and contains much of his own special brand of passionate emotion. Yet somehow it fails to thrill and inspire as it should. For this, Reinick's poem is to blame. It reads well enough at first glance, as an account of some fine lordly feeling; but the verse is pedestrian and pretentious.

Despite this handicap Wolf's admirable music achieves a strong and true rhetoric, and for anyone who admires rhetoric the song will be a lasting favourite. The climax at the word 'Siegen' (conquer), spread over three and a half bars of moderate $\frac{6}{8}$ time with a bright top G sharp and an exultant accompaniment, can sound inspiring.

NOTES. 1. In the Mörike song *Der Genesene an die Hoffnung* (13) the word 'Sieg' is set to the same top note in the same key; and with, partly, the same harmonies.

2. At the mention of angels, after 'fliegen', there is heard an echo of the exquisite phrase allotted to the angels of that much more humble song *Wir haben beide* (205).

3. This song is one of the clearest examples of the use of mediant key-changes to stand for increasing intensity of light (motif 24).

254

235. Skolie: A stirrup cup

1st August 1889

Hand me the cup full of sparkling wine. Give me your red lips to kiss. Let the spirit-stirring music start! The wine, your kisses, the music, fill me with fire. Let the waves of battle engulf me, the waves of love lift me to the clouds. Life, I greet you in exultation!

Wolf's music, lacking the austere technical refinement and control of his last period, does nothing to redeem Reinick's tepid verses. There is fire and bravura in plenty, and dramatic effect; and the song finely sung and played would win deserved plaudits. But to read through the music is to be struck by the uncanny accuracy with which Wolf reproduces not only the élan but the essential witlessness of the poem.

Four songs to words by Heine, Shakespeare and Byron

[Peters Edition 3154, Nos. 19–22]

---

236. 'Wo wird einst . . .'
24th January 1888

Where shall the weary wanderer find his last resting place? Under southern palms? Under the lindens on the Rhine? In some desert, or by the sea? Wherever it be, God's skies will always be over me, and at night the stars will swing their funeral torches high.

The main point of interest about this song is the date of its composition. In this attempt to reproduce the romantic tragedy of a well-known poem by Heine, the Wolfian touches are unmistakable, but, for the most part, spiritless mannerisms. One sees why he despaired of ever having a serious creative gift. Yet less than a month later he was to begin the Mörike songs.

NOTES. 1. The narrative-reflective motif 21 at bars 1–2.
   2. For the piano part at bar 3, etc., see 37, note 2.

237. Lied des transferierten Zettel: Bottom's song from 'Midsummer Night's Dream'
1st May 1889

> *The finch, the sparrow and the lark,*
> *The plain-song cuckoo gray,*
> *Whose notes full many a man doth mark*
> *And dares not answer, nay.*

The song is introduced in Shakespeare thus (Act III, Scene 1):

(Re-enter Bottom, with an ass's head)

Quince: Bless thee, Bottom, bless thee! Thou art translated.

Bottom: I see their knavery, this is to make an ass of me; to fright me if they could. But I will not stir from this place, do what they can: I will walk up and down here, and I will sing, that they shall hear I am not afraid.

The German text is Bottom freely translated, by A. W. von Schlegel. The second verse of the song, quoted above, is expanded into two, and incorporates a chorus of explanatory hee-haws.

Wolf had considered the *Dream* as the basis of an operatic libretto; his charming setting for solo, chorus and orchestra, of the fairies' song *Ye spotted snakes with double tongue* also dates from 1889. This explains why, in one of the great song years, he spared time from writing masterpieces to produce this agreeable but not very important song. Even so, the dramatic idea of uneasy bravado finds no particular expression in this music, which is related to the words not the situation. The piano part of the second verse in particular is crammed with cuckoo calls.

NOTES. I. The braying of a donkey is depicted in a similar way and in the same key in *Schweig einmal still* (229) written seven years later.

2. An uneasy laughter may be indicated by the acciaccature (motif 4).

238. 'Sonne der Schlummerlosen . . .'
18th December 1896

> *Sun of the sleepless! melancholy star!*
> *Whose tearful beam glows tremulously far,*
> *Thou show'st the darkness thou canst not dispel,*
> *How like thou art to joy remembered well!*
> *So gleams the past, the light of other days,*
> *Which shines, but warms not with its powerless rays;*
> *A night-beam Sorrow watcheth to behold,*
> *Distinct but distant – clear, but oh, how cold.*

239. 'Keine gleicht von allen Schönen . . .'
29th December 1896

> *There be none of Beauty's daughters*
> *With a magic like thee;*
> *And like music on the waters*
> *Is thy sweet voice to me:*
> *When, as if its sound were causing*
> *The charmed ocean's pausing,*
> *The waves lie still and gleaming,*
> *And the lull'd winds seem dreaming:*
>
> *And the midnight moon is weaving*
> *Her bright chain o'er the deep;*
> *Whose breast is gently heaving,*
> *As an infant's asleep:*

So the spirit bows before thee,
To listen and adore thee:
With a full but soft emotion,
Like the swell of Summer's ocean.

The words of both Byron poems here are quite literally translated (by Otto Gildemeister); yet Wolf finds in them more than is readily apparent in a reading of the English originals.

The first is an unfamiliar set of album-verses addressed to the moon; the second a much-loved anthology piece. Wolf very typically finds an essence in each and re-creates it. The first lyric is stripped and left shivering in clear cold music; the second is wrapped up in rich and sumptuous material.

These songs belong to the last years of Wolf's creative life, and are far from negligible. Each contains moments of rare beauty, coinciding with the key phrases of each poem – 'ach wie kalt' at the end of the first and 'eingelullte Winde träumen' (and the lull'd winds seem dreaming) in the second. But on the whole they seem to lack depth and penetration. They give the impression of two adjacent pictures in a gallery; a winter moonscape, and a summer seascape, of flawless academic perfection, but somehow lacking in that rich inner life which Wolf at his most characteristic never fails to convey.

NOTES (to 238). 1. There is in the rhythm a reminiscence of *Alle gingen* (167), in the texture a hint of *Wie glänzt der helle Mond* (186) and in the harmony a foretaste of *Alles endet* (241).

2. At bar 4 in the piano is an indication of the wakefulness of motif 17.

3. C sharp minor is Wolf's nocturnal tonality.

NOTE (to 239). In the piano postlude is an analogue of motif 18 in its context here reminiscent of the end of *Verschwiegene Liebe* (68).

The Michelangelo songs

[Peters Edition No. 3155]

Michelangelo Buonarroti (1475–1564) was not only sculptor, painter and architect but a considerable poet.

Wolf had intended to set several of Walter Robert-Tornow's translations; but only the following three songs were satisfactorily completed before the composer's breakdown in September 1897.

240. 'Wohl denk' ich oft . . .'
18th March 1897

I often think of my past life as it was before my love for you. Then no one paid heed to me; each day was lost for me. I thought I would dedicate myself to the art of song, and withdraw from the world. . . . Today men speak my name, whether in praise or dispraise; and all the world knows I am here.

This song is noble and convincing, if a shade conventional. Solemn octaves in the piano lead into a sad reverie of the past, with a beautifully modulated and expressive vocal line throughout and a resigned yet strong piano part. The music becomes more withdrawn until, in the contrasting final section, its latent strength becomes magnificently vigorous. The voice rings out finely, while the accompaniment bursts into a paean of exultant fanfare. A strong tonic major chord is heard for the first time at 'da bin' (am here) and makes fame suddenly vivid.

NOTES. 1. The motif stated unequivocally in the piano at 'ein jeder Tag verloren' and the following bars is the 'sorrow' motif 22. In bars 11–14 this lends itself to the cyclic treatment already noted in 143 and 218, and is thematically transformed into the final trumpet flourish.

2. The harmonies at this point ('da bin wissen alle Leute') have been heard before in the same key in bars 15–16 of the love-song *Wenn du mich* (224). The change from sorrow to exaltation here owes something to love, as the poem says, as well as to renown.

241. 'Alles endet, was entstehet . . .'

20th March 1897

All created things have an end; all things pass away. For time passes, and the sun sees that all things pass away; thought, speech, grief and joy. And our children's children have vanished like darkness in daylight, like mists in the wind. Once we too were men, gay and sad, just as you. And now we are dead, we are but dust, as you see. All created things have an end; all things pass away.

This strange and terrifying work is a unique masterpiece; but it is not a song one can live with or love. Perhaps the music, in following the poem, goes beyond our reach. It is among the dead, speaking the language of the dead. The language seems almost forgotten through disuse. Dark octaves grope for expression; lifeless chords strain agonized after a semblance of melody. The voice enters, disembodied: 'Alles endet, was entstehet; alles, alles, rings vergehet.' Now a metrical pulse begins to beat. Gradually a faint spark of life kindles in the music. The piano's bass octaves find and hold the melodic line which has already been hinted at. The pulse quickens at 'und die wir zu Enkeln hatten' (our grandchildren). There is even a glimpse of emotion at 'wie ein Dunst im Windeshauch' (like mists in the wind), and then in the warmth of E major, now heard for the first time, real human regret, the more moving for its simplicity of expression, at 'Menschen waren wir ja auch' (once we too were men). But now the warmth dies away from the music; the lifeless language resumes; and with it the implacable vision of dry bones singing returns until in the piano postlude death itself dies away.

NOTES. 1. The articulation of this music, achieved by the bare minimum of a rising and a falling semitone, repays close study.

2. C sharp minor was Wolf's tonality for music of night and darkness.

3. The opening octaves recall the menace of the prelude to *Der Genesene an die Hoffnung* (13) in the same key.

242. 'Fühlt meine Seele . . .'

22nd–28th March 1897

What is this light that my spirit feels? Is it the longed-for light of God, or some new beauty of this vale of tears, waking my memories? Is it a sound, or a vision in a dream, that fills my heart and eyes with unfathomable burning grief? I cannot tell. This light I long for, this light that guides me, is not in me. Where shall I find it?

In this light you are revealed to me, my love. It has shone about me ever since I saw you. I am in torments of yes and no, of sweet and bitter; and to this I am brought, lady, by your eyes.

It is difficult to agree with the usual verdict that this song is the least satisfactory of the Michelangelo group. The poem is not always clear; but great sorrow and great love are clearly in it, and Wolf's music expresses them finely.

The piano prelude seems to be groping its way upwards out of darkness. The voice enters quietly questioning. The piano part continues subdued; the vocal phrases are not very far-ranging melodically. Yet it is impossible to perform or hear this first page without receiving the impression of a monumental force lifting and sustaining the music, seeking enlightenment. As the voice goes on with its questioning – 'ist es ein Klang, ein Traumgesicht?' (is it a sound, a vision in a dream?) the piano begins to speak, in Wolf's own special language, of passionate and enduring love. The music rises to a climax, then falls back; 'Ich weiss es nicht' sings the voice resignedly (I cannot tell). Now comes a series of masterstrokes of unconscious art. The searching music of the first page was dominated by the tonality of E minor and voice and piano melodies moving mainly stepwise. The love-themes inclined to E major, with a fuller chordal accompaniment and wider-ranging melodic phrases. In what now follows at 'Was ich ersehne' (what I long for) the piano right hand combines the minor tonality and texture of the first themes with the rhythm of the second. The two ideas of longing and love, already unified by the left-hand rhythm ♪ ♩ ♪ are taken onwards as one single passionate quest.

First, half the truth is perceived – 'ist nicht in mir' (is not in me). Then the searching resumes, and, in the piano, climbs ever higher to a fantastic climax; the moment of waking, of truth, of revelation. Then it is as if the truth is realized and accepted, with an acquiescence of deep piano semibreves. The voice returns with the first themes at 'Mir zeigt es wohl', etc. (you are revealed to me). The problem once solved, the love-themes are recalled, suffused with warmth, and bursting out in overwhelming love until the final words 'daran sind, Herrin, deine Augen Schuld' and the cherishing postlude.

This is not a perfect work, nor is it easy to grasp at first hearing. But the workmanship is so exquisite, the emotion so intense, that a man might be immortal for having written this one song. It was Wolf's last.

NOTES. 1. The love-music of this song, e.g. bars 12–13, is a finely character-istic example of motif 13.

    2. The unifying rhythm ♪ ♩ ♪, etc., is the self-surrendering motif 1.

    3. See 44, note 2.

Index A   The songs

(Main page references are shown in bold type)

Index B   General

Allegory, 26, 104, 126, 183, 199

Bach, 180
Beethoven, 34, 92, 122, 125, 175
Brahms, 27, 50 54, 105, 106, 169, 177, 206, 207
Bruckner, 111
Byron, 258

Chopin, 28, 66, 136, 188, 193, 195, 229
Corregidor, Der, 1, 150, 177, 185

Declamation, 1, 3, 4, 72
Decsey, Ernst, 12, 56, 128

Effects, 6–7. Bells, 84, 85; birds, 26, 123, 206, 257; braying, 247, 248, 257; disappearance, 77, 245; drums, 43, 196, 197, 225, 226; guns, 79, 110; hammering, 131, 157, 199; heartbeats, 191, 192, 201; hollowness, 130, 131; military bands, marches, 106, 107, 128, 196, 226, 232; processional exits, 106, 107, 135, 146, 197, 232; seascape, 112; stringed instruments, 102, 109, 178, 191, 198, 199, 230, 234; thunder, 79; whips, 84, 93 254; winds, 28, 45, 77, 86, 168
Eichendorff, 1, 97, 99–114 *passim*
Equivalents, 2, 20, 21, 57, 66, 185, 221. defiance, 128, 157, 158, 217, 230; transparency, 87, 245

Fauré, 137
Form, 2, 63, 66, 72, 76, 85, 169, 179, 209

Geibel, 1, 163, 165–200 *passim*
Gildemeister, Otto, 258

Goethe, 1, 31–33, 65, 115, 117–161 *passim*
Goldmark, Carl, 128
Goldschmidt, A. von, 128

Haberlandt, Dr Michael, 34
Harmony, 4, 5, 20–1, 131, 139, 165, 166, 191, 214. colour effects of, 56, 101, 145; four-part, 17, 20, 231; tonic major delayed, 51, 56, 122, 147, 154, 167, 228
Hebbel, 26
Heine, 256
Heyse, 1, 21, 163, 165–200 *passim*, 211, 241

Invention, fertility of, 43, 57, 106, 220
Italian Serenade, 103, 195, 197

Keller, 1, 21, 35, 203, 205–9
Kerner, 34
Keys, associations with, 6. A flat major, 19, 28, 69, 75, 170, 234; A major, 44, 181, 207, 244; A minor, 45, 87, 104, 122, 141, 166, 190, 200, 244; B minor, 83, 184, 188, 195, 197; C major, 103; C sharp minor, 37, 55, 60, 258, 260; D major, 25, 49, 131, 144, 159, 186, 246; D minor, 131, 150, 246; E flat major, 19, 228; F major, 165, 170, 192; F sharp major, 33, 49, 50, 140, 146, 176, 177, 184, 197, 200, 222

Liszt, 125
Loewe, 89, 122

Maler Nolten, 59, 73, 88
Manuel Venegas, 1, 31, 82, 244

267